GUN FODDER

Major A. Hamilton Gibbs, R. A.

GUN FODDER

THE DIARY OF
FOUR YEARS OF WAR

BY

A. HAMILTON GIBBS
MAJOR, R.A.

WITH INTRODUCTION BY PHILIP GIBBS

BOSTON
LITTLE, BROWN, AND COMPANY
1924

Copyright, 1919,
BY A. HAMILTON GIBBS.

All rights reserved

INTRODUCTION

THERE seems no reason to me why I should write a preface to my brother's book except that I have been, as it were, a herald of war proclaiming the achievements of Knights and men-at-arms in this great conflict that has passed, and so may take up my scroll again on his behalf, because here is a good soldier who has told, in a good book, his story of

> "most disastrous chances of moving accidents by flood and field; of hair-breadth 'scapes i' the imminent-deadly breach."

That he was a good soldier I can say not because my judgment is swayed by brotherly partiality, but because I saw him at his job, and heard the opinions of his fellow officers, which were immensely in his favor. "Your brother is a born soldier," said my own Chief who was himself a gallant officer and had a quick eye for character. I think that was true. The boy whom once I wheeled in a go-cart when he was a shock-headed Peter and I the elder brother with a sense of responsibility towards him, had grown up before the war into a strong man whose physical prowess as an amateur pugilist, golfer, archer (in any old sport) was quite outside my sphere of activities, which were restricted to watching the world spin round and recording its movements by quick penmanship. Then the war came and like all the elder brothers of England I had a quick kind of heart-beat when I knew that the kid brother had joined up and in due time would have to face the music being played by the great orchestra of death across the fields of life.

I saw the war before he did, knew the worst before he guessed at the lesser evils of it, heard the crash of shell fire, went into burning and bombarded towns, helped to carry dead and wounded, while he was training in England under foul-mouthed sergeants — training to learn how to fight, and, if need be, how to die, like a little gentleman. But I from the first was only the onlooker, the recorder, and he was to be, very quickly, one of the actors in the drama, up to his neck in the "real thing." His point of view was to be quite different from mine. I saw the war in the mass, in its broad aspects and movements from the front line trenches to the Base, from one end of the front to the other. I went into dirty places, but did not stay there. I went from one little corner of hell to another, but did not dwell in its narrow boundaries long enough to get its intimate details of hellishness burnt into my body and soul. He did. He had not the same broad vision of the business of war — appalling in its vastness of sacrifice and suffering, wonderful in its mass-heroism — but was one little ant in a particular muck-heap for a long period of time, until the stench of it, the filth of it, the boredom of it, the futility of it, entered into his very being, and was part of him as he was part of it. His was the greater knowledge.

INTRODUCTION

He was the sufferer, the victim. Our ways lay apart for a long time. He became a ghost to me, during his long spell in Salonica, and I thought of him only as a ghost figure belonging to that other life of mine which I had known "before the war", that far-off period of peace which seemed to have gone forever. Then one day I came across him again out in Flanders in a field near Armentières, and saw how he had hardened and grown, not only in years but in thoughtfulness and knowledge. He was a commander of men, with the power of life and death over them. He was a commander of guns with the power of death over human creatures lurking in holes in the earth, invisible creatures beyond a hedge of barbed wire and a line of trench. But he also was under the discipline of other powers with higher command than his — who called to him on the telephone and told him to do things he hated to do, but had to do, things which he thought were wrong to do, but had to do; and among those other powers, disciplining his body and soul was German gun-power from that other side of the barbed-wire hedge, always a menace to him, always teasing him with the chance of death, — a yard this way, a yard that, as I could see by the shell-holes round about his gun-pits, following the track of his field-path, clustering in groups outside the little white house in which he had his mess. I studied this brother of mine curiously. How did he face all the nerve-strain under which I had seen many men break? He was merry and bright (except for sudden silences and a dark look in his eyes at times).

He had his old banjo with him and tinkled out a tune on it. How did he handle his men and junior officers? They seemed to like him "this side idolatry", yet he had a grip on them, and demanded obedience, which they gave with respect. Queer! My kid-brother had learned the trick of command. He had an iron hand under a velvet glove. The line of his jaw, his straight nose (made straighter by that boxing in his old Oxford days) were cut out for a job like this. He looked the part. He was born to it. All his training had led up to this soldier's job in the field, though I had not guessed so when I wheeled him in that old go-cart.

For me he had a slight contempt, which he will deny when he reads this preface. Though a writer of books before the war, he had now the soldier's scorn of the chronicler. It hurt him to see my green arm-bands, my badge of shame. That I had a motor-car seemed to him, in his stationary exile, the sign of a soft job — as, compared with his it was — disgraceful in its luxury. From time to time I saw him, and, in spite of many narrow escapes under heavy shelling, he did not change, but was splendidly cheerful. Even on the eve of the great German offensive in March of 1918, when he took me to see the graves dug in under the embankment south of St. Quentin, he did not seem apprehensive of the awful ordeal ahead of him. I knew more than he did about that. I knew the time and place of its coming, and I knew that he was in a very perilous position. We said "so long" to each other at parting, with a grip of hands, and I thought it might be the last time I should see him. It was I think ten days later when I saw him, and in that time much had happened, and all that time I gave him up as lost. Under the overwhelming weight of numbers — 114 Divisions to 48 — the British line had broken, and, fighting desperately, day by day, our men fell back mile after mile with the enemy outflanking them, cutting off broken battalions, threatening to cut off vast bodies of men. Every day I was in the swirl of that Retreat, pushing up to its rearguards, seeing with increasing dismay the fearful wreckage of our organization and machine of war which became for a little while like the broken springs of a watch, with Army, Corps, and Divisional staffs entirely out of tune with the fighting units owing to the break-down of all lines of communication. In that tide of traffic, of men, and guns, and transport, I made a few enquiries about that brother of mine. Nobody had seen, or heard of his battery. I must have been close to him at times in Noyon, and Guiscard and Ham, but one individual was like a needle in a bunch of hay, and the enemy had rolled over in a tide, and there did not seem to me a chance of his escape. Then, one morning, in a village near Poix, when I asked a gunner-officer whether he had seen my brother's battery, he said, "Yes — two villages up that road." "Do you happen to know Major Gibbs?" "Yes . . . I saw him walking along there a few minutes ago."

It was like hearing that the dead had risen from the grave.

Half an hour later we came face to face.

He said:

"Hulloa, old man!"

And I said:

"Hulloa, young fellow!"

Then we shook hands on it, and he told me some of his adventures, and I marvelled at him, because after a wash and shave he looked as though he had just come from a holiday at Brighton instead of from the Valley of Death. He was as bright as ever, and I honestly believe even now that in spite of all his danger and suffering, he had enjoyed the horrible thrills of his adventures. It was only later when his guns were in action near Albert that I saw a change in him. The constant shelling, and the death of some of his officers and men, had begun to tell on him at last. I saw that his nerve was on the edge of snapping, as other men's nerves had snapped after less than his experiences, and I decided to rescue him by any means I could. . . . I had the luck to get him out of that hole in the earth just before the ending of the war.

Now I have read his book. It is a real book. Here truthfully, nakedly, vividly, is the experience not only of one soldier in the British Army, but of thousands, and hundreds of thousands. All our men went through the training he describes, were shaped by its hardness and its roughness, were trampled into obedience of soul and body by its heavy discipline. Here is the boredom of war, as well as its thrill of horror, that devastating long-drawn Boredom which is the characteristic of war and the cause of much of its suffering. Here is the sense of futility which sinks into the soldier's mind, tends to sap his mental strength and embitters him, so that the edge is taken off his enthusiasm, and he abandons the fervor of the ideal with which he volunteered.

There is a tragic bitterness in the book, and that is not peculiar to the temperament of the author, but a general feeling to be found among masses of demobilized officers and men, not only of the British Armies, but of the French, and I fancy, also, of the American forces. What is the cause of that? Why this spirit of revolt on the part of men who fought with invincible courage and long patience? It will seem strange to people who have only seen war from afar that an officer like this, decorated for valour, early in the field, one of the old stock and tradition of English loyalty, should utter such fierce words about the leaders of the war, such ironical words about the purpose and sacrifice of the world conflict. He seems to accuse other enemies than the Germans, to turn round upon Allied statesmen, philosophers, preachers, mobs and say, "You too were guilty of this fearful thing. Your hands are red also with the blood of youth. And you forget already those who saved you by their sacrifice."

That is what he says, clearly, in many passionate paragraphs; and I can bear witness that his point of view is shared by many other soldiers who fought in France. These men were thinking hard when day by day they were close to death. In their dug-outs and ditches they asked of their own souls enormous questions. They asked whether the war was being fought really for Liberty, really to crush Militarism, really on behalf of Democracy, or whether to bolster up the same system on our side of the lines which had produced the evils of the German menace. Was it not a conflict between rival Powers imbued with exactly the same philosophy of Imperialism and Force? Was it not the product of commercial greed, diplomatic fears and treacheries and intrigues (conducted secretly over the heads of the peoples) and had not the German people been led on to their villainy by the same spell-words and "dope" which had been put over our peoples, so that the watch-words of "patriotism", "defensive warfare" and "Justice" had been used to justify this massacre in the fields of Europe by the Old Men of all nations, who used the Boys as pawns in their Devil's game? The whole structure of Europe had been wrong. The ministers of the Christian churches had failed Christ by supporting the philosophy of Force, and diplomatic wickedness and old traditions of hatred. All nations were involved in this hark-back to the jungle-world, and Germany was only most guilty because first to throw off the mask, most efficient in the mechanism of Brute-government, most logical in the damnable laws of that philosophy which poisoned the spirit of the modern world.

That was the conclusion to which, rightly or wrongly — I think rightly — many men arrived in their secret conferences with their own souls when death stood near the door of their dug-outs.

That sense of having fought for ideals which were not real in the purpose of the war embittered them; and they were most bitter on their home coming, after Armistice, or after Peace, when in England they found that the victory they had won was being used not to inaugurate a new era of liberty, but to strengthen the old laws of "Might and Right", the old tyrannies of government without the consent of peoples, the old Fetish worship of hatred masking under the divine name of Patriotism. Disillusionment, despair, a tragic rage, filled the hearts of fighting men who after all their sacrifices found themselves unrewarded, unemployed, and unsatisfied in their souls. Out of this psychological distress have come civil strife and much of the unrest which is now at work.

My brother's book reveals something of this at work in his own mind, and, as such, is a revelation of all his comrades. I do not think he has yet found the key to the New Philosophy which will arise out of all that experience, emotion, and thought; just as the mass of fighting men are vague about the future which must replace the bad old past. They are perplexed, illogical, passionate without a clear purpose. But undoubtedly out of their perplexities and passion the New Era will be born.

So I salute my "kid-brother" as one of the makers of History greater than that which crushed German militarism and punished German crimes (which were great), and I wish him luck with this book, which is honest, vital, and revealing.

PHILIP GIBBS.

CONTENTS

	PAGE
INTRODUCTION BY PHILIP GIBBS	v

PART I
THE RANKS 1

PART II
UBIQUE 83

PART III
THE WESTERN FRONT 139

PART IV
THE ARMISTICE 303

PART I

THE RANKS

GUN FODDER

I. THE RANKS

1.

IN June, 1914, I came out of a hospital in Philadelphia after an operation, faced with two facts. One was that I needed a holiday at home in England, the second that after all hospital expenses were paid I had five dollars in the world. But there was a half-finished novel in my trunk and the last weeks of the theatrical tour which had brought me to Philadelphia would tide me over. A month later the novel was bought by a magazine and the boat that took me to England seemed to me to be the tangible result of concentrated will power. "Man proposes. . . ." My own proposal was to return to America in a month or six weeks to resume the task of carving myself a niche in the fiction market.

The parting advice of the surgeon had been that I was not to play ball or ride a horse for at least six months. The green sweeping uplands of Buckinghamshire greeted me with all their fragrance and a trig golf course gave me back strength while I thought over ideas for a new novel.

Then like a thunderbolt the word "War" crashed out. Its full significance did not break through the ego of one who so shortly would be leaving Europe far behind and to whom a personal career seemed of vital importance. England was at war. The Army would be buckling on its sword, running out its guns; the Navy clearing decks for action. It was their job, not mine. The Boer War had only touched upon my childish consciousness as a shouting in the streets, cheering multitudes and brass bands. War, as such, was something which I had never considered as having any personal meaning for me. Politics and war were the business of politicians and soldiers. My business was writing and I went up to London to arrange accommodations on the boat to New York.

London was different in those hot August days. Long queues waited all day, — not outside theatres, but outside recruiting offices, — city men, tramps, bricklayers, men of all types and ages with a look in their eyes that puzzled me. Every taxi hoot drew one's attention to the flaring poster on each car "Young Men of England, Your King and Country need you!"

How many millions of young men there were who would be glad to answer that call to adventure, — an adventure which surely could not last more than six months? It did not call me. My adventure lay in that wonderland of sprouting towers that glistened behind the Statue of Liberty.

But day by day the grey wave swept on, tearing down all veils from before the altar of reality. Belgian women were not merely bayoneted.

"Why don't we stop this? What is the Army

doing?" How easy to cry that out from the leafy lanes of Buckinghamshire. A woman friend of mine travelled up in the train with me one morning, a friend whose philosophy and way of life had seemed to me more near the ideal than I had dreamed of being able to reach. She spoke of war, impersonally and without recruiting propaganda. All unconsciously she opened my eyes to the unpleasant fact that it was *my* war too. Suppose I had returned to New York and the Germans had jumped the tiny Channel and "bayoneted" her and her children? Could I ever call myself a man again?

I took a taxi and went round London. Every recruiting office looked like a four-hour wait. I was in a hurry. So I went by train to Bedford and found it crowded with Highlanders. When I asked the way to the recruiting office they looked at me oddly. Their speech was beyond my London ear but a pointing series of arms showed it to me.

By a miracle the place was empty except for the doctor and an assistant in khaki.

"I want to join the Cavalry," said I.

"Very good, sir. Will you please take off your clothes."

It was the last time a sergeant called me sir for many a long day.

I stripped, was thumped and listened to and gave description of tattoo marks which interested that doctor greatly. The appendix scar didn't seem to strike him. "What is it?" said he, looking at it curiously, and when I told him merely grunted. Shades of Shaw! I thought with a jump of that

Philadelphia surgeon. "Don't ride a horse for six months." Only three had elapsed.

I was passed fit. I assured them that I was English on both sides, unmarried, not a spy, and was finally given a bundle of papers and told to take them along to the barracks.

The barracks were full of roughnecks and it occurred to me for the first time, as I listened to them being sworn in, that these were my future brother soldiers. What price Mulvaney, Learoyd and Ortheris? thought I.

I repeated the oath after an hour's waiting and swore to obey orders and respect superior officers and in short do my damnedest to kill the King's enemies. I've done the last but when I think of the first two that oath makes me smile.

However, I swore, received two shillings and threepence for my first two days' pay and was ordered to report at the Cavalry Depot, Woolwich, the following day, September 3, 1914.

The whole business had been done in a rush of exaltation that didn't allow me to think. But when I stepped out into the crowded streets with that two shillings rattling in my pocket I felt a very sober man. I knew nothing whatever of soldiering. I hardly even knew a corporal from a private or a rifle from a ramrod, and here I was Trooper A. H. Gibbs, 9th Lancers, with the sullen rumble of heavy guns just across the Channel — growing louder.

THE RANKS

2.

Woolwich!

Bad smells, bad beer, bad women, bad language! — Those early days! None of us who went through the ranks will ever forget the tragedy, the humour, the real democracy of that period. The hand of time has already coloured it with the glow of romance, but in the living it was crude and raw, like waking up to find your nightmare real.

Oxford University doesn't give one much of an idea of how to cope with the class of humanity at that Depot in spite of Ruskin Hall, the workingman's college, of which my knowledge consisted only of climbing over their wall and endeavoring to break up their happy home. But the Ruskin Hall man was a prince by the side of those recruits. They came with their shirts sticking out of trousers seats, naked toes showing out of gaping boots, and their smell — We lay at night side by side on adjoining bunks, fifty of us in a room. They had spent their two days' pay on beer, bad beer. The weather was hot. Most of them were stark naked. I'd had a bath that morning. They hadn't.

The room was enormous. The windows had no blinds. The moon streamed in on their distorted bodies in all the twistings of uneasy sleep. Some of them smoked cigarettes and talked. Others blasphemed them for talking but the bulk snored and ground their teeth in their sleep.

A bugle rang out.

Aching in every limb from the unaccustomed hardness of the iron bed it was no hardship to answer the call. There were lavatories outside each room and amid much sleepy blasphemy we shaved, those of us who had razors, and washed, and in the chill of dawn went down to a misty common. It was too early for discipline. There weren't enough N.C.O.'s, so for the first few days we hung about waiting for breakfast instead of doing physical jerks.

Breakfast! One thinks of a warm room with cereals and coffee and eggs and bacon with a morning paper and, if there's a soot in our cup, a sarcastic reference as to cleanliness. That was before the war.

We lined up before the door of a gun shed, hundreds of us, shivering, filing slowly in one by one and having a chunk of bread, a mug of tea and a tin of sardines slammed into our hands, the sardines having to be divided among four.

The only man in my four who possessed a jackknife to open the tin had cleaned his pipe with it, scraped the mud off his boots, cleaned out his nails and cut up plug tobacco. Handy things, jackknives. He proceeded to hack open the tin and scoop out sardines. It was only my first morning and my stomach wasn't strong in those days. I disappeared into the mist, alone with my dry bread and tea. Hunger has taught me much since then.

The mist rolled up later and daylight showed us to be a pretty tough crowd. We were presently taken in hand by a lot of sergeants who divided us into groups, made lists of names and began to teach us how to march in files, and in sections, —

the elements of soldiering. Some of them didn't seem to know their left foot from their right but the patience of those sergeants was only equalled by the cunning of their blasphemy and the stolidity of their victims.

After an hour of it we were given a rest for fifteen minutes, this time to get a handful of tobacco. Then it went on again and again, — and yet again.

The whole of that first period of seven days was a long jumble of appalling happenings; meals served by scrofulitic hands on plates from which five other men's leavings and grease had to be removed; bread cut in quarter loaves; meat fat, greasy, and stewed — always stewed, tea, stewed also, without appreciable milk, so strong that a spoon stood up in it unaided; sleeping in one's clothes and inadequate washing in that atmosphere of filth indescribable; of parades to me childish in their elementariness; of long hours in the evening with nothing to do, no place to go, no man to talk to, — a period of absolute isolation in the middle of those thousands broken only by letters which assumed a paramount importance, constituting as they did one's only link with all that one had left behind, that other life which now seemed like a mirage.

Not that one regretted the step. It was a firsthand experience of life that only Jack London or Masefield could have depicted. It was too the means of getting out to fight the Boche. A monotonous means, yes, but every day one learnt some new drill and every day one was thrilled with the absolute cold-blooded reality of it all. It was good to be alive, to be a man, to get one's teeth right into things. It was a bigger part to play than that of the boy in "The Blindness of Virtue."

3.

Two incidents stand out in that chrysalis stage of becoming soldiers.

One was a sing-song, spontaneously started among the gun sheds in the middle of the white moonlight. One of the recruits was a man who had earned his living — hideously sarcastic phrase! — by playing a banjo and singing outside public houses. He brought his banjo into the army with him. I hope he's playing still!

He stuck his inverted hat on the ground, lit a candle beside it in the middle of the huge square, smacked his dry lips and drew the banjo out of its baize cover.

"Perishin' thirsty weather, Bill."

He volunteered the remark to me as to a brother.

"Going to play for a drink?" I asked.

He was already tuning. He then sat down on a large stone and began to sing. His accompaniment was generous and loud and perhaps once he had a voice. It came now with but an echo of its probable charm, through a coating of beer and tobacco and years of rough living.

It was extraordinary. Just he sitting on the stone, and I standing smoking by his side, and the candle flickering in the breeze, and round us the hard black and white buildings and the indefinable rumble of a great life going on somewhere in the distance.

Presently, as though he were the Pied Piper, men came in twos and threes and stood round us, forming a circle.

"Give us the 'Little Grey 'Ome in the West', George!"

And "George", spitting after the prolonged sentiment of Thora, struck up the required song. At the end of half an hour there were several hundred men gathered round joining in the choruses, volunteering solos, applauding each item generously. The musician had five bottles of beer round his inverted hat and perhaps three inside him, and a collection of coppers was taken up from time to time.

They chose love ballads of an ultra-sentimental nature with the soft pedal on the sad parts, — these men who to-morrow would face certain death. How little did that thought come to them then. But I looked round at their faces, blandly happy, dirty faces, transformed by the moon and by their oath of service into the faces of crusaders.

How many of them are alive to-day, how many buried in nameless mounds somewhere in that silent desolation? How many of them have suffered mutilation? How many of them have come out of it untouched, to the waiting arms of their women? Brothers, I salute you.

The other incident was the finding of a friend, a kindred spirit in those thousands which accentuated one's solitude.

We had been standing in a long queue outside the Quartermaster's store, being issued with khaki one by one. I was within a hundred yards of getting outfitted when the Q.M. came to the door in person and yelled that the supply had run out. I think we all swore. The getting of khaki meant a vital step nearer to the Great Day when we should cross the Channel. As the crowd broke away in disorder, I heard a voice with an 'h' say "How perfectly ruddy!" I could have fallen on the man's neck with joy. The owner of it was a comic sight. A very battered straw hat, a dirty handkerchief doing the duty of collar, a pair of grey flannel trousers that had been slept in these many nights. But the face was clear and there was a twinkle of humorous appreciation in the blue eye. I made a bee-line for that man. I don't remember what I said, but in a few minutes we were swapping names, and where we lived and what we thought of it, and laughing at our mutually draggled garments.

We both threw reserve to the wind and were most un-English, except perhaps that we may have looked upon each other as the only two white men in a tribe of savages. In a sense we were. But it was like finding a brother and made all that difference to our immediate lives. There was so much pent-up feeling in both of us that we hadn't been able to put into words. Never have I realized the value and comfort of speech so much, or the bond established by sharing experiences and emotions.

4.

My new-found "brother's" name was Bucks. After a few more days of drilling and marching and sergeant grilling, we both got khaki and spurs and cap badges and bandoliers, and we both bought white lanyards and cleaning appliances. Smart? We made a point of being the smartest recruits of the whole bunch. We felt we were the complete soldier at last and although there wasn't a horse in Woolwich we clattered about in spurs that we burnished to the glint of silver.

And then began the second chapter of our military career. We all paraded one morning and were told off to go to Tidworth or the Curragh.

Bucks and I were for Tidworth and marched side by side in the great squad of us who tramped in step, singing "Tipperary" at the top of our lungs, down to the railway station.

That was the first day I saw an officer, two officers as a matter of fact, subalterns of our own regiment. It gave one for the first time the feeling of belonging to a regiment. In the depot at Woolwich were 9th Lancers, 5th Dragoon Guards, and 16th Lancers. Now we were going to the 9th Lancer barracks and those two subalterns typified the regiment to Bucks and me. How we eyed them, those two youngsters, and were rather proud of the aloof way in which they carried themselves. They were specialists. We were novices beginning at the bottom of the ladder and I wouldn't have changed places with them at that moment had it been possible. As an officer I shouldn't have known what to do with the mob of which I was one. I should have been awkward, embarrassed.

It didn't occur to me then that there were hundreds,

thousands, who knew as little as we did about the Army, who were learning to be second lieutenants as we were learning to be troopers.

We stayed all day in that train, feeding on cheese and bread which had been given out wrapped in newspapers, and buns and biscuits bought in a rush at railway junctions at which we stopped from time to time. It was dark when we got to Tidworth, that end-of-the-world siding, and were paraded on the platform and marched into barracks whose thousand windows winked cheerily at us as we halted outside the guardroom.

There were many important people like sergeant majors waiting for us, and sergeants who called them "sir" and doubled to carry out their orders. These latter fell upon us and in a very short time we were divided into small groups and marched away to barrack rooms for the night. There was smartness here, discipline. The chaos of Woolwich was a thing of the past.

Already I pictured myself being promoted to lance corporal, the proud bearer of one stripe, picking Boches on my lance like a row of pigs, — and I hadn't even handled a real lance as yet!

5.

Tidworth, that little cluster of barrack buildings on the edge of the sweeping downs, golden in the early autumn, full of a lonely beauty like a green Sahara with springs and woods, but never a house for miles, and no sound but the sighing of the wind and the mew of the peewit! Thus I came to know it first. Later the rain turned it into a sodden stretch of mud, blurred and terrible, like a drunken streetwoman blown by the wind, filling the soul with shudders and despair. — The barrack buildings covered perhaps a square mile of ground, ranged orderly in series, officers' quarters — as far removed from Bucks and me as the Carlton Hotel — married quarters, sergeants' mess, stables, canteen, riding school, barrack rooms, hospital; like a small city, thriving and busy, dropped from the blue upon that patch of country.

The N.C.O.'s at Tidworth were regulars, time-serving men who had learnt their job in India and who looked upon us as a lot of "perishin' amatoors." It was a very natural point of view. We presented an ungodly sight, a few of us in khaki, some in "blues", those terrible garments that make their wearers look like an orphans' home, but most in civilian garments of the most tattered description. Khaki gave one standing, self-respect, cleanliness, enabled one to face an officer feeling that one was trying at least to be a soldier.

The barrack rooms were long and whitewashed, a stove in the middle, rows of iron beds down either side to take twenty men in peace times. As it was we late comers slept on "biscuits", square hard mattresses, laid down between the iron bunks, and mustered nearly forty in a room. In charge of each room was a lance corporal or corporal whose job it was to detail a room orderly and to see furthermore that he did his job, *i.e.*, keep the room swept and garnished, the lavatory basins washed, the fireplace blackleaded, the windows cleaned, the step swept and whitewashed.

Over each bed was a locker (without a lock, of course) where each man kept his small kit, — razor, towel, toothbrush, blacking and his personal treasures. Those who had no bed had no locker and left things beneath the folded blankets of the beds.

How one missed one's household goods! One learnt to live like a snail, with everything in the world upon one's person, — everything in the world cut down to the barest necessities, pipe and baccy, letters, a photograph, knife, fork and spoon, toothbrush, bit of soap, tooth paste, one towel, one extra pair of socks. Have you ever tried it for six months — a year? Then don't. You miss your books and pictures, the bowl of flowers on the table, the table-cloth. All the things of everyday life that are taken for granted become a matter of poignant loss when you've got to do without them. But it's marvellous what can be done without when it's a matter of necessity.

Bucks unfortunately didn't get to the same room with me. All of us who had come in the night before were paraded at nine o'clock next morning before the Colonel and those who had seen service or who could ride were considered sheep and separated from the goats who had never seen service nor a horse. Bucks was a goat. I could ride, — although the sergeant major took fifteen sulphuric minutes to tell me he didn't think so. And so Bucks and I were separated by the space of a barrack wall, as we thought then. It was a greater separation

THE RANKS

really, for he was still learning to ride when I went out to France to reinforce the fighting regiment which had covered itself with glory in the retreat from Mons. But before that day came we worked through to the soul of Tidworth, and of the sergeant major, if by any stretch of the imagination he may be said to have had a soul. I think he had but all the other men in the squadron dedicated their first bullet to him if they saw him in France. What a man! He stands out among all my memories of those marvellous days of training when everything was different from anything I had ever done before. He stands before me now, a long, thin figure in khaki, with a face that had been kicked in by a horse, an eye that burnt like a branding iron, and picked out unpolished buttons like a magnet. In the saddle he was a centaur, part of the horse, wonderful. His long, thin thighs gripped like tentacles of steel. He could make an animal grunt, he gripped so hard. And his language! Never in my life had I conceived the possibilities of blasphemy to shrivel a man's soul until I heard that sergeant major. He ripped the Bible from cover to cover. He defied thunderbolts from on high and referred to the Almighty as though he were a scullion, — and he's still doing it. Compared to the wholesale murder of eight million men it was undoubtedly a pin-prick but it taught us how to ride!

6.

Reveille was at 5.30.

Grunts, groans, curses, a kick, — and you were

sleepily struggling with your riding breeches and puttees.

The morning bath? Left behind with all the other things.

There were horses to be groomed and watered and fed, stables to be "mucked out", much hard and muscular work to be done before that pint of tea and slab of grease called bacon would keep body and soul together for the morning parade. One fed first and shaved and splashed one's face, neck, and arms with water afterwards. Have you ever cleaned out a stable with your bare hands and then been compelled to eat a meal without washing?

By nine o'clock one paraded with cleaned boots, polished buttons and burnished spurs and was inspected by the sergeant major. If you were sick you went before the doctor instead. But it didn't pay to be sick. The sergeant major cured you first. Then as there weren't very many horses in barracks as yet, we were divided half into the riding school, half for lance and sword drill.

Riding school was invented by the Spanish Inquisition. Generally it lasted an hour by which time one was broken on the rack and emerged shaken, bruised and hot, blistered by the sergeant major's tongue. There were men who'd never been on a horse more than twice in their lives but most of us had swung a leg over a saddle. Many in that ride were grooms from training stables, riders of steeplechasers. But their methods were not at all those desired in His Majesty's Cavalry and they suffered like the rest of us. But the sergeant major's tongue never stopped and we either learned the essentials in double-quick time or got out to a more elementary ride.

It was a case of the survival of the fittest. Round and round that huge school, trotting with and without stirrups until one almost fell off from sheer agony, with and without saddle over five-foot jumps pursued by the hissing lash of the sergeant major's tongue and whip, jumping without reins, saddle or stirrups. The agony of sitting down for days afterwards!

Followed a fifteen-minute break, after the horses were led back to the stables and off-saddled, and then parade on the square with lance and sword. A lovely weapon the lance — slender, irresistible — but after an hour's concentrated drill one's right wrist became red-hot and swollen and the extended lance points drooped in our tired grasp like reeds in the wind. At night in the barrack room we used to have competitions to see who could drive the point deepest into the door panels.

Then at eleven o'clock "stables" again: caps and tunics off, braces down, sleeves rolled up. We had a magnificent stamp of horse but they came in ungroomed for days and under my inexpert methods of grooming took several days before they looked as if they'd been groomed at all.

Dinner was at one o'clock and by the time that hour struck one was ready to eat anything. Each squadron had its own dining rooms, concrete places with wooden tables and benches, but the eternal stew went down like caviar.

The afternoon parades were marching drill, physical exercises, harness cleaning, afternoon stables and finish for the day about five o'clock, unless one were wanted for guard or picquet. Picquet meant the care of the horses at night, an unenviable job. But guard was a twenty-four hours' duty, two hours on, four hours off, much coveted after a rough passage in the riding school. It gave one a chance to heal.

Hitherto everything had been a confused mass of men without individuality but of unflagging cheerfulness. Now in the team work of the squadron and the barrack room individuality began to play its part and under the hard and fast routine the cheerfulness began to yield to grousing.

The room corporal of my room was a reënlisted man, a schoolmaster from Scotland, conscientious, liked by the men, extremely simple. I've often wondered whether he obtained a commission. The other troopers were ex-stable boys, labourers, one a golf caddy and one an ex-sailor who was always singing an interminable song about a highly immoral donkey. The caddy and the sailor slept on either side of me. They were a mixed crowd and used filthy language as naturally as they breathed, but as cheery and stout a lot as you'd wish to meet. Under their grey shirts beat hearts as kindly as many a woman's. I remember the first time I was inoculated and felt like nothing on earth.

"Christ!" said the sailor. "Has that perishin' doctor been stickin' his perishin' needle into you, Mr. Gibbs?" — For some reason they always called

THE RANKS

me Mr. Gibbs. — "Come over here and get straight to bed before the perishin' stuff starts workin'. I've 'ad some of it in the perishin' navy." And he and the caddy took off my boots and clothes and put me to bed with gentle hands.

The evening's noisiness was given up. Everybody spoke in undertones so that I might get to sleep. And in the morning, instead of sweeping under my own bed as usual, they did it for me and cleaned my buttons and boots because my arm was still sore.

Can you imagine men like that nailing a kitten by its paws to a door as a booby-trap to blow a building sky high, as those Boches have done? Instead of bayoneting prisoners the sailor looked at them and said, "Ah, you poor perishin' tikes!" and threw them his last cigarettes.

They taught me a lot, those men. Their extraordinary acceptation of unpleasant conditions, their quickness to resent injustice and speak of it at once, their continual cheeriness, always ready to sing, gave me something to compete with. On wet days of misery when I'd had no letters from home there were moments when I damned the war and thought with infinite regret of New York. But if these fellows could stick it, well, I'd had more advantages than they'd had and, by Jove, I was going to stick it too. It was a matter of personal pride.

Practically they taught me many things as well. It was there that they had the advantage of me. They knew how to wash shirts and socks and do all the menial work which I had never done. I had to learn. They knew how to dodge "fatigues" by removing themselves just one half-minute before the sergeant came looking for victims. It didn't take me long to learn that.

Then one saw gradually the social habit emerge, called "mucking in." Two men became pals and paired off, sharing tobacco and pay and saddle soap and so on. For a time I "mucked in" with Sailor — he was always called Sailor — and perforce learned the song about the Rabelaisian donkey. I've forgotten it now. Perhaps it's just as well. Then when the squadron was divided up into troops Sailor and I were not in the same troop and I had to muck in with an ex-groom. He was the only man who did not use filthy language.

It's odd about that language habit. While in the ranks I never caught it, perhaps because I considered myself a bit above that sort of thing. It was so childish and unsatisfying. But since I have been an officer I think I could sometimes have almost challenged the sergeant major!

7.

As soon as one had settled into the routine the days began to roll by with a monotony that was, had we only known it, the beginning of knowledge. Some genius has defined war as "months of intense boredom punctuated by moments of intense fear." We had reached the first stage. It was when the day's work was done that the devil stalked into one's soul and began asking insidious questions. The work itself was hard, healthy, of real enjoyment. Shall I ever forget those golden autumn dawns

THE RANKS

when I rode out, a snorting horse under me, upon the swelling downs, the uplands touched by the rising sun; but in the hollows the feathery tops of trees poked up through the mist which lay in velvety clouds and everywhere a filigree of silver cobwebs, like strung seed pearls. It was with the spirit of crusaders that we galloped cross-country with slung lances, or charged in line upon an imaginary foe with yells that would demoralise him before our lance points should sink into his fat stomach. The good smells of earth and saddlery and horse flesh, the lance points winking in the sun, were all the outward signs of great romance and one took a deep breath of the keen air and thanked God to be in it. One charged dummies with sword and lance and hacked and stabbed them to bits. One leaped from one's horse at the canter and lined a bank with rifles while the numbers three in each section galloped the horses to a flank under cover. One went over the brigade jumps in troop formation, taking pride in riding so that all horses jumped as one, a magnificent bit of team work that gave one a thrill.

It was on one of those early morning rides that Sailor earned undying fame. Remember that all of the work was done on empty stomachs before breakfast and that if we came back late, a frequent occurrence, we received only scraps and a curse from the cook. On the morning in question the sergeant major ordered the whole troop to unbuckle their stirrup leathers and drop them on the ground. We did so.

"Now," said he, "we're going to do a brisk little cross-country follow-my-leader. I'm the leader and (a slight pause with a flash from the steely eye) God help the weak-backed, herring-gutted sons of — who don't perishin' well line up when I give the order to halt. Half sections right! walk, march!"

We walked out of the barracks until we reached the edge of the downs and then followed such a ride as John Gilpin or the Baron Munchausen would have revelled in — perhaps. The sergeant major's horse could jump anything and what it couldn't jump it climbed over. It knew better than to refuse. We were indifferently mounted, some well, some badly. My own was a good speedy bay. The orders were to keep in half sections — two and two. For a straight half-mile we thundered across the level, drew rein slightly through a thick copse that lashed one's face with pine branches and then dropped over a precipice twenty feet deep. That was where the half-section business went to pieces, especially when the horses clambered up the other side. We had no stirrups. It was a case of remaining in the saddle somehow. Had I been alone I would have ridden five miles to avoid the places the sergeant major took us over, through, and under, — bramble hedges that tore one's clothes and hands, ditches that one had to ride one's horse at with both spurs, banks so steep that one almost expected the horse to come over backwards, spinneys where one had to lie down to avoid being swept off. At last, breathless, aching and exhausted, those of us who were left were halted and dismounted, while the sergeant major, who hadn't turned a hair, took note of who was missing.

Five unfortunates had not come in. The sergeant major cast an eye towards the open country and remained ominously silent. After about a quarter of an hour the five were seen to emerge at a walk from behind a spinney. They came trotting up, an anxious expression on their faces, all except Sailor, who grinned from ear to ear. Instead of being allowed to fall in with us they were made to halt and dismount by themselves, facing us. The sergeant major looked at them, slowly, with an infinite contempt, as they stood stiffly to attention. Then he began.

"Look at them!" he said to us. "Look at those five . . ." and so on in a stinging stream, beneath which their faces went white with anger.

As the sergeant major drew breath, Sailor stepped forward. He was no longer grinning from ear to ear. His face might have been cut out of stone and he looked at the sergeant major with a steady eye.

"That's all right, Sergeant Major," he said. "We're all that and a perishin' lot more perhaps but not you nor Jesus Christ is going to make me do a perishin' ride like that and come back to perishin' barracks and get no perishin' breakfast and go on perishin' parade again at nine with not a perishin' thing in my perishin' stomach."

"What do you mean?" asked the sergeant major.

"What I says," said Sailor, standing to his guns while we, amazed, expected him to be slain before our eyes. "Not a perishin' bit of breakfast do we get when we go back late."

"Is that true?" The sergeant major turned to us.

"Yes," we said, "perishin' true!"

"Mount!" ordered the sergeant major without another word and we trotted straight back to barracks. By the time we'd watered, off-saddled and fed the horses we were as usual twenty minutes late for breakfast. But this morning the sergeant major, with a face like a black cloud, marched us into the dining hall and up to the cook's table.

We waited, breathless with excitement. The cook was in the kitchen, a dirty fellow.

The sergeant major slammed the table with his whip. The cook came, wiping a chewing mouth with the back of his hand.

"Breakfast for these men, quick," said the sergeant major.

"All gone, sir," said the cook, "we can't —"

The sergeant major leaned over with his face an inch from the cook's. "Don't you perishin' well answer me back," he said, "or I'll put you somewhere where the Almighty couldn't get you out until I say so. Breakfast for these men, you fat, chewing swine, or I'll come across the table and cut your tripes out with my riding whip and cook *them* for breakfast! Jump, you foul-feeder!" and down came the whip on the table like a pistol shot.

The cook swallowed his mouthful whole and retired, emerging presently with plenty of excellent breakfast and hot tea. We laughed.

"Now," said the sergeant major, "if you don't

get as good a breakfast as this to-morrow and every to-morrow, tell me, and I'll drop this lying bastard into his own grease trap."

Sailor got drunk that night. We paid.

8.

The evenings were the hardest part. There was only Bucks to talk to, and it was never more than twice a week that we managed to get together. Generally one was more completely alone than on a desert island, a solitude accentuated by the fact that as soon as one ceased the communion of work which made us all brothers on the same level, they dropped back, for me at least, into a seething mass of rather unclean humanity whose ideas were not mine, whose language and habits never ceased to jar upon one's sensitiveness. There was so little to do. The local music hall, intensely fifth rate, only changed its programme once a week. The billiard tables in the canteen had an hour-long waiting list always.

The Y.M.C.A. hadn't developed in those early days to its present manifold excellence. There was no gymnasium. The only place one had was one's bed in the barrack room on which one could read or write, not alone, because there was always a shouting incoming and outgoing crowd and cross fire of elementary jokes and horseplay. It seemed that there was never a chance of being alone, of escaping from this "lewd and licentious soldiery." There were times when the desert island called irresistibly in this eternal isolation of mind but not of body.

All that one had left behind, even the times when one was bored and out of temper, because perhaps one was off one's drive at the Royal and Ancient, or some other trivial thing like that, became so glorious in one's mind that the feel of the barrack blanket was an agony. Had one *ever* been bored in that other life? Had one been touchy and said sarcastic things that were meant to hurt? Could it be possible that there was anything in that other world for which one wouldn't barter one's soul now? How little one had realised, appreciated, the good things of that life! One accepted them as a matter of course, as a matter of right.

Now in the barrack-room introspections their real value stood out in the limelight of contrast and one saw oneself for the first time: a rather selfish, indifferent person, thoughtless, hurrying along the road of life with no point of view of one's own, doing things because everybody else did them, accepting help carelessly, not realising that other people might need one's help in return, content with a somewhat shallow second-hand philosophy because untried in the fire of reality. This was reality, this barrack life. This was the first time one had been up against facts, the first time it was a personal conflict between life and oneself with no mother or family to fend off the unpleasant; a fact that one hadn't attempted to grasp.

The picture of oneself was not comforting. To find out the truth about oneself is always like taking a pill without its sugar coating; and it was doubly bitter in those surroundings.

Hitherto one had never been forced to do the unpleasant. One simply avoided it. Now one had to go on doing it day after day without a hope of escape, without any more alleviation than a very occasional week-end leave. Those week-ends were like a mouthful of water to Dives in the flames of hell, — but which made the flames all the fiercer afterwards! One prayed for them and loathed them.

The beating heart with which one leaped out of a taxi in London and waited on the doorstep of home, heaven. The glory of a clean body and more particularly, clean hands. It was curious how the lack of a bath ceased after a time to be a dreadful thing but the impossibility of keeping one's hands clean was always a poignant agony. They were always dirty, with cracked nails and a cut or two, and however many times they were scrubbed, they remained appalling. But at home on leave, with hot water and stacks of soap and much manicuring, they did not at least make one feel uncomfortable.

The soft voices and laughter of one's people, their appearance — just to be in the same room, silent with emotion — God, will one ever forget it? Thin china to eat off, a flower on the table, soft lights, a napkin. — The little ones who came and fingered one's bandolier and cap badge and played with one's spurs with their tiny, clean hands — one was almost afraid to touch them, and when they puckered up their tiny mouths to kiss one good night. — I wonder whether they ever knew how near to tears that rough looking soldier-man was?

And then in what seemed ten heart-beats one was saying good-by to them all. Back to barracks again by way of Waterloo and the last train at 9 P.M. — its great yellow lights and awful din, its surging crowd of drunken soldiers and their girls who yelled and hugged and screamed up and down the platform, and here and there an officer diving hurriedly into a first-class compartment. Presently whistles blew and one found oneself jammed into a carriage with about twelve other soldiers who fought to lean out of the window and see the last of their girls until the train had panted its way out of the long platform. Then the foul reek of Woodbine cigarettes while they discussed the sexual charms of those girls — and then a long snoring chorus for hours into the night, broken only by some one being sick from overmuch beer.

The touch of the rosebud mouth of the baby girl who had kissed me good-by was still on my lips.

9.

It was in the first week of November that, having been through an exhaustive musketry course in addition to all the other cavalry work, we were "passed out" by the Colonel. I may mention in passing that in October, 1914, the British Cavalry were armed, for the first time in history, with bayonets in addition to lance, sword and rifle. There was much sarcastic reference to "towies", "foot-sloggers", "P.B.I." — all methods of the mounted man to designate infantry; and when an infantry sergeant was lent to teach us bayonet

THE RANKS

fighting it seemed the last insult, even to us recruits, so deeply was the cavalry spirit already ingrained in us.

The "passing out" by the Colonel was a day in our lives. It meant that, if successful, we were considered good enough to go and fight for our country: France was the Mecca of each of us.

The day in question was bright and sunny with a touch of frost which made the horses blow and dance when, with twinkling lance-points at the carry, we rode out with the sergeant major, every bright part of our equipment polished for hours overnight in the barrack room amid much excited speculation as to our prospects.

The sergeant major was going to give us a half-hour's final rehearsal of all our training before the Colonel arrived. Nothing went right and he damned and cursed without avail, until at last he threatened to ride us clean off the plain and lose us. It was very depressing. We knew we'd done badly, in spite of all our efforts, and when we saw, not far off, the Colonel, the Major and the Adjutant, with a group of other people riding up to put us through our paces, there wasn't a heart that didn't beat faster in hope or despair. We sat to attention like Indians while the officers rode round us, inspecting the turnout.

Then the Colonel expressed the desire to see a little troop drill.

The sergeant major cleared his throat and like an 18-pounder shell the order galvanised us into action. We wheeled and formed and spread out and reformed without a hitch and came to a halt in perfect dressing in front of the Colonel again, without a fault. Hope revived in despairing chests.

Then the Colonel ordered us over the jumps in half sections, and at the order each half section started away on the half-mile course — walk, trot, canter, jump, steady down to trot, canter, jump — *e da capo* right round about a dozen jumps, each one over a different kind of obstacle, each half section watched far more critically perhaps by the rest of the troop than by the officers. My own mount was a bay mare which I'd ridden half a dozen times. When she liked she could jump anything. Sometimes she didn't like.

This day I was taking no chances and drove home both spurs at the first jump. My other half section was a lance corporal. His horse was slow, preferring to consider each jump before it took it.

Between jumps, without moving our heads and looking straight in front of us, we gave each other advice and encouragement.

Said he, "Not so perishin' fast. Keep dressed, can't you."

Said I, "Wake your old blighter up! What've you got spurs on for. — Hup! Over. Steady, man, steady."

Said he, "Nar, then, like as we are. Knee to knee. Let's show 'em what the perishin' Kitchener's mob perishin' well *can* do." And without a refusal we got round and halted in our places.

When we'd all been round, the Colonel, with a faint smile on his face, requested the sergeant major to take us round as a troop — sixteen lancers knee to knee in the front rank and the same number behind.

It happened that I was the centre of the front rank — technically known as centre guide — whose job it was to keep four yards from the tail of the troop leader and on whom the rest of the front rank "dressed."

When we were well away from the officers and about to canter at the first jump the sergeant major's head turned over his shoulder.

"Oh, *you*'re centre guide, Gibbs, are you! Well, you keep your distance proper, that's all, and by Christ, if you refuse —"

I don't know what fate he had in store for me had I missed a jump but there I was with a knee on either side jammed painfully hard against mine as we came to the first jump. It was the man on either flank of the troop who had the most difficult job. The jumps were only just wide enough and they had to keep their horses from swinging wide of the wings. It went magnificently. Sixteen horses as one in both ranks rose to every jump, settled down and dressed after each and went round the course without a hitch, refusal or fall, and at last we sat at attention facing the Colonel, awaiting the verdict which would either send us back for further training or out to — what? Death, glory, or maiming?

The Major looked pleased and twisted his moustache with a grin. He had handled our squadron and on the first occasion of his leading us in a charge, he in front with drawn sword, we thundering behind with lances menacing his back in a glittering row, we got so excited that we broke ranks and flowed round him, yelling like cowboys. How he damned us!

The Colonel made a little speech and complimented us on our work and the sergeant major for having trained us so well, — us, the first of Kitchener's "mob" to be ready. Very nice things he said and our hearts glowed with appreciation and excitement. We sat there without a movement but our chests puffed out like a row of pouter pigeons.

At last he saluted us — saluted *us*, he, the Colonel — and the officers rode away, — the Major hanging behind a little to say with a smile that was worth all the cursings the sergeant major had ever given us, "Damn good, you fellows! *Damn* good!" We would have followed him to hell and back at that moment.

And then the sergeant major turned his horse and faced us. "You may *think* you're perishin' good soldiers after all that, but by Christ, I've never seen such a perishin' awful exhibition of carpet-baggers."

But there was an unusual twinkle in his eye and for the first time in those two months of training he let us "march at ease", *i.e.*, smoke and talk, on the way back to stables.

10.

That was the first half of the ordeal.

The second half took place in the afternoon in the barrack square when we went through lance drill and bayonet exercises while the Colonel and the officers walked round and discussed us. At last we were dismissed, trained men, recruits no longer; and didn't we throw our chests out in the canteen that night! It made me feel that the Nobel prize was futile beside the satisfaction of being a fully trained trooper in His Majesty's Cavalry, and in a crack regiment too, which had already shown the Boche that the "contemptible little army" had more "guts" than the Prussian Guards regiments and anything else they liked to chuck in.

I foregathered with Bucks that night and told him all about it. Our ways had seemed to lie apart during those intensive days, and it was only on Sundays that we sometimes went for long cross-country walks with biscuits and apples in our pockets if we were off duty. About once a week too we made a point of going to the local music hall where red-nosed comedians knocked each other about and fat ladies in tights sang slushy love songs; and with the crowd we yelled choruses and ate vast quantities of chocolate.

Two other things occurred during those days which had an enormous influence on me; one indeed altered my whole career in the army.

The first occurrence was the arrival in a car one evening of an American girl whom I'd known in New York. It was about a week after my arrival at Tidworth. She, it appeared, was staying with friends about twenty miles away.

The first thing I knew about it was when an orderly came into stables about 4.30 P.M. on a golden afternoon and told me that I was wanted at once at the Orderly Room.

"What for?" said I, a little nervous.

The Orderly Room was where all the scallawags were brought up before the Colonel for their various crimes, — and I made a hasty examination of conscience.

However, I put on my braces and tunic and ran across the square. There in a car was the American girl whom I had endeavoured to teach golf in the days immediately previous to my enlistment. "Come on out and have a picnic with me," said she. "I've got some perfectly luscious things in a basket."

The idea was heavenly, but it occurred to me I ought to get permission. So I went into the Orderly Room.

There were two officers and a lot of sergeants. I tiptoed up to a sergeant and explaining that a lady had come over to see me, asked if I could get out of camp for half an hour? I was very raw in those days, — half an hour!

The sergeant stared at me. Presumably ladies in motor cars didn't make a habit of fetching cavalry privates. It wasn't "laid down" in the drill book. However, he went over to one of the officers, — the Adjutant, I discovered later.

The Adjutant looked me up and down as I repeated my request, asked me my name and which ride I was in and finally put it to the other officer, who said "yes" without looking up. So I thanked the Adjutant, clicked to the salute and went out. As I walked round the front of the car, while the chauffeur cranked up, the door of the Orderly Room opened and the Adjutant came on to the step. He took a good look at the American girl and said, "Oh — er — Gibbs! You can make it an hour if you like."

It may amuse him to know, if the slaughter hasn't claimed him, that I made it exactly sixty minutes, much as I should have liked to make it several hours, and was immensely grateful to him both for the extra half hour and for the delightful touch of humour.

What a picnic it was! We motored away from that place and all its roughness and took the basket under a spinney in the afternoon sun which touched everything in a red glow.

It wasn't only tea she gave me, but sixty precious minutes of great friendship, letting fall little remarks which helped me to go back all the more determined to stick to it. She renewed my faith in myself and gave me renewed courage, — for which I was unable to thank her. We British are so accursedly tongue-tied in these matters. I did try, but of course made a botch of it.

There are some things which speech cannot deal with. Your taking me out that day, oh, American girl, and the other days later, are numbered among them.

11.

The other occurrence was also brought about by a woman, *the* woman for whom I joined up. It was a Sunday morning on which fortunately I was not detailed for any fatigues and she came to take me out to lunch. We motored to Marlborough, lunched at the hotel and after visiting a racing stable some distance off came back to the hotel for tea, a happy day unflecked by any shadow. In the corner of the dining room were two officers with two ladies. I, in the bandolier and spurs of a trooper, sat with my back to them and my friend told me that they seemed to be eyeing me and making remarks. It occurred to me that as I had no official permission to be away from Tidworth they might possibly be going to make trouble. How little I knew what was in their minds. When we'd finished and got up to go one of the officers came across as we were going out of the room and said, "May I speak to you a moment?"

We both stopped. "I see you're wearing the numerals of my regiment," said he and went on to ask why I was in the ranks, why I hadn't asked for a commission, and strongly advised me to do so.

I told him that I hadn't ever thought of it because I knew nothing about soldiering and hadn't the faintest idea of whether I should ever be any good as an officer. He waved that aside and advised me to apply. Then he added that he himself was going out to France one day in the following week and would I like to go as his servant? Would I? My whole idea was to get to France; and this happened before I had been passed out by the Colonel. So he took down my name and particulars and said he would ask for me when he came to Tidworth, which he proposed to do in two days' time.

Whether he ever came or not I do not know. I

never saw him again. Nor did I take any steps with regard to a commission. My friend and I talked it over and I remember rather laughing at the idea of it.

Not so she, however. About a fortnight later I was suddenly sent for by the Colonel.

"I hear you've applied for a commission," said he.

It came like a bolt from the blue. But through my brain flashed the meeting in the Marlborough Hotel and I saw in it the handiwork of my friend.

So I said, "Yes, sir."

He then asked me where I was educated and whether I spoke French and what my job was in civil life, and finally I was sent off to fill up a form and then to be medically examined.

And there the matter ended. I went on with the daily routine, was passed out by the Colonel and a very few days after that heard the glorious news that we were going out as a draft to France on active service.

We were all in bed in the barrack room one evening when the door opened and a sergeant came in and flicked on the electric light, which had only just been turned out.

"Wake up, you bloodthirsty warriors," he cried. "Wake up. You're for a draft to-morrow, all of you on this list," and he read out the names of all of us in the room who had been passed out. "Parade at the Quartermaster's store at nine o'clock in the morning." And out went the light, and the door slammed and a burst of cheering went up.

And while I lay on my "biscuits", imagining

France and hearing in my mind the thunder of guns and wondering what our first charge would be like, the machinery which my friend had set in motion was rolling slowly (shades of the War Office!) but surely. My name had been submerged in the "usual channels", but was receiving first aid, all unknown to me, of a most vigorous description.

12.

Shall I *ever* forget that week-end, with all its strength of emotions running the gamut from exaltation to blank despair and back again to the wildest enthusiasm?

We paraded at the Quartermaster's stores and received each a kit bag, two identity discs — the subject of many gruesome comments — a jackknife, mess tin, water bottle, haversack, and underclothes. Thus were we prepared for the killing.

Then the Major appeared and we fell in before him.

"Now which of you men want to go to the front?" said he. "Any man who wants to, take one pace forward."

As one man the whole lot of us, about thirty, took one pace forward.

The Major smiled. "Good," said he. "Any man *not* want to go — prove."

No man proved.

"Well, look here," said the Major, "I hate to disappoint anybody, but only twenty-eight of you can go. You'll have to draw lots."

Accordingly bits of paper were put into a hat,

thirty scraps of paper, two of them marked with crosses. Was it a sort of inverted omen that the two who drew the crosses would never find themselves under little mounds in France?

We drew in turn, excitement running high as paper after paper came out blank. My heart kicked within me. How I prayed not to draw a cross. But I did!

Speechless with despair the other man who drew a cross and I received the good-natured chaff of the rest.

I saw them going out, to leave this accursed place of boredom and make-believe, for the real thing, the thing for which we had slaved and sweated and suffered. We two were to be left. We weren't to go on sharing the luck with these excellent fellows united to us by the bonds of fellow-striving, whom we knew in sickness and health, drunk and sober.

We had to remain behind, eating our hearts out to wait for the next draft — a lot of men whom we did not know, strangers with their own jokes and habits — possibly a fortnight of hanging about. The day was a Friday and our pals were supposed to be going at any moment. The other unlucky man and myself came to the conclusion that consolation might be found in a long week-end leave and that if we struck while the iron of sympathy was hot the Major might be inclined to lend a friendly ear. This indeed he did and within an hour we were in the London train on that gloomy Friday morning, free as any civilian till midnight of the following Tuesday. Thus the Major's generosity. The only proviso was that we had both to leave telegraphic addresses in case —

But in spite of that glorious week-end in front of us, we refused to be consoled, yet, and insisted on telling the other occupants of the carriage of our rotten luck. We revelled in gloom and extraneous sympathy until Waterloo showed up in the murk ahead. Then I'm bound to confess my own mental barometer went up with a jump and I said good-by to my fellow lancer, who was off to pursue the light o' love in Stepney, with an impromptu Te Deum in my heart.

My brother, with whom I spent all my week-ends in those days, had a house just off the Park. He put in his time looking like a rather tired admiral, most of whose nights were passed looking for Zeppelins and yearning for them to come within range of his beloved "bundooks", which were in the neighbourhood of the Admiralty. Thither I went at full speed in a taxi — they still existed in those days — and proceeded to wallow in a hot bath, borrowing my brother's bath salts (or were they his wife's?), clean "undies" and hair juice with a liberal hand. It was a comic sight to see us out together in the crowded London streets, he all over gold lace, me just a Tommy with a cheap swagger stick under my arm. Subalterns, new to the game, saluted him punctiliously. I saluted them. And when we met generals or a real admiral we both saluted together. The next afternoon, Saturday, at tea time a telegram came. We were deep in armchairs in front of a gorgeous fire, with muffins sitting in the hearth and softly shaded electric lights throwing a glow over pictures and backs of books and the piano which, after the barrack room, made up as near heaven as I've ever been. The telegram was for me, signed by the Adjutant.

"Return immediately."

It was the echo of a far-off boot and saddle. — I took another look round the room. Should I ever see it again? My brother's eye met mine and we rose together.

"Well, I must be getting along," said I. "Cheero, old son."

"I'll come with you to the station," said he.

I shook my head. "No, please don't bother. — Don't forget to write."

"Rather not. — Good luck, old man."

"Thanks."

We went down to his front door. I put on my bandolier and picked up my haversack.

"Well — so long."

We shook hands.

"God bless you."

I think we said it together and then the door closed softly behind me.

Partir, c'est mourir un peu. — Un peu. — God!

13.

The next day, Sunday, we all hung about in a sort of uneasy waiting, without any orders.

It gave us all time to write letters home. If I rightly remember, absolute secrecy was to be maintained, so we were unable even to hint at our departure or to say good-by. It was probably just as well, but they were difficult letters to achieve. So we tied one identity disc to our braces and slung the other round our necks on a string and did rather more smoking than usual.

Next morning, however, all was bustle. The orders had come in and we paraded in full fighting kit in front of the guardroom.

The Colonel came on parade and in a silence that was only broken by the beating of our hearts told us we were going out to face the Boche for our King and Country's sake, to take our places in the ranks of a very gallant regiment, and he wished us luck.

We gave three rather emotional cheers and marched away with our chins high, followed by the cheers of the whole barracks who had turned out to see us off. Just as we were about to entrain, the Major trotted up on his big charger and shook us individually by the hand and said he wished he were coming with us. His coming was a great compliment and every man of us appreciated it to the full.

The harbour was a wonderful sight when we got in late that afternoon. Hundreds of arc lights lit up numbers of ships and at each ship was a body of troops entraining, — English, Scotch and Irish, cavalry, gunners and infantry. At first glance it appeared a hopeless tangle, a babel of yelling men all getting into each other's way. But gradually the eye tuned itself up to the endless kaleidoscope and one saw that absolute order prevailed. Every single man was doing a job and the work never ceased.

We were not taking horses and marched in the charge of an officer right through the busy crowd and halted alongside a boat which already seemed packed with troops. But after a seemingly endless wait we were marched on board and, dodging men stripped to the waist who were washing in buckets, we climbed down iron ladders into the bowels of the hold, were herded into a corner and told to make ourselves comfortable. Tea would be dished out in half an hour.

Holds are usually iron. This was. Furthermore it had been recently red-leaded. Throw in a strong suggestion of garlic and more than a hint of sea-sickness and you get some idea of the perfume that greeted us, friendly-like.

The comments, entirely good-natured, were unprintable. There were no bunks. We had one blanket each and a greatcoat. My thoughts turned to the first-class stateroom of the *Caronia* in which only four months previously I had had no thought of war. The accepted form of romance and the glamour of war have been altered. There are no cheering crowds and fluttering handkerchiefs and brass bands. The new romance is the light of the moon flickering on darkened ships that creep one after the other through the mine barrier out into deep waters, turning to silver the foam ripped by the bows, picking out the white expressionless faces of silent thousands of khaki-clad men lining the rail, following the will-o'-the-wisp which beckoned to a strange land.

How many of them knew what they were going

to fight for? How many of them realised the unforgetable hell they were to be engulfed in, the sacrifice which they so readily made of youth, love, ambition, life itself — and to what end? To give the lie to one man who wished to alter the face of the world? To take the part of the smaller country trampled and battered by the bully? To save from destruction the greasy skins of dirty-minded politicians, thinking financially or even imperially, but staying at home?

God knows why most of us went.

But the sting of the Channel wind as we set our faces to the enemy drove all reason from the mind and filled it with a mighty exultation. If Death were there to meet us, well, it was all in the game.

14.

We climbed up from the hold next morning to find ourselves in Portsmouth harbour. The word submarines ran about the decks. There we waited all day, and again under cover of dark made our way out to open water, reaching Havre about six o'clock next morning.

We were marched ashore in the afternoon and transferred to another boat. Nobody knew our destination and the wildest guesses were made. The new boat was literally packed. There was no question of going down into a hold. We were lucky to get sufficient deck space to lie down on, and just before getting under way, it began to rain. There were some London Scottish at our end of the deck who, finding that we had exhausted our rations, shared theirs with us. There was no question of sleeping. It was too cold and too uncomfortable. So we sang. There must have been some two thousand of us on board and all those above deck joined in choruses of all the popular songs as they sat hunched up or lying like rows of sardines in the rain. Dawn found us shivering, passing little villages on either bank of the river as we neared Rouen. The early-rising inhabitants waved and their voices came across the water, "*Vivent les Anglais! A bas les Boches!*" And the sun came out as we waved our shaving brushes at them in reply. We eventually landed in the old cathedral city and formed up and marched away across the bridge, with everybody cheering and throwing flowers until we came to La Bruyère camp.

Hundreds of bell tents, thousands of horses, and mud over the ankles! That was the first impression of the camp. It wasn't until we were divided off into tents and had packed our equipment tight round the tent pole that one had time to notice details.

We spent about nine days in La Bruyère camp and we groomed horses from 6 A.M. to 6 P.M. every day, wet or fine. The lines were endless and the mud eternal. It became a nightmare, relieved only by the watering of the horses. The water was about a kilometer and a half distant. We mounted one horse and led two more each and in an endless line splashed down belly-deep in mud past the hospital where the slightly wounded leaned over the rail and exchanged badinage. Sometimes the sisters gave us cigarettes, for which we called down blessings on their heads.

It rained most of the time and we stood ankle-deep all day in the lines, grooming and shovelling away mud. But all the time jokes were hurled from man to man although the rain dripped down their faces and necks. We slept, if I remember rightly, twenty men in a tent, head outwards, feet to the pole, piled on top of each other, — wet, hot, aching. Oh, those feet, the feet of tired heroes, but unwashed. And it was impossible to open the tent flap because of the rain. — Fortunately it was cold those nights and one smoked right up to the moment of falling asleep. Only two per cent of passes to visit the town were allowed, but the camp was only barb-wired and sentried on one side. The other side was open to the pine woods, and very pretty they were as we went cross-country towards the village of St. Etienne from which a tramcar ran into Rouen in about twenty minutes. The military police posted at the entrance to the town either didn't know their job or were good fellows of Nelsonian temperament, content to turn a blind eye. From later experience I judge that the former was probably the case. Be that as it may, several hundreds of us went in without official permission nearly every night and, considering all things, were most orderly. Almost the only man I ever saw drunk was, paradoxically enough, a policeman. He tried to place my companion and myself under arrest, but was so far gone that he couldn't write down our names and numbers and we got off. The hand of Fate was distinctly

THE RANKS

in it for had I been brought up and crimed for being loose in the town without leave it might have counted against me when my commission was being considered.

One evening, the night before we left for the front, we went down for a bath, the last we should get for many a day. On our way we paid a visit to the cathedral. It was good to get out of the crowded streets into the vast gloom punctured by pin points of candlelight, with only faint footfalls and the squeak of a chair to disturb the silence. For perhaps half an hour we knelt in front of the high altar, — quite unconsciously the modern version of that picture of a knight in armour kneeling, holding up his sword as a cross before the altar. It is called the Vigil, I believe. We made a little vigil in khaki and bandoliers and left the cathedral with an extraordinary confidence in the morrow. There was a baby being baptised at the font. It was an odd thing seeing that baby just as we passed out. It typified somewhat the reason of our going forth to fight.

The bath was amusing. The doors were being closed as we arrived and I had just the time to stick my foot in the crack, much to the annoyance of the attendant. I blarneyed him in French and at last pushed into the hall, only to be greeted by a cry of indignation from the lady in charge of the ticket office. She was young, however, and pretty, and, determined to get a bath, I played upon her feelings to the extent of my vocabulary. At first she was adamant. The baths were closed. I pointed out that the next morning we were going to the front to fight for France. She refused to believe it. I asked her if she had a brother. She said she hadn't. I congratulated her on not being agonised by the possibilities of his death from hour to hour. She smiled.

My heart leaped with hope and I reminded her that as we were possibly going to die for her the least she could do was to let us die clean. She looked me straight in the eye. There was a twinkle in hers. "You will not die," she said. Somehow one doesn't associate the selling of bath tickets with the calling of prophet. But she combined the two. And the bath was gloriously hot.

15.

That nine days at La Bruyère did not teach us very much, — not even the realisation of the vital necessity of patience. We looked upon each day as wasted because we weren't up the line. Everywhere were preparations of war, but we yearned for the sound of guns. Even the blue-clad figures who exchanged jokes with us over the hospital railing conveyed nothing of the grim tragedy of which we were only on the fringe. They were mostly convalescent. It is only the shattered who are being pulled back to life by a thread who make one curse the war. We looked about like new boys in a school, interested but knowing nothing of the workings, reading none of the signs. This all bored us. We wanted the line with all the persistence of the completely ignorant.

The morning after our bath we got it. There was much bustle and running and cursing and finally we had our saddles packed, and a day's rations in our haversacks and a double feed in the nose bags.

The cavalry man in full marching order bears a strange resemblance to a travelling ironmonger and rattles like the banging of old tins. The small man has almost to climb up the near foreleg of his horse, so impossible is it to get a leg anywhere near the stirrup iron with all his gear on. My own method was to stick the lance in the ground by the butt, climb with infinite labour and heavings into the saddle and come back for the lance when arranged squarely on the horse.

Eventually everything was accomplished and we were all in the saddle and were inspected to see that we were complete in every detail. Then we rode out of that muddy camp in sections — four abreast — and made our way down towards the station. It was a real touch of old-time romance, that ride. The children ran shouting, and people came out of the shops to wave their hands and give us fruit and wish us luck, and the girls blew kisses, and through the hubbub the clatter of our horses over the cobbles and the jingle of stirrup striking stirrup made music that stirred one's blood.

There was a long train of cattle trucks waiting for us at the station and into these we put our horses, eight to each truck, fastened by their ropes from the head collar to a ring in the roof. In the two-foot space between the two lots of four horses facing each other were put the eight saddles and blankets and a bale of hay.

Two men were detailed to stay with the horses in each truck while the rest fell in and were marched away to be distributed among the remaining empty trucks. I didn't altogether fancy the idea of looking after eight frightened steeds in that two-foot alleyway, but before I could fall in with the rest I was detailed by the sergeant.

That journey was a nightmare. My fellow stableman was a brainless idiot who knew even less about the handling of horses than I did.

The train pulled out in the growing dusk of a cold November evening, the horses snorting and starting at every jolt, at every signal and telegraph pole that we passed. When they pawed with their front feet we, sitting on the bale of hay, had to dodge with curses. There was no sand or bedding and it was only the tightness with which they were packed together that kept them on their feet. Every light that flashed by drew frightened snorts. We spent an hour standing among them, saying soothing things and patting their necks. We tried closing the sliding doors, but at the end of five minutes the heat splashed in great drops of moisture from the roof and the smell was impossible. Eventually I broke the bale of hay and threw some of that down to give them a footing.

There was a lamp in the corner of the truck. I told the other fellow to light it. He said he had no matches. So I produced mine and discovered that I had only six left. We used five to find out that

THE RANKS 53

the lamp had neither oil nor wick. We had just exhausted our vocabularies over this when the train entered a tunnel. At no time did the train move at more than eight miles an hour and the tunnel seemed endless. At times I still dream of that tunnel and wake up in a cold sweat.

As our truck entered, great billows of smoke rushed into it. The eight horses tried as one to rear up and crashed their heads against the roof. The noise was deafening and it was pitch dark. I felt for the door and slid it shut while the horses blew and tugged at their ropes in a blind panic. Then there was a heavy thud, followed by a yell from the other man and a furious squealing.

"Are you all right?" I shouted, holding on to the head collar of the nearest beast.

"Christ!" came the answer. "There's a 'orse down and I'm jammed up against the door 'ere. Come and get me out, for Christ's sake."

My heart was pumping wildly.

The smoke made one gasp and there was a furious stamping and squealing and a weird sort of blowing gurgle which I could not define.

Feeling around I reached the next horse's head collar and staggered over the pile of saddlery. As I leaned forward to get to the third, something whistled past my face and I heard the sickening noise of a horse's hoof against another horse, followed by a squeal. I felt blindly and touched a flank where a head should have been. One of them had swung round and was standing with his fore feet on the fallen horse and was lashing out with both hind feet, while my companion was jammed against the wall of the truck by the fallen animal presumably.

And still that cursed tunnel did not come to an end. I yelled again to see if he were all right and his fruity reply convinced me that at least there was no damage done. So I patted the kicker and squeezed in to his head and tried to get him round. It was impossible to get past, over or under, and the brute wouldn't move. There was nothing for it but to remain as we were until out of the tunnel. And then I located the gurgle. It was the fallen horse, tied up short by the head collar to the roof, being steadily strangled. It was impossible to cut the rope. A loose horse in that infernal mêlée was worse than one dead — or at least choking. But I cursed and pulled and heaved in my efforts to get him up.

By this time there was no air and one's lungs seemed on the point of bursting. The roof rained sweat upon our faces and every moment I expected to get a horse's hoof in my face.

How I envied that fellow jammed against the truck. At last we came out into the open again, and I slid back the door, and shoved my head outside and gulped in the fresh air. Then I untied the kicker and somehow, I don't know how, got him round into his proper position and tied him up, with a handful of hay all round to steady their nerves.

The other man was cursing blue blazes all this time, but eventually I cut the rope of the fallen horse, and after about three false starts he got on his feet again and was retied. The man was not hurt. He had been merely wedged. So we gave some more hay all round, cursed a bit more to ease ourselves and then went to the open door for air. A confused shouting from the next truck reached us. After many yells we made out the following, "Pass the word forward that the train's on fire."

All the stories I'd ever heard of horses being burnt alive raced through my brain in a fraction of a second.

We leaned to the truck in front and yelled. No answer. The truck was shut.

"Climb on the roof," said I, "and go forward." The other man obeyed and disappeared into the dark.

Minutes passed, during which I looked back and saw a cloud of smoke coming out of a truck far along the train.

Then a foot dropped over from the roof and my companion climbed back.

"Better go yourself," he said. "I carnt mike 'im understand. He threw lumps of coal at me from the perishin' engine."

So I climbed on to the roof of the swaying coach, got my balance and walked forward till a yard-wide jump to the next roof faced me in the darkness.

"Lord!" thought I, "if I didn't know that other lad had been here, I shouldn't care about it. However —" I took a strong leap and landed, slipping to my hands and knees.

There were six trucks between me and the engine and the jumps varied in width. I got there all right and screamed to the engine driver, "*Incendie! — Incendie!*"

He paused in the act of throwing coal at me and I screamed again. Apparently he caught it, for first peering back along all the train, he dived at a lever and the train screamed to a halt. I was mighty thankful. I hadn't looked forward to going back the way I came and I climbed quickly down to the rails. A sort of guard with a lantern and an official appearance climbed out of a box of sorts and demanded to know what was the matter, and when I told him, called to me to follow and began doubling back along the track.

I followed. The train seemed about a mile long but eventually we reached a truck, full of men and a rosy glare, from which a column of smoke bellied out. The guard flashed his lantern in.

The cursed thing wasn't on fire at all. The men were burning hay in a biscuit tin, singing merrily, just keeping themselves warm.

I thought of the agony of those jumps in the dark from roof to roof and laughed. But I got my own back. They couldn't see us in the dark, so in short snappy sentences I ordered them to put the fire out immediately. And they thought I was an officer and did so.

16.

The rest of the night passed in an endeavour to get to sleep in a sitting position on the bale of hay. From time to time one dozed off, but it was too cold and the infernal horses would keep on pawing.

Never was a night so long and it wasn't till eight o'clock in the morning that we ran into Hazebrouck

THE RANKS

and stopped. By this time we were so hungry that food was imperative. On the station was a great pile of rifles and bandoliers and equipment generally, all dirty and rusty, and in a corner some infantry were doing something round a fire.

"Got any tea, chum?" said I.

He nodded a Balaklava helmet.

We were on him in two leaps with extended dixies. It saved our lives, that tea. We were chilled to the bone and had only bully beef and biscuits, of course, but I felt renewed courage surge through me with every mouthful.

"What's all that stuff?" I asked, pointing to the heap of equipments.

"Dead men's weapons," said he, lighting a "gasper." Somehow it didn't sound real. One couldn't picture all the men to whom that had belonged dead. Nor did it give one anything of a shock. One just accepted it as a fact without thinking, "I wonder whether *my* rifle and sword will ever join that heap?" The idea of my being *killed* was absurd, fantastic. Any of these others, yes, but somehow not myself. Never at any time have I felt anything but extreme confidence in the fact — yes, fact — that I should come through, in all probability, unwounded. I thought about it often but always with the certainty that nothing would happen to me.

I decided that *if* I were killed I should be most frightfully angry! There were so many things to be done with life, so much beauty to be found, so many ambitions to be realised, that it was impossible that I should be killed. All this dirt and discomfort was just a necessary phase to the greater appreciation of everything.

I can't explain it. Perhaps there isn't any explanation. But never at any time have I seen the shell or bullet with my name on it, — as the saying goes. And yet somehow that pile of broken gear filled one with a sense of the pity of it all, the utter folly of civilization which had got itself into such an unutterable mess that blood-letting was the only way out. — I proceeded to strip to the waist and shave out of a horse-bucket of cold water.

There was a cold drizzle falling when at last we had watered the horses, fed and saddled them up, and were ready to mount. It increased to a steady downpour as we rode away in half sections and turned into a muddy road lined with the eternal poplar. In the middle of the day we halted, numbed through, on the side of a road, and watered the horses again, and snatched a mouthful of biscuit and bully and struggled to fill a pipe with icy fingers. Then on again into the increasing murk of a raw afternoon.

Thousands of motor lorries passed like an endless chain. Men muffled in greatcoats emerged from farmhouses and faintly far came the sound of guns.

The word went round that we were going up into the trenches that night. Heaven knows who started it, but I found it a source of spiritual exaltation that helped to conquer the discomfort of that ride. Every time a trickle ran down one's neck one thought, "It doesn't matter. This is the real thing. We

THE RANKS 59

are going up to-night," and visualised a Hun over the sights of one's rifle.

Presently the flames of fires lit up the murk and shadowy forms moved round them which took no notice of us as we rode by.

At last in pitch darkness we halted at a road crossing and splashed into a farmyard that was nearly belly deep in mud. Voices came through the gloom, and after some indecision and cursing we off-saddled in a stable lit by a hurricane lamp, hand-rubbed the horses, blanketed them and left them comfortable for the night.

We were given hot tea and bread and cheese and shepherded into an enormous barn piled high with hay. Here and there twinkled candles in biscuit tins and everywhere were men sitting and lying on the hay, the vague whiteness of their faces just showing. It looked extremely comfortable.

But when we joined them — the trench rumour was untrue — we found that the hay was so wet that a lighted match thrown on it fizzled and went out. The rain came through innumerable holes in the roof and the wind made the candles burn all one-sided. However, it was soft to lie on, and when my "chum" and I had got on two pairs of dry socks each and had snuggled down together with two blankets over our tunics and greatcoats, and mufflers round our necks, and Balaklava helmets over our heads we found we could sleep warm till reveille.

The sock question was difficult. One took off soaking boots and puttees at night and had to put them on again still soaking in the morning. The result was that by day our feet were always ice-cold and never dry. We never took anything else off except to wash, or to groom horses.

The next morning I had my first lesson in real soldiering. The results were curious.

The squadron was to parade in drill order at 9 A.M. We had groomed diligently in the chilly dawn. None of the horses had been clipped, so it consisted in getting the mud off rather than really grooming, and I was glad to see that my horse had stood the train journey and the previous day's ride without any damage save a slight rubbing of his tail. At about twenty minutes to nine, shaved and washed, I went to the stables to saddle up for the parade. Most of the others in that stable were nearly ready by the time I got there and to my dismay I found that they had used all my gear. There was nothing but the horse and the blanket left, — no saddle, no head collar and bit, no rifle, no sword, no lance. Everything had disappeared. I dashed round and tried to lay hands on some one else's property. They were too smart and eventually they all turned out, leaving me. The only saddle in the place hadn't been cleaned for months and I should have been ashamed to ride it. Then the sergeant appeared, a great, red-faced, bad-tempered-looking man.

I decided on getting the first blow in. So I went up and told him that all my things had been "pinched." Could he tell me where I could find some more?

His reply would have blistered the paint off a door. His adjectives concerning me made me want to hit him. But one cannot hit one's superior officer in the army — more's the pity — on occasions like that. So we had a verbal battle. I told him that if he didn't find me everything down to lance buckets I shouldn't appear on parade and that if he chose to put me under arrest, so much the better, as the Major would then find out how damned badly the sergeant ran his troop.

It was a good bluff. Bit by bit he hunted up a head collar, a saddle, sword, lance, etc. Needless to say they were all filthy and I wished all the bullets in Germany on the dirty dog who had pinched my clean stuff. However, I was on parade just half a minute before the Major came round to inspect us. He stopped at me, his eye taking in the rusty bit and stirrup irons, the coagulations on the bridle, the general damnableness of it all. It wasn't nice.

"Did you come in last night?" The voice was hard.

"Yes, sir."

"Did you come up from the base with your appointments in that state?"

"No, sir."

"What do you mean?"

The sergeant was looking apoplectic behind him.

"These aren't my things, sir," said I.

"Whose are they?"

"I don't know, sir."

"Where are your things?"

"They were in the stables at reveille, sir, but they'd all gone when I went to saddle up. The horse is the only thing I brought with me, sir."

The whole troop was sitting at attention, listening, and I hoped that the man who had stolen everything heard this dialogue and was quaking in his wet boots.

The Major turned. "What does this mean, Sergeant?"

There was a vindictive look in the sergeant's eye as he spluttered out an unconvincing reply that "these new fellows wanted nursemaids and weren't 'alf nippy enough in lookin' arter 'emselves."

The Major considered it for a moment, told me that I must get everything clean for the next parade and passed on.

At least I was not under arrest, but it wasn't good enough on the first morning to earn the Major's scorn through no fault of my own. I wanted some one's blood.

Each troop leader, a subaltern, was given written orders by the Major and left to carry them out. Our own troop leader didn't seem to understand his orders and by the time the other three troops had ridden away he was still reading his paper. The Major returned and explained, asked him if all was clear, and getting yes for an answer, rode off.

The subaltern then asked the sergeant if he had a map!

What was even more curious, the sergeant said yes. The subaltern said we had to get to a place called Flêtre within three quarters of an hour and they proceeded to try and find it on the sergeant's map without any success for perhaps five minutes.

During that time the troopers around me made remarks in undertones, most ribald remarks. We had come through Flêtre the previous day and I remembered the road. So I turned to a lance corporal on my right and said, "Look here, I know the way. Shall I tell him?"

"Yes, tell him for Christ's sake!" said the lance corporal. "It's too perishin' cold to go on sitting 'ere."

So I took a deep breath and all my courage in both hands and spoke. "I beg your pardon, sir," said I. "I know Flêtre."

The subaltern turned round on his horse. "Who knows the place?" he said.

"I do, sir," and I told him how to get there.

Without further comment he gave the word to advance in half sections and we left the parade ground, but instead of turning to the left as I had said, he led us straight on at a good sharp trot.

More than half an hour later, when we should have been at the pin point in Flêtre, the subaltern halted us at a crossroads in open country and again had a map consultation with the sergeant. Again it was apparently impossible to locate either the crossroads or the rendezvous.

But in the road were two peasants coming towards us. He waited till they came up and then asked them the way in bad German. They looked at him blankly, so he repeated his question in worse French. His pronunciation of Flêtre puzzled them but at last one of them guessed it and began a stream of explanations and pointings.

"What the hell are they talking about?" said the subaltern to the sergeant.

The lance corporal nudged me. "Did *you* understand?"

"Yes," said I.

"Tell him again," he said. "Go on."

So again I begged his pardon and explained what the peasants had told him. He looked at me for a moment oddly. I admit that it wasn't usual for a private to address his officer on parade without being first spoken to. But this was war, the world war, and the old order changeth. Anyhow I was told to ride in front of the troop as guide and did and brought the troop to the rendezvous about twenty minutes late.

The Major was not pleased.

Later in the day the subaltern came around the stables and, seeing me, stopped and said, "Oh — er — you!"

I came to attention behind the horse.

"What's your name?" said he.

I told him.

"Do you talk French?"

"Yes, sir."

"Where were you educated?"

"France and Oxford University, sir."

"Oh!" slightly surprised. "Er — all right, get on with your work" — and whether it was he or the sergeant I don't know, but I had four horses to groom that morning instead of two.

From that moment I decided to cut out being intelligent and remain what the French call a "simple" soldier.

By a strange coincidence there was a nephew of

THE RANKS

that subaltern in the Brigade of Gunners to which I was posted when I received a commission. It is curious how accurately nephews sum up uncles.

17.

When we did not go out on drill orders like that we began the day with what is called rough exercise. It was. In the foggy dawn, swathed in scarfs and Balaklava helmets, one folded one's blanket on the horse, bitted him, mounted, took another horse on either side and in a long column followed an invisible lance corporal across ploughed fields, over ditches, and along roads at a good stiff trot that jarred one's spine. It was generally raining and always so cold that one never had the use of either hands or feet. The result was that if one of the unbitted led horses became frolicsome it was even money that he would pull the rope out of one's hands and canter off blithely down the road, — for which one was cursed bitterly by the sergeant on one's return. The rest of the day was divided between stables and fatigues in that eternal heart-breaking mud. One laid brick paths and brushwood paths and within twenty-four hours they had disappeared under mud. It was shovelled away in sacks and wheelbarrows and it oozed up again as if by magic. One made herring-bone drains and they merged in the mud. There seemed to be no method of competing with it. In the stables the horses stood in it knee-deep. As soon as one had finished grooming, the brute seemed to take a diabolical pleasure in lying down in it. It became a nightmare.

The sergeant didn't go out of his way to make things easier for any of us and confided most of the dirtier, muddier jobs to me. There seemed to be always something unpleasant that required "intelligence", so he said, and in the words of the army I "clicked." The result was that I was happiest when I was on guard, a twenty-four-hour duty which kept me more or less out of the mud and entirely out of his way.

The first time I went on I was told by the N.C.O. in charge that no one was to come through the hedge that bounded the farm and the road after lights out and if any one attempted to do so I was to shoot on sight. So I marched up and down my short beat in the small hours between two and four, listening to the far-off muttering of guns and watching the Verey lights like a miniature firework display, praying that some spy would try and enter the gap in the hedge. My finger was never very far from the trigger and my beat was never more than two yards from the hedge. I didn't realise then that we were so far from the line that the chances of a strolling Hun were absurd. Looking back on it I am inclined to wonder whether the N.C.O. didn't tell me to shoot on sight because he knew that the sergeant's billet was down that road and the hedge was a short cut. The sergeant wasn't very popular.

There was an *estaminet* across the road from the farm and the officers had arranged for us to have the use of the big room. It was a godsend, that *estaminet*, with its huge stove nearly red-hot, its

THE RANKS

bowls of coffee and the single glass of raw cognac which they were allowed to sell us. The evenings were the only time one was ever warm and although there was nothing to read except some old and torn magazines we sat there in the fetid atmosphere just to keep warm.

The patron talked vile French but was a kindly soul, and his small boy Gaston, aged about seven, became a great friend of mine. He used to bring me my coffee, his tiny dirty hands only just big enough to hold the bowl, and then stand and talk while I drank it, calling me "thou."

"*T'es pas anglais, dis?*"

And I laughed and said I was French.

"*Alors comment qu' t'es avec eux, dis?*"

And when one evening he came across and looked over my shoulder as I was writing a letter he said, "*Qué que t'écris, dis?*"

I told him I was writing in English.

He stared at me and then called out shrilly, "*Papa! V'là l'Français qu'écrit en anglais!*"

He had seen the Boche, had little Gaston, and told me how one day the Uhlans had cleaned the *estaminet* out of everything, — wine, cognac, bread, blankets, sheets — *les sales Boches!*

As the days dragged muddily through it was borne in on me that this wasn't fighting for King and Country. It was just Tidworth over again with none of its advantages and with all its discomforts increased a thousandfold. Furthermore the post-office seemed to have lost me utterly and weeks went by before I had any letters at all. It was heartbreaking to see the mail distributed daily and go away empty-handed. It was as though no one cared, as though one were completely forgotten, as though in stepping into this new life one had renounced one's identity. Indeed every day it became more evident that it was not I who was in that mud patch. It was some one else on whom the real me looked down in infinite amazement. I heard myself laugh in the farm at night and join in choruses; saw myself dirty and unbathed, with a scarf around my stomach and another round my feet and a woollen helmet over my head; standing in the mud stripped to the waist, shaving without a looking-glass; drinking coffee and cognac in that *estaminet.* — Was it I who sometimes prayed for sleep that I might shut it all out and slip into the land of dreams where there is no war and no mud? Was it I who when the first letters arrived from home went out into the rainy night with a candle-end to be alone with those I loved? And was it only the rain which made it so difficult to read them?

18.

The culminating point was reached when I became ill.

Feeling sick, I couldn't eat any breakfast and dragged myself on parade like a mangy cat. I stuck it till about three in the afternoon, when the horse which I was grooming receded from me and the whole world rocked. I remember hanging on to the horse till things got a bit steadier and then asked the sergeant if I might go off parade. I suppose I must have looked pretty ill, because he said yes at once.

For three days I lay wrapped up on the straw in the barn, eating nothing; and only crawling out to see the doctor each morning at nine o'clock. Of other symptoms I will say nothing. The whole affair was appalling but I recovered sufficient interest in life on the fourth morning to parade sick, although I felt vastly more fit. Indeed the argument formed itself, "since I am a soldier I'll play the 'old soldier' and see how long I can be excused duty." And I did it so well that for three more days I was to all intents and purposes a free man. On one of the days I fell in with a corporal of another squadron and he and I got a couple of horses and rode into Bailleul, which was only about three miles south of us, and we bought chocolates and candles and books and exchanged salutes with the Prince of Wales who was walking in the town. Then we came back with our supplies after an excellent lunch at the hotel in the square, the Faucon, and had tea with the officers' servants in a cosy little billet with a fire and beds. The remarks they made about their officers were most instructive and they referred to them either as "my bloke" or "'is lordship."

And there it was I met again a man I had spoken to once at Tidworth, who knew French and was now squadron interpreter. He was a charming man of considerable means, with a large business, who had joined up immediately on the outbreak of war. But being squadron interpreter he messed with the officers, had a billet in a cottage, slept on a bed, had a private hip bath and hot water and was in heaven, comparatively. He suggested to me that as my squadron lacked an interpreter (he was doing the extra work) and I knew French it was up to me.

"But how the devil's it to be done?" said I, alight with the idea.

"Why don't you go and see the Colonel?" he suggested.

I gasped. The Colonel was nearly God.

He laughed. "This is 'Kitchener's Army'," he said, "not the regular Army. Things are a bit different." They were indeed!

So I slept on the idea and every moment it seemed to me better and better, until the following evening after tea, instead of going to the *estaminet*, I went down to squadron headquarters. For about five minutes I walked up and down in the mud, plucking up courage. I would rather have faced a Hun any day.

At last I went into the farmyard and knocked at the door. There were lights in the crack of the window shutters.

A servant answered the door.

"Is the Colonel in?" said I boldly.

He peered at me. "What the perishin' 'ell do *you* want to know for?"

"I want to see him," said I.

"And what the 'ell do *you* want to see him for?"

I was annoyed. It seemed quite likely that this confounded servant would do the St. Peter act and refuse me entrance into the gates.

THE RANKS

"Look here," I said, "it doesn't matter to you what for or why. You're here to answer questions. Is the Colonel *in?*"

The man snorted. "Oh! I'm 'ere to answer questions, am I? Well, if you want to know, the Colonel ain't in. — Anything else?"

I was stumped. It seemed as if my hopes were shattered. But luck was mine — as ever. A voice came from the inner room. "Thomson! Who is that man?"

The servant made a face at me and went to the room door.

"A trooper, sir, from one of the squadrons, askin' to see the Colonel."

"Bring him in," said the voice.

My heart leapt.

The servant returned to me and showed me into the room.

I saw three officers, one in shirt sleeves, all sitting around a fire. Empty tea things were still on a table. There were a sofa and armchairs and bright pictures, a pile of books and magazines on a table, and a smell of Egyptian cigarettes. They all looked at me as I saluted.

"Thomson tells me you want to see the Colonel," said the one whose voice I had heard, the one in shirt sleeves. "Anything I can do?"

It was good to hear one's own language again and I decided to make a clean breast of it.

"It's awfully kind of you, sir," said I. "Perhaps you can. I came to ask for the interpretership of my squadron. We haven't got one and I can talk

French. If you could put in a word for me I should be lastingly grateful."

His next words made him my brother for life. "Sit down, won't you," he said, "and have a cigarette."

Can you realise what it meant after those weeks of misery, with no letters and the eternal adjective of the ranks which gets on one's nerves till one could scream, to be asked to sit down and have a cigarette in that officers' mess?

Speechless I took one, although I dislike cigarettes and always stick to a pipe. But that one was a link with all that I'd left behind and was the best I've ever smoked in my life. He proceeded to ask me my name and where I was educated and said he would see what he could do for me, and after about ten minutes I went out again into the mud a better soldier than I went in. That touch of fellow feeling helped enormously. And he was as good as his word. For the following morning the Major sent for me.

19.

The rain had stopped and there had been a hard frost in the night which turned the roads to ice. The horses were being walked round and round in a circle and the Major was standing watching them when I came up and saluted.

"Yes, what is it?" he said.

"You sent for me, sir."

"Oh — you're Gibbs, are you? — Yes, let's go in out of this wind." He led the way into the mess and stood with his back to the fire.

THE RANKS

Every detail of that room lives with me yet. One went up two steps into the room. The fireplace faced the door with a window to the right of the fireplace. There was a table between us with newspapers on it and tobacco and pipes. And two armchairs faced the fire.

He asked me what I wanted the interpretership for. I told him I was sick of the ranks, that I had chucked a fascinating job to be of use to my King and country and that any fool trooper could shovel mud as I did day after day.

He nodded. "But interpreting is no damned good, you know," he said. "It only consists in looking after the forage and going shopping with those officers who can't talk French. — That isn't what you want, is it?"

"No, sir," said I.

"Well, what other job would you like?"

That floored me completely. I didn't know what jobs there were in the squadron and told him so.

"Well, come and have dinner to-night and we'll talk about it," said he.

Have dinner! My clothes reeked of stables and I had slept in them ever since I arrived.

"That doesn't matter," said the Major. "You come along to-night at half-past seven. You've been sick all this week. How are you? Pretty fit again?"

He's Brigadier General now and has forgotten all about it years ago. I don't think I ever shall.

There were the Major, the Captain and one subaltern at dinner that night — an extraordinary dinner

— the servant who a moment previously had called me "chum" in the kitchen gradually getting used to waiting on me at the meal, and I, in the same dress as the servant, gradually feeling less like a fish out of water as the officers treated me as one of themselves. It was the first time I'd eaten at a table covered with a white table-cloth for over two months, the first time I had used a plate or drunk out of a glass, the first time I had been with my own kind. — It was very good.

The outcome of the dinner was that I was to become squadron scout, have two horses, keep them at the cottage of the interpreter where I was to live, and ride over the country gathering information which I was to bring as a written report every night at six o'clock. While the squadron was behind the lines it was of course only a matter of training myself before other men were given me to train. But when we went into action, — vistas opened out before me of dodging Uhlan patrols and galloping back with information through a rain of bullets. It was a job worth while and I was speechless with gratitude.

It was not later than seven o'clock the following morning, Christmas Eve, 1914, that I began operations. I breakfasted at the cottage to which I had removed my belongings overnight, and went along towards the stables to get a horse.

The man with whom I had been mucking in met me outside the farm. He was in the know and grinned cheerily.

"The sergeant's lookin' for you," he said. "He's over in the stables."

I went across. He was prowling about near the forage.

"Good morning, Sergeant," said I.

He looked at me and stopped prowling. "Where the —" and he asked me in trooperese where I had been and why I wasn't at early morning stables. I told him I was on a special job for the Major.

He gasped and requested an explanation.

"I'm knocked off all rolls and parades and fatigues," I said. "You've got to find me a second horse. They are both going to be kept down the road and I shall come and see you from time to time when I require forage."

He was speechless for the first and only time. It passed his comprehension.

At that moment the sergeant major came in and proceeded to tell him almost word for word what I had told him. It was a great morning, a poetic revenge, and eventually I rode away leading the other horse, the sergeant's pop eyes following me as I gave him final instructions as to where to send the forage.

Later, as I started out on my first expedition as squadron scout, he waved an arm at me and came running. His whole manner had changed and he said in a voice of honey, "If you *should* 'appen to pass through Ballool would you mind gettin' me a new pipe? — 'Ere's five francs."

I got him a pipe and in Bailleul sought out every likely looking English signaller or French officer and dropped questions, and eventually at 6 P.M., having been the round of Dramoutre, Westoutre, and Locre, took in a rather meagre first report to the Major. How I regretted that I had never been a newspaper reporter! However, it was a beginning.

The following morning was Christmas Day, cold and foggy, and before starting out I went about a mile down the road to another farm and heard Mass in a barn. An odd little service for Christmas morning. The altar was made of a couple of biscuit boxes in an open barn. The priest wore his vestments and his boots and spurs showed underneath. About half a dozen troopers with rifles were all the congregation and we knelt on the damp ground.

The first Christmas at Bethlehem came to mind most forcibly. The setting was the same. An icy wind blew the wisps of straw and the lowing of a cow could be heard in the byre. Where the Magi brought frankincense and myrrh we brought our hopes and ambitions and laid them at the Child's feet, asking Him to take care of them for us while we went out to meet the great adventure. What a contrast to the previous Christmas in the gold and sunshine of Miami, Florida, splashed with the scarlet flowers of the bougainvillea, and at night the soft feathery palms leaning at a curious angle in the hard moonlight as though a tornado had once swept over the land.

The farm people sold me a bowl of coffee and a slice of bread and I mounted and rode away into the fog with an apple and a piece of chocolate in my pocket, the horse slipping and sliding on the icy road. Not a sound broke the dead silence except the blowing of my horse and his hoofs on the road.

Every gun was silent during the whole day as though the Child had really brought peace and good will.

I got to within a couple of miles of Ypres by the map and saw nothing save a few peasants who emerged out of the blanket of fog on their way to Mass. A magpie or two flashed across my way and there was only an occasional infantryman muffled to the eyes when I passed through the scattered villages.

About midday I nibbled some chocolate and watered my horse and gave him a feed, feeling more and more miserable because there was no means of getting any information. My imagination drew pictures of the Major, on my return with a blank confession of failure, telling me that I was no good and had better return to duty. As the short afternoon drew in my spirits sank lower and lower. They were below zero when at last I knocked reluctantly at the door of the mess and stood to attention inside. To make things worse all the officers were there.

"Well, Gibbs?" said the Major.

"It isn't well, sir," said I. "I'm afraid I'm no damn good. I haven't got a thing to report," and I told him of my ride.

There was silence for a moment. The Major flicked off the ash of his cigarette. "My dear fellow," he said quietly, "you can't expect to get the hang of the job in five minutes. Don't be impatient with it. Give it a chance."

It was like a reprieve to a man awaiting the hangman.

20.

The squadron, having been on duty that day, had not celebrated Christmas, but the *estaminet* was a mass of holly and mistletoe in preparation for tomorrow, and talk ran high on the question of the dinner and concert that were to take place. There were no letters for me but in spite of it I felt most unaccountably and absurdly happy as I left the *estaminet* and went back to my billet and got to bed.

The interpreter came in presently. He had been dining well and Christmas exuded from him as he smoked a cigar on the side of his bed.

"Oh, by the way," he said, "your commission has come through. They were talking about it in mess to-night. Congratulations."

Commission! My heart jumped back to the Marlborough Hotel.

"I expect you'll be going home to-morrow," he went on; "lucky devil."

Home! Could it be? Was it possible that I was going to escape from all this mud and filth? Home. What a Christmas present! No more waiting for letters that never came. No more of the utter loneliness and indifference that seemed to fill one's days and nights.

The dingy farm room and the rough army blanket faded and in their place came a woman's face in a setting of tall red pines and gleaming patches of moss and high bracken and a green lawn running up to a little house of gables, with chintz-curtained

THE RANKS

windows, warm tiles and red chimneys, and a shining river twisting in stately loops. And instead of the guns which were thundering the more fiercely after their lull, there came the mewing of sandpipers, and the gurgle of children's laughter, and the voice of that one woman who had given me the vision. —

21.

The journey home was a foretaste of the return to civilisation, of stepping not only out of one's trooper's khaki but of resuming one's identity, of counting in the scheme of things. In the ranks one was a number, like a convict, — a cipher indeed, and as such it was a struggle to keep one's soul alive. One had given one's body. They wanted one's soul as well. By "they", I mean the system, that extraordinary self-contained world which is the Army, where the private is marched to church whether he have a religion or not, where he is forced to think as the sergeant thinks, and so on, right up to the General commanding. How few officers realise that it is in their power to make the lives of their juniors and men a hell or a heaven.

It was a merciful thing for me that I was able to escape so soon, to climb out of that mental and physical morass and get back to myself.

From the squadron I went by motor lorry to Hazebrouck and thence in a first-class carriage to Boulogne, and although the carriage was crowded I thought of the horse truck in which I'd come up from Rouen and chuckled. At Boulogne I was able to help the Major, who was going on leave.

He had left a shirt case in the French luggage office weeks before and by tackling the porter in his own tongue I succeeded in digging it out in five minutes. It was the only thing I've ever been able to do to express the least gratitude, — and how ridiculously inadequate.

We spent the night in a hotel and caught the early boat, horribly early. But it was worth it. We reached London about two in the afternoon, a rainy, foggy, depressing afternoon, but if it had snowed ink I shouldn't have minded. I was above mere weather, sailing in the blue ether of radiant happiness. In this case the realisation came up to and even exceeded the expectation. Miserable-looking policemen in black waterproof capes were things of beauty. The noise of the traffic was sweetest music. The sight of dreary streets with soaked pedestrians made one's eyes brim with joy. The swish of the taxi round abrupt corners made me burst with song. I was glad of the rain and the sort of half-fog. It was so typically London, and when the taxi driver stopped at my brother's house and said to me as I got out, "Just back from the front, chum?" I laughed madly and scandalously overtipped him. No one else would ever call me chum. That was done with. I was no longer 7205 Trooper A. H. Gibbs, 9th Lancers. I was Second Lieutenant A. Hamilton Gibbs, R.F.A., and could feel the stars sprouting.

My brother wasn't at home. He was looking like an admiral still and working like the devil. But his wife was and she most wisely lent me dis-

THE RANKS

tant finger tips and hurried me to a bath, what time she telephoned to my brother.

That bath! I hadn't had all my clothes off more than once in six weeks and had slept in them every night. Ever tried it? Well, if you really want to know just how I felt about that first bath, you try it.

I stayed in it so long that my sister-in-law became anxious and tapped at the door to know if I were all right. All right! Before I was properly dressed — but running about the house most shamelessly for all that — my brother arrived.

It was good to see him again, — very good. We "foregathered", — what?

And the next morning, scandalously early, the breakfast things still on the table, found me face to face once more with the woman who had brought me back to life. All that nightmare was immediately washed away for ever. It was past. The future was too vague for imaginings but the present was the most golden thing I had ever known.

PART II

UBIQUE

II. UBIQUE

1.

THE Division of Field Artillery to which I was posted by the War Office was training at Bulford up to its neck in mud, but the brigade had moved to Fleet two days before I joined. By that time — it was a good fifteen days since I had come home — I had grown accustomed to the feel and splendour of a Sam Browne belt and field boots and the recurring joy of being saluted not merely by Tommies but by exalted beings like sergeants and sergeant majors; and I felt mentally as well as physically clean.

At the same time I arrived at the Fleet Golf Club, where most of the officers were billeted, feeling vastly diffident. I'd never seen a gun, never given a command in my life and hadn't the first or foggiest idea of the sort of things gunners did, and my only experience of an officers' mess was my dinner with the Major in France. Vaguely I knew that there was a certain etiquette demanded. It was rather like a boy going to a new school.

It was tea time and dark when the cab dropped me at the door and the place was practically empty. However, an officer emerged, asked me if I'd come to join, and led me in to tea. Presently, however, a crowd swarmed in, flung wet mackintoshes and caps about the hall and began devouring bread and jam in a way that more and more resembled school. They looked me over with the unintentional insolence of all Englishmen and one or two spoke. They were a likely-looking lot, mostly amazingly young and full of a vitality that was like an electric current. One, a fair willowy lad with one or two golden fluffs that presumably did duty as a moustache, took me in hand. He was somewhat fancifully called Pot-face but he had undoubtedly bought the earth and all things in it. Having asked and received my name he informed me that I was posted to his battery and introduced me to the other subaltern, also of his battery. This was a pale, blue-eyed, head-on-one-side, sensitive youth who was always just a moment too late with his repartee. Pot-face, who possessed a nimble, sarcastic tongue, took an infinite delight in baiting him to the verge of tears. His nickname, to which incidentally he refused to answer, was the Fluttering Palm.

The others did not assume individualities till later. It was an amusing tea and afterwards we adjourned to the big club room with two fireplaces and straw armchairs and golfing pictures. The senior officers were there and before I could breathe Pot-face had introduced me to the Colonel, the Adjutant, and the Captain commanding our battery, a long, thin, dark man with India stamped all over him and a sudden infectious laugh that crinkled all his face. He turned out to be the owner of a vitriolic tongue.

A lecture followed, one of a series which took

place two or three evenings a week attended by all the officers in the brigade, a good two thirds of whom were billeted in the village and round about. Of technical benefit I don't think I derived any, because I knew no gunnery, but it helped me to get to know everybody. A further help in that respect was afforded by my Captain, who on that first evening proposed getting up a concert. Having had two years on the stage in America I volunteered to help and was at once made O. C. Concert. This gave me a sort of standing, took away the awful newness and entirely filled my spare time for two weeks. The concert was a big success and from that night I felt at home.

To me, after my experience in the ranks, everything was new and delightful. We were all learning, subalterns as well as men. Only the Colonel and the Battery Commanders were regulars and every single officer and man was keen. The work therefore went with a will that surprised me. The men were a different class altogether to those with whom I had been associated. There were miners, skilled men, clerks, people of some education and distinct intelligence. Then too the officers came into much closer contact with them than in the Cavalry. Our training had been done solely under the sergeant major. Here in the Gunners the officers not only took every parade and lecture and stable hour and knew every man and horse by name, but played in all the inter-battery football matches. It was a different world, much more intimate and much better organised. We worked hard and played hard.

Riding was of course most popular because each of us had a horse. But several had motor-bicycles and went for joy-rides half over the south of England between tattoo and reveille. Then the Golf Club made us honorary members, and the Colonel and I had many a match, and he almost invariably beat me by one hole.

My ignorance of gunnery was monumental and it was a long time before I grasped even the first principles. The driving drill part of it didn't worry me. The Cavalry had taught me to feel at home in the saddle and the drawing of intricate patterns on the open country with a battery of four guns was a delightful game soon learnt. But once they were in action I was lost. It annoyed me to listen helplessly while children of nineteen with squeaky voices fired imaginary salvos on imaginary targets and got those gunners jumping. So I besought the Colonel to send me on a course to Shoebury and he did.

Work? I'd never known what it meant till I went to Shoebury and put on a canvas duck suit. We paraded at ungodly hours in the morning, wet or fine, took guns to bits and with the instructor's help put them together again; did gun drill by the hour and learnt it by heart from the handbook and shouted it at each other from a distance; spent hours in the country doing map-reading and re-section; sat through hours of gunnery lectures where the mysteries of a magic triangle called T.O.B. became more and more unfathomable; knocked out countless churches on a miniature range with a precision that was quite Boche-like; waded through a

ghastly tabloid book called F.A.T. and flung the
thing in despair at the wall half a dozen times a
day; played billiards at night when one had been
clever enough to arrive first at the table by means of
infinite manœuvring; ate like a Trojan, got dog-
tired by 9 P.M., slept like a child; dashed up to
London every week-end and went to the theatre,
and became in fact the complete Shoeburyite.

Finally I returned to the brigade extraordinarily
fit, very keen and with perhaps the first glimmerings
of what a gun was. A scourge of a mysterious skin
disease ran through the horses at that time. It
looked like ringworm and wasn't, — according to
the Vet. But we subalterns vied with each other
in curing our sections and worked day and night on
those unfortunate animals with tobacco juice, sulphur
and every unpleasant means available until they
looked the most wretched brutes in the world.

Little by little the training built itself up. From
standing gun drill we crept to battery gun drill and
then took the battery out for the day and lost it
round Aldershot in that glorious pine country,
coming into action over and over again.

The Colonel watched it all from a distance with a
knowledgeable eye and at last took a hand. Brigade
shows then took place, batteries working in con-
junction with each other and covering zones.

Those were good days in the early spring with all
the birds in full chorus, clouds scudding across a
blue sky, and the young green feathering all the trees,
days of hard physical work with one's blood running
free and the companionship of one's own kind; in-

spired by a friendly rivalry in doing a thing just a little bit better than the other fellow — or trying to: with an occasional week-end flung in like a sparkling jewel.

And France? Did we think about it? Yes, when the lights were turned out at night and only the point of the final cigarette like a glowworm marked the passage of hand to mouth. Then the talk ran on brothers "out there" and the chances of our going soon. None of them had been except me, but I could only give them pictures of star-shell at night and the heart-breaking mud, and they wanted gunner talk.

It was extraordinary what a bond grew up between us all in those days, shared, I think, by the senior officers. We declared ourselves the first brigade in the Division, and each battery was of course hotly the finest in the brigade; our Colonel was miles above any other Colonel in the Army and our Battery Commanders the best fellows that ever stepped. By God, we'd show Fritz! —

We had left Fleet and the golf club and moved into hutments at Deepcut about the time I returned from the gunnery course. Now the talk centred round the firing practice when every man and officer would be put to the test and one fine morning the order came to proceed to Trawsfynydd, Wales.

We "proceeded" by train, taking only guns, firing battery wagons and teams and after long, long hours found ourselves tucked away in a camp in the mountains with great blankets of mist rolling down and blotting everything out, the ground a squelching bog of tussocks with outcrops of rock sprouting up everywhere. A strange, hard, cold country, with unhappy houses, grey-tiled and lonely, and peasants whose faces seemed marked by the desolation of it all.

The range was a rolling stretch of country falling away from a plateau high above us, reached by a corkscrew path that tore the horses to pieces, and cut up by stone walls and nullahs which after an hour's rain foamed with brown water. Through glasses we made out the targets — four black dots representing a battery, a row of tiny figures for infantry, and a series of lines indicating trenches. For three days the weather prevented us from shooting but at last came a morning when the fog blanket rolled back and the guns were run up, and little puffs of cotton wool appeared over the targets, the hills ringing with countless echoes as though they would never tire of the firing.

Each subaltern was called up in turn and given a target by the Colonel who, lying silently on his stomach, watched results through his glasses and doubtless in his mind summed each of us up from the methods of our orders to the battery, the nimbleness and otherwise with which we gauged and corrected them. A trying ordeal which was, however, all too short. Sixteen rounds apiece were all that we were allowed. We would have liked six hundred, so fascinating and bewildering was the new game. It seemed as if the guns took a malignant pleasure in disobeying our orders, each gun having its own particular devil to compete with.

In the light of to-day the explanation is simple. There was no such thing as calibration then, that exorciser of the evil spirit in all guns.

And so, having seen at last a practical demonstration of what I had long considered a fact — that the Gunners' Bible F.A.T. (the handbook of Field Artillery Training) was a complete waste of time, we all went back to Deepcut even more than ever convinced that we were the finest brigade in England. And all on the strength of sixteen rounds apiece!

Almost at once I was removed from the scientific activities necessitated by being a battery subaltern. An apparently new establishment was made, a being called an Orderly Officer, whose job was to keep the Colonel in order and remind the Adjutant of all the things he forgot. In addition to those two matters of supreme moment there were one or two minor duties like training the brigade signallers to lay out cables and buzz messages, listen to the domestic troubles of the regimental sergeant major, whose importance is second only to that of the Colonel, look after some thirty men and horses and a cable wagon and endeavour to keep in the good books of the Battery Commanders.

I got the job — and kept it for over a year.

Colonel, didn't I keep you in order?

Adj, did I *ever* do any work for you?

Battery Commanders, didn't I come and cadge drinks daily — and incidentally wasn't that cable which I laid from Valandovo to Kajali the last in use before the Bulgar pushed us off the earth?

2.

So I forgot the little I ever knew about gunnery and laid spiders' webs from my cable wagon all over Deepcut, and galloped for the Colonel on Divisional training stunts with a bottle of beer and sandwiches in each wallet against the hour when the General, feeling hungry, should declare an armistice with the opposing force and Colonels and their Orderly Officers might replenish their inner men. Brave days of great lightheartedness, untouched by the shadow of what was to come after.

May had put leaves on all the trees and called forth flowers in every garden. Then came June to perfect her handiwork and with it the call to lay aside our golf clubs and motor-cycles, to say good-by to England in all her beauty and go out once more to do our bit.

There was much bustle and packing of kits and writing of letters and heartburnings over last week-end leaves refused and through it all a thirst for knowledge of where we were going. Everything was secret, letters severely censored. Rumour and counter-rumour chased each other through the camp until, an hour before starting, the Captain in whose battery I had begun appeared with a motor car full of topees.

Then all faces like true believers were turned towards the East and on every tongue was the word Gallipoli.

Avonmouth was the port of embarkation and there we filled a mass of waiting boats, big and little.

The Colonel, the Adjutant and I were on one of the biggest. My horses had been handed over to a battery for the voyage and I had only the signallers to look after. Everything was complete by ten o'clock in the morning. The convoy would not sail till midnight, so some of us got leave to explore and took train to Bristol, lunching royally for the last time in a restaurant, buying innumerable novels to read on board, sending final telegrams home.

How very different it was to the first going out! No red lead. No mud. The reality had departed. It seemed like going on a picnic, a merry outing with cheery souls, a hot sun trickling down one's back; and not one of us but heard the East a-calling.

A curious voyage that was when we had sorted ourselves out. The mornings were taken up with a few duties, — physical jerks, chin inspection and Grand Rounds when we stood stiffly to attention, rocking with the sway of the boat while the two commanders of the sister services inspected the ship; life-boat drill, a little signalling; and then long hours in scorching sunshine, to lie in a deck chair gazing out from the saloon deck upon the infinite blue, trying to find the answer to the why of it all, arguing the alpha and omega with one's pals, reading the novels we had bought in Bristol, writing home, sleeping. Torpedoes and mines? We never thought about them.

Boxing competitions and sports were organised for the men and they hammered each other's faces to pulp with the utmost good fellowship.

Then we passed The Rock and with our first

glimpse of the African coast — a low brown smudge — we began to stir restlessly and think of terra firma. It broke the spell of dreams which had filled the long days. Maps were produced and conferences held, and we studied eagerly the contours of Gallipoli, discussed the detail of landings and battery positions, wagon lines and signalling arrangements, even going so far as to work off our bearing of the line of fire. Fragments of war news were received by wireless and a *communiqué* was posted daily but it all seemed extraordinarily unreal, as though it were taking place in another world.

One night we saw a fairyland of piled-up lights which grew swiftly as we drew nearer and took shape in filigreed terraces and arcades when our anchor at last dropped with a mighty roar in Valetta harbour. Tiny boats like gondolas were moored at the water's edge in tight rows, making in the moonlight a curious scalloped fringe. People in odd garments passed in noiseless swarms up and down the streets, cabs went by, shop doors opened and shut, and behind all those lights loomed the impenetrable blackness of the land towering up like a mountain. From the distance at which we were anchored no sound could be heard save that of shipping, and those ant-sized people going about their affairs, regardless of the thousands of eyes watching them, gave one the effect of looking at a stage from the gallery through the wrong end of an opera glass.

Coaling began within an hour, and all that night bronze figures naked to the waist and with bare feet slithered up and down the swaying planks, tireless, unceasing, glistening in the arc light which spluttered from the mast of the coaling vessel; the grit of coal dust made one's shoes crunch as one walked the decks in pyjamas, filled one's hair and neck, and on that stifling night became as one of the plagues of Pharaoh.

A strange discordant chattering waked one next morning as though a tribe of monkeys had besieged the ship. Then one leaped to the porthole to get a glimpse of Malta, to us the first hint of the mysterious East. There it was, glistening white against the turquoise blue, built up in fascinating tiers with splashes of dark green trees clinging here and there as though afraid of losing their hold and toppling into the sea. All round the ship the sea was dotted with boats and dark people yelling and shouting, all reds and blues and bright yellows; piles of golden fruit and coloured shawls; big boats with high snub noses, the oarsmen standing, showing rows of gleaming teeth; baby boats the size of walnut shells with naked brown babies uttering shrill cries and diving like frogs for silver coins.

Was it possible that just a little farther on we should meet one end of the line of death that made a red gash right across Europe?

We laughed a little self-consciously under the unusual feel of our topees and went ashore to try and get some drill khaki. Finding none we drank cool drinks and bought cigars and smiled at the milk sellers with their flocks of goats and the *café au lait* coloured girls, some of whom moved with extraordinary grace and looked very pretty under their black mantillas. The banks distrusted us and would give us no money and the Base cashier refused to undo his purse strings. We cursed him and tried unsuccessfully to borrow from each other, having only a few pounds in our pockets. Down a back street we found a Japanese tattooist and in spite of the others' ridicule I added a highly coloured but pensive parrot to my collection. But the heat was overwhelming and our puttees and tunics became streaked with sweat. We were glad to get back to the boat and lie in a cold bath and climb languidly into the comparative coolness of slacks. The men had not been allowed ashore but hundreds of them dived overboard and swam round the boat, and the native fruit sellers did a thriving trade.

After dinner we went ashore again. It was not much cooler. We wandered into various places of amusement. They were all the same, large dirty halls with a small stage and a piano and hundreds of marble-topped tables where one sat and drank. Atrociously fat women appeared on the stage and sang four songs apiece in bad French. It didn't matter whether the first song was greeted with stony silence or the damning praise of one sarcastic laugh. Back came each one until she'd finished her repertoire. Getting bored with that I collected a fellow sufferer and together we went out and made our way to the top of the ramparts. The sky looked as if a giant had spilt all the diamonds in the world. They glittered and changed colour. The sea was also powdered as if little bits of diamond dust had dropped from the sky. The air smelled sweet and a little strange and in that velvety darkness which one could almost touch one's imagination went rioting.

As if that were not enough a guitar somewhere down below was suddenly touched with magic fingers and a little love song floated up in a soft lilting tenor. — We were very silent on the old wall.

3.

The next morning on waking up, that song still echoing in our ears, we were hull down. Only a vague disturbance in the blue showed where Malta had been, and but for the tattoo which irritated slightly, it might have been one of the Thousand and One Nights. We arrived at last at Alexandria instead of Gallipoli. The shore authorities lived up to the best standards of the Staff.

They said, "Who the devil are you?"

And we replied, "The — Division."

And they said, "We've never heard of you, don't know where you come from, have no instructions about you, and you'd better buzz off again."

But we beamed at them and said, "To hell with you. We're going to land," — and landed.

There were no arrangements for horses or men; and M.L.O.'s in all the glory of staff hats and armlets chattered like impotent monkeys. We were busy, however, improvising picketing-ropes from ships' cables borrowed from the amused ships' commander and we smiled politely and said, "Yes, it *is* hot," and went on with the work. Never heard of the — Division? Well, well!

Hot? We had never known what heat was before. We thought we did lying about on deck, but when it came to working for hours on end, — tunics disappeared and collars and ties followed them. The horses looked as if they had been out in the rain and left a watery trail as we formed up and marched out of the harbour and through the town. We bivouacked for the night in a rest camp called Karaissi where there wasn't enough room and tempers ran high until a couple of horses broke loose in the dark and charged the tent in which there were two Colonels. The tent ropes went with a ping and camp beds and clothing and Colonels were mixed up in the sand. No one was hurt, so we emptied the Colonels' pyjamas, called their servants and went away and laughed.

Then we hooked in and marched again, and in the middle of the afternoon found Mamoura — a village of odd smells, naked children, filthy women and pariah dogs — and pitched camp on the choking sand half a mile from the seashore.

By this time the horses were nearly dead and the only water was a mile and a half away and full of sand. But they drank it, poor brutes, by the gallon, — and two days after we had our first case of sand colic.

The Staff were in marquees on the seashore. Presumably being bored, having nothing earthly to do, they began to exhibit a taste for design, and each day the camp was moved, twenty yards this way, fifteen that, twelve and a half the other, until, thank God, the sun became too much for them and they retired to suck cool drinks through straws and think up a new game.

By this time the Colonel had refused to play and removed himself, lock, stock, and barrel, to the hotel in the village. The Adjutant was praying aloud for the mud of Flanders. The Orderly Officer made himself scarce and the Battery Commanders were telling Indian snake stories at breakfast. The sergeants and the men, half naked and with tongues hanging out, were searching for beer.

The days passed relentlessly, scorching hot, the only work, watering the horses four times a day, leaving everybody weak and exhausted. At night a damp breeze sighed across the sand from the sea, soaking everything as though it had rained. The busiest men in the camp were the Vet. and the doctor.

Sand colic ran through the Division like a scourge, and dysentery began to reduce the personnel from day to day. The flies bred in their billions, in spite of all the doctor's efforts, loyally backed up by us. The subalterns' method of checking flies was to catch salamanders and walk about, holding them within range of guy ropes and tent roofs where flies swarmed, and watch their coiled tongues uncurl like a flash of lightning and then trace the passage of the disgruntled fly down into the salamander's interior. Battery Commanders waking from a fly-pestered siesta would lay their piastres eagerly on "Archibald" versus "Yussuf." Even Wendy would have admitted that it was "frightfully fascinating."

Every morning there was a pyjama parade at six o'clock when we all trooped across to the sea and went in as nature made us. Or else we rode the horses with snorts and splashings. The old hairy enjoyed it as much as we did and, once in, it was difficult to get him out again, even with bare heels drumming on his ribs.

The infantry, instead of landing at Alexandria, had gone straight to the Dardanelles, and after we had been in camp about a fortnight the two senior brigades of Gunners packed up and disappeared in the night, leaving us grinding our teeth with envy and hoping that they wouldn't have licked the Turk until we got there too.

Five full months and a half we stayed in that camp! One went through two distinct phases.

The first was good, when everything was new, different, romantic, delightful, from the main streets of Alexandria with European shops and Oriental people, the club with its white-burnoused waiters with red sash and red fez, down to the unutterable filth and foul smells of the back streets where every disease lurked in the doorways. There were early morning rides to sleepy villages across the desert, pigeons fluttering round the delicate minarets, one's horse making scarcely any sound in the deep sand until startled into a snort by a scuttling salamander or iguana as long as one's arm. Now and then one watched breathless a string of camels on a distant skyline disappearing into the vast silence. Then those dawns, with opal colours like a rainbow that had broken open and splashed itself across the world! What infinite joy in all that riot of colour. The sunsets were too rapid: one great splurge of blood and then darkness, followed by a moonlight that was as hard as steel mirrors. Buildings and trees were picked out in ghostly white but the shadows by contrast were darker than the pit, made gruesome by the howling of pariah dogs which flitted silently like damned souls.

The eternal mystery of the yashmak caught us all, — two deep eyes behind that little veil, the lilting, sensuous walk, the perfect balance and rhythm of those women who worshipped other gods.

Then there was the joy of mail day. Letters and papers arrived regularly, thirteen days old but more precious because of it. How one sprang to the mess-table in the big marquee, open to whatever winds that blew, when the letters were dumped on it, and danced with impatience while they were being sorted, and retired in triumph to one's reed hut like a dog with a bone to revel in all the little happenings at home that interested us so vitally, to marvel at the amazingly different points of view and to thank God that, although thousands of miles away, one "belonged."

Then came the time when we had explored everything, knew it all backwards, and the colours didn't seem so bright. The sun seemed hotter, the flies thicker and the days longer. Restlessness attacked everybody and the question, "What the devil are we doing here?" began to be asked, only to draw bitter answers. Humour began to have a tinge of sarcasm, remarks tended to become personal, and people disappeared precipitately after mess instead of playing the usual rubbers. The unfortunate subaltern who was the butt of the mess — a really excellent and clever fellow — relapsed into a morose silence, and every one who had the least tendency to dysentery went gladly to hospital. Even the brigade laughter-maker lost his touch. It had its echo in the ranks. Sergeants made more frequent arrests, courts-martial cropped up and it was more difficult to get the work done in spite of concerts, sports and boxing contests. Interest flagged utterly. Mercifully the Staff held aloof.

The courts-martial seemed to me most Hogarthian versions of justice, satirical and damnable. One in particular was held on a poor little rat of an infantryman who had missed the boat for Gallipoli and was being tried for desertion. The reason of his missing the boat was that she sailed before her time and he, having had a glass or two — and why not? — found that she had already gone when he arrived back in the harbour five minutes before the official time for her departure. He immediately reported to the police.

I am convinced that she was the only boat who ever sailed before her time during the course of the war!

However, I was under instruction — and learnt a great deal. The heat was appalling. The poor little prisoner, frightened out of his life, utterly lost his head, and the Court, after hours of formal scribbling on blue paper, brought him in guilty. Having obtained permission to ask a question I requested to know whether the Court was convinced that he had the intention of deserting.

The Court was quite satisfied on that point and, besides, there had been so many cases of desertion lately from the drafts for Gallipoli that really it was time an example was made of some one. He got three years!

Supposing I'd hit that bullying sergeant in the eye in Flanders?

4.

Two incidents occurred during that lugubrious period that helped to break the dead monotony.

The first was the sight of a real live eunuch, according to all the specifications of the Arabian Nights. We were to give a horse show and as the flag of residence was flying from the Sultan's palace I asked the Colonel if I might invite the Sultan. The Colonel was quite in favour of it. So with an extra polish on my buttons and saddlery I collected a pal and together we rode through the great gateway into the grounds of the palace, ablaze with tropical vegetation and blood-red flowers. Camped among the trees on the right of the drive was a native guard of about thirty men. They rose as one man, jabbered at the sight of us but remained stationary. We rode on at a walk with all the dignity of the British Empire behind us. Then we saw a big Arab come running towards us from the palace, uttering shrill cries and waving his arms. We met him and would have passed but he made as though to lay hands upon our bits. So we halted and listened to a stream of Arabic and gesticulation.

Then the eunuch appeared, a little man of immense shoulders and immense stomach, dressed in a black frock coat and stiff white collar, yellow leather slippers and red fez and sash. He was about five feet tall and addressed us in a high squeaky voice like a fiddle string out of tune. His dignity was surprising and he would have done justice to the Court of Haroun al Raschid. We were delighted with him and called him Morgiana.

He didn't understand that so I tried him in French, whereupon he clapped his hands twice, and from an engine room among the outbuildings came running an Arab mechanic in blue jeans. He spoke a sort of hybrid Levantine French and conveyed our invitation of the Sultan to the eunuch, who bowed and spoke again. The desire to laugh was appalling.

It appeared that the Sultan was absent in Alexandria and only the Sultana and the ladies were here and it was quite forbidden that we should approach nearer the palace.

Reluctantly, therefore, we saluted, which drew many salaams and bowings in reply, and rode away, followed by that unforgetable little man's squeaks.

The other incident covered a period of a week or so. It was a question of spies.

The village of Mamoura consisted of a railway terminus and hotel round which sprawled a dark and smelly conglomeration of hovels out of which sprouted the inevitable minaret. The hotel was run by people who purported to be French but who were of doubtful origin, ranging from half-caste

Arab to Turk by way of Greek and Armenian Jew. But they provided dinner and cooling drinks and it was pleasant to sit under the awninged verandah and listen to the frogs and the sea or to play their ramshackle piano and dance with the French residents of Alexandria who came out for week-ends to bathe.

At night we used to mount donkeys about as big as large beetles and have races across the sands back to camp, from which one could see the lights of the hotel. Indeed we thought we saw what they didn't intend us to, for there were unmistakable Morse flashings out to sea from that cool verandah. We took it with grim seriousness and lay for hours on our stomachs with field glasses glued to our eyes. I posted my signalling corporal in a drinking house next door to the hotel, gave him late leave and paid his beer so that he might watch with pencil and notebook. But always he reported in the morning that he'd seen nothing.

The climax came when one night an orderly burst into the hut which the Vet. and I shared and said, "Mr. —— wants you to come over at once, sir. He's taken down half a message from the signalling at the hotel."

I leapt into gum boots, snatched my glasses and ran across to the sand mound from where we had watched.

The other subaltern was there in a great state of excitement.

"Look at it," he said. "Morsing like mad."

I looked, — and looked again.

There was a good breeze blowing and the flag on the verandah was exactly like the shutter of a signalling lamp!

5.

Having sat there all those months, the order to move, when it did finally come, was of the most urgent nature. It was received one afternoon at tea time and the next morning before dawn we were marching down the canal road.

Just before the end we had done a little training, more to get the horses in draught than anything else. With that and the horse shows it wasn't at all a bad turnout.

Once more we didn't know for certain where we were bound for but the betting was about five to four on Greece. How these things leak out is always a puzzle but leak out they do. Sure enough we made another little sea voyage and in about three days steamed up the Ægean, passing many boats loaded with odd-looking soldiers in khaki who turned out to be Greek, and at last anchored outside Salonica in a mass of shipping, French and English troopships, destroyers and torpedo boats and an American battleship with Eiffel-tower masts.

From the sea Salonica was a flashing jewel in a perfect setting. Minarets and mosques, white and red, sprouted everywhere from the white, brown and green buildings. Trees and gardens nestled within the crumbling old city wall. Behind it ran a line of jagged peaks, merging with the clouds, and here and there ran a little winding ribbon of road, climbing up and up only to lose itself suddenly by falling over a precipice.

Here again the M.L.O. had not quite the Public School and Varsity manner and we suffered accordingly. However, they are a necessary evil presumably, these quay-side warriors. The proof undoubtedly lies in the number of D.S.O.'s they muster, — but I don't remember to have seen any of them with wound stripes. Curious, that.

We marched through mean streets, that smelled worse than Egypt, and a dirty populace, poverty-stricken and covered with sores; the soldiers in khaki that looked like brown paper, and leather equipments that were a good imitation of cardboard. Most of the officers wore spurs like the Three Musketeers and their little tin swords looked as if they had come out of toy shops. None of them were shaved. If first impressions count for anything then God help the Greeks.

Our camp was a large open field some miles to the northwest of the town, on the lower slopes of a jagged peak. The tinkle of cow bells made soft music everywhere. Of accommodation there was none of any sort, no tents, nothing but what we could improvise. The Colonel slept under the lee of the cook's cart. The Adjutant and the doctor shared the Maltese cart, and the Vet. and I crept under the forage tarpaulin, from which we were awakened in the dark by an unrestrained cursing and the noise of a violent rainfall.

Needless to say everybody was soaked, fires wouldn't light, breakfast didn't come, tempers as well as appetites became extremely sharp and things were most unpleasant, — the more so since it went on raining for three weeks almost without stopping. Although we hadn't seen rain for half a year it didn't take us five minutes to wish we were back in Egypt. Fortunately we drew bell tents within forty-eight hours and life became more bearable. But once more we had to go through a sort of camp drill by numbers, — odd numbers too, for the order came round that tents would be moved first, then vehicles, and lastly the horses.

Presumably we had to move the guns and wagons with drag-ropes while the horses watched us, grinning into their nose bags.

Anyhow, there we were, half the artillery in Greece, all eighteen-pounders, the other half and the infantry somewhere in the Dardanelles. It appeared, however, that the — Division had quite a lot of perfectly good infantry just up the road but their artillery hadn't got enough horses to go round. So we made a sort of Jack Sprat and his wife arrangement and declared ourselves mobile.

About four days after we'd come into camp the *Marquette* was wrecked some thirty miles off Salonica. It had the — Divisional Ammunition Column on board and some nurses. They had an appalling time in the water and many were lost. The surviving officers, who came dressed in the most motley garments, poor devils, were split up amongst the brigade.

On the Headquarter Staff we took to our bosoms a charming fellow who was almost immediately given the name of Woodbine, — jolly old Woodbine, one of the very best, whom we left behind with infinite regret while we went up country. I'd like to know what his golf handicap is these days.

The political situation was apparently delicate. Greece was still sitting on the fence, waiting to see which way the cat would jump, and here were we and our allies, the French, marching through their neutral country.

Slight evidences of the "delicacy" of the times were afforded by the stabbing of some half dozen Tommies in the dark streets of the town and by the fact that it was only the goodly array of guns which prevented them from interning us. I don't think we had any ammunition as yet, so we couldn't have done very much. However that may be and whatever the political reasons, we sat on the roadside day after day, watching the French streaming up country, — infantry, field guns, mountain artillery and pack transport, — heedless of Tino and his protests. Six months in Egypt, and now this! We *were* annoyed.

However, on about the twentieth day things really happened. "Don" battery went off by train, their destination being some unpronounceable village near the firing line. We, the Headquarters Staff, and "AC" battery followed the next day. The railway followed the meanderings of the Vardar through fertile land of amazing greenness and passed mountains of stark rock where not even live oak grew. The weather was warm for November, but that ceaseless rain put a damper on everything, and when we finally arrived we found "Don" battery sitting gloomily in a swamp on the side of the road. We joined them.

6.

The weather changed in the night and we were greeted with a glorious sunshine in the morning that not only dried our clothes but filled us with optimism.

Just as we were about to start, the pole of my G.S. wagon broke. Everybody went on, leaving me in the middle of nowhere with a broken wagon, no map, and instructions to follow on to the "i" of Causli in a country whose language I couldn't speak and with no idea of the distance. Fortunately I kept the brigade artificer with me and a day's bully beef and biscuits, for it was not till two o'clock in the afternoon that we at last got that wagon mended, having had to cut down a tree and make a new pole and drive rivets. Then we set off into the unknown through the most glorious countryside imaginable. The autumn had stained all the trees red and the fallen leaves made a royal carpet. Vaguely I knew the direction was north by east and once having struck the road out of the village which led in that direction I found that it went straight on through beds of streams, between fields of maize and plantations of mulberries and tumbled villages tenanted only by starving dogs. The doors of nearly every house were splashed with a blue cross, — reminiscences of a plague of typhus. From time to time we met refugees trudging behind ox-drawn wagons laden with everything they possessed in the world, including their babies, — sad-faced, wild-looking peasants, clad in picturesque rags of all colours with eyes that had looked upon fear. I confess to having kept my revolver handy. For all I knew they might be Turks, Bulgars, or at least brigands.

The sense of solitude was extraordinary. There was no sign of an army on the march, not even a bully beef tin to mark the route, nothing but the purple hills remaining always far away and sending out a faint muttering like the beating of drums heard in a dream. The road ahead was always empty when I scanned it through my glasses at hour intervals, the sun lower and lower each time. Darkness came upon us as it did in Egypt, as though some one had flicked off the switch. There was no sign of the village which might be Causli and in the dark the thought which had been uneasily twisting in my brain for several hours suddenly found utterance in the mouth of the artificer sergeant.

"D'you think we're on the right road, sir?"

The only other road we could have taken was at the very start. Ought I to have taken it? In any case there was nothing to be done but go on until we met some one French or English, but the feeling of uncertainty was distinctly unpleasant. I sent the corporal on ahead scouting and we followed silently, very stiff in the saddle.

At last I heard a shout, "Brigade 'Eadquarters?" I think both the team drivers and myself answered "Yes" together.

The corporal had found a guide sent out by the Adjutant, who turned us off across fields and led us on to another road, and round a bend we saw lights twinkling and heard the stamp and movement of picketed horses and answered the challenge of sentries. Dinner was over, but the cook had kept some hot for me, and my servant had rigged up my bivvy, a tiny canvas tent just big enough to take a camp bed. As there was a touch of frost I went to the bivvy to get a woollen scarf, heard a scuffle, and saw two green eyes glaring at me.

I whipped out my revolver and flicked on an electric torch. Crouched down on the bed was a little tortoise-shell kitten so thin that every rib stood out and even more frightened than I was. I caught it after a minute. It was ice cold so I tucked it against my chest under the British warm and went to dinner. After about five minutes it began to purr and I fed it with some bits of meat which it bolted ravenously. It followed that up by standing in a saucer of milk, growling furiously and lapping for dear life. Friendship was established. It slept in the British warm, purring savagely when I stroked it, as though starved of affection as well as food; followed close to my heels when I went out in the morning but fled wildly back to the bivvy if any one came up to me, emerging arched like a little caterpillar from under the bed, uttering cries of joy when I lifted the bivvy flap.

It was almost like finding a refugee child who had got frightened and lost and trusted only the hand that had done it a kindness.

7.

The "i" of Causli showed itself in the morning to be a stretch of turf in a broad green trough between two rows of steep hills. Causli was somewhere tucked behind the crest in our rear and the road on which I had travelled ran back a couple of miles, doubled in a hairpin twist and curved away on the other side of the valley until it lost itself behind a belt of trees that leaped out of the far hill. Forward the view was shut in by the spur which sheltered us, but our horses were being saddled and after breakfast the Colonel took me with him to reconnoitre. Very soon the valley ceased and the road became a mountain path with many stone bridges taking it over precipitous drops. Looking over, one saw little streams bubbling in the sunlight. After about three miles of climbing we came upon a signal station on the roadside ,with linesmen at work. It was the first sign of any troops in all that country, but miles behind us, right back to Salonica, the road was a long chain of troops and transport. Our brigade was as yet the only one up in action.

The signal station proved to be infantry headquarters. It was the summit of the pass, the mountains opening like a great V in front through which further mountains appeared, with that one endless road curling up like a white snake. There was a considerable noise of firing going on and we were just in time to see the French take a steep crest, — an unbelievable sight. We lay on our stomachs miles behind them and through glasses watched puffs of cotton wool, black and white, sprout out of a far-away hill, followed by a wavering line of blue dots. Presently the cotton wool sprouted closer to the crest and the blue dots climbed steadily. Then the cotton wool disappeared over the top and the blue dots gave chase. Now and then one stumbled and fell. Breathless one watched to see if he would get up again. Generally he didn't, but the line didn't stop and presently the last of it had disappeared over the crest. The invisible firing went on and the only proof that it wasn't a dream was the motionless bundles of blue that lay out there in the sun. —

It was the first time I'd seen men killed and it left me silent, angry. Why "go out" like that on some damned Serbian hill? What was it all about that everybody was trying to kill everybody else? Wasn't the sun shining and the world beautiful? What was this disease that had broken out like a scab over the face of the world? — Why did those particular dots have to fall? Why not the ones a yard away? What was the law of selection? Was there a law? *Did* every bullet have its billet? Was there a bullet for the Colonel? — For *me?* — No. It was impossible! But then, why those others and which of us? —

I think I've found the answer to some of those questions now. But on that bright November day, 1915, I was too young. It was all in the game, although from that moment there was a shadow on it.

8.

"Don" battery went into action first.

The Headquarters moved up close to the signalling station — and I lost my kitten — but "Don" went down the pass to the very bottom and cross-country to the east, and dug themselves in near a deserted farmhouse on the outskirts of Valandovo. "Beer" and "C" batteries came up a day or two later and sat down with "AC." There seemed to be no hurry. Our own infantry were not in the line. They were in support of the French, and, with supine ignorance or amazing pluck, but anyhow a total disregard of the laws of warfare, proceeded to dig trenches of sorts in full daylight *and* in full view of the Bulgar. We shouldn't have minded so much but our O.P. happened to be on the hill where most of these heroes came to dig.

The troops themselves were remarkably ill-chosen. Most of those who were not Irish were flat-footed "brickees" from Middlesex, Essex and the dead-level east coast counties, so their own officers told me, where they never raise one ankle above the other. Now they were chosen to give imitations of chamois in these endless hills. Why not send an aviator to command a tank? Furthermore, the only guns were French 75's and our eighteen-pounders and, I think, a French brigade of mountain artillery, when obviously howitzers were indicated. And there were no recuperators in those days. Put a quadrant angle of 28° and some minutes on an old pattern eighteen-pounder and see how long you stay in action, — with spare springs at a premium and the nearest workshops sixty miles away. My own belief is that a couple of handfuls of Gurkhas and French Tirailleurs would have cleaned up Serbia in a couple of months. As it was. —

The French gave us the right of the line from northwest of Valandovo to somewhere east of Kajali in the blue hills, over which, said the Staff, neither man nor beast could pass. We needn't worry about our right, they said. Nature was doing that for us. But apparently Nature had allowed not less than eight Greek divisions to march comfortably over that impassable right flank of ours in the previous Græco-Bulgarian dust-up. Of course the Staff didn't find it out till afterwards. It only cost us a few thousand dead and the Staff were all right in Salonica, so there was no great harm done! Till then the thing was a picnic. On fine mornings the Colonel and I rode down the pass to see Don battery, climbed the mountain to the stone sangar which was their O.P. and watched them shoot — they were a joyous unshaven crowd — went on down the other side to the French front line and reconnoitred the country for advanced positions and generally got the hang of things.

As I knew French there were occasions when I was really useful, otherwise it was simply a joy-ride for me until the rest of the batteries came into action. One morning the Colonel and I were right forward watching a heavy barrage on a village occupied by the Bulgar. The place selected by the Colonel from which to enjoy a really fine view was only ten yards from a dead Bulgar who was in a kneeling position in a shallow trench with his hands in his pockets, keeled over at an angle. He'd been there many days and the wind blew our way. But the Colonel had a cold. I fled to a flank. While we watched, two enemy batteries opened. For a long time we tried to locate their flash. Then we gave it up and returned up the pass to where a French battery was tucked miraculously among holly bushes just under the crest. One of their officers was standing on the sky line, also endeavouring to locate those new batteries. So we said we'd have another try, climbed up off the road, lay upon our stomachs and drew out our glasses. Immediately a pip-squeak burst in the air about twenty yards away. Another bracketed us and the empty shell went whining down behind us. I thought it was rather a joke and but for the Colonel would have stayed there.

He, however, was a regular Gunner, thank God, and slithered off the mound like an eel. I followed him like his shadow and we tucked ourselves half crouching, half sitting, under the ledge, with our feet on the road.

For four hours the Bulgar tried to get that French battery. If he'd given five minutes more right he'd have done it, — and let us alone. As it was he plastered the place with battery fire every two seconds. — Shrapnel made pockmarks in the road, percussion bursts filled our necks with dirt from the ledge and ever the cases whined angrily into the ravine. We smoked many pipes.

It was my first experience under shell fire. I found

it rather like what turning on the quarter current in the electric chair must be, — most invigorating, but a little jumpy. One never knew. Thank heaven they were only pip-squeaks. During those crouching hours two French poilus walked up the pass — it was impossible to go quickly because it was so steep — and without turning a hair or attempting to quicken or duck walked through that barrage with a *sangfroid* that left me gasping. Although in a way I was enjoying it, I was mighty glad to be under that ledge, and my heart thumped when the Colonel decided to make a run for it and went on thumping till we were a good thousand yards to a flank.

The worst of it was, it was the only morning that I hadn't brought sandwiches.

9.

When the other three batteries went into action and the ammunition column tucked itself into dry nullahs along the road we moved up into Valandovo and established Brigade Headquarters in a farmhouse and for many days the signallers and I toiled up and down mountains, laying air lines. It was an elementary sort of war. There were no balloons, no aeroplanes and camouflage didn't seem to matter. Infantry pack transport went up and down all day long. It was only in the valley that the infantry were able to dig shallow trenches. On the hills they built sangars, stone breastwork affairs. Barbed wire I don't remember to have seen. There were no gas shells, no 5.9's, nothing bigger than pip-squeaks. The biggest artillery the Allies possessed were two

120-centimetre guns called respectively Crache Mort and Chasse Boche. One morning two Heavy Gunners blew in and introduced themselves as being on the hunt for sixty-pounder positions. They were burning to lob some over into Strumnitza. We assisted them eagerly in their reconnaissance and they went away delighted, promising to return within three days. They were still cursing on the quayside when we came limping back to Salonica. Apparently there was no one qualified to give them the order to come up and help. In those days Strumnitza was the Bulgar railhead, and they could have pounded it to bits.

As it was, our brigade was the only English Gunner unit in action, and the Battery Commanders proved conclusively to the French (and the Bulgar) that the eighteen-pounder was a handy little gun. The French General ordered one of the 75 batteries to advance to Kajali. They reconnoitred the hills and reported that it was impossible without going ten miles round. The General came along to see for himself and agreed. The Captain of "C" battery, however, took a little walk up there and offered to get up if the Colonel would lend him a couple of hundred infantry. At the same time he pointed out that coming down in a hurry was another story, absolutely impossible. However, it was discussed by the powers that were and the long and short of it was that two of our batteries were ordered forward. "C" was the pioneer; and with the two hundred infantry — horses were out of the question — and all the gunners they laboured from 4.30 P.M. to

6 A.M. the next morning, at which hour they reported themselves in action again. It was a remarkable feat, brought about by sheer muscle and will power, every inch of the way a battle, up slopes that were almost vertical, over small boulders, round big ones with straining drag ropes for about two miles and a half. The 75's refused to believe it until they had visited the advanced positions. They bowed and said "Touché!"

Then the snow came in blinding blizzards that blotted out the whole world and everybody went underground and lived in overcoats and stoked huge fires, — everybody except the infantry whose rifle bolts froze stiff, whose rations didn't arrive and who could only crouch behind their stone sangars. The cold was intense and they suffered terribly. When the blizzard ceased after about forty-eight hours the tracks had a foot of snow over them and the drifts were over one's head.

Even in our little farmhouse where the Colonel and I played chess in front of a roaring fire, drinks froze solid on the mantelpiece and we remained muffled to the eyes. Thousands of rock pigeons appeared round the horse lines, fighting for the dropped grain, and the starving dogs became so fierce and bold that it was only wise to carry a revolver in the deserted villages. Huge brutes some of them, the size of Arab donkeys, a cross between a mastiff and a great Dane. Under that clean garment of snow which didn't begin to melt for a fortnight, the country was of an indescribable beauty. Every leaf on the trees bore its little white burden, firm and crisp, and a cold sun appeared and threw wonderful lights and shadows. The mountains took on a virgin purity.

But to the unfortunate infantry it was one long stretch of suffering. Hundreds a day came down on led mules in an agonised string, their feet bound in straw, their faces and hands blue like frozen meat. The hospitals were full of frost-bite cases, and dysentery was not unknown in the brigade. Potface in particular behaved like a hero. He had dysentery very badly but absolutely refused to let the doctor send him down.

Our rations were none too good, and there were interminable spells of bully beef, fried, hashed, boiled, rissoled, *au naturel* with pickles, and bread became a luxury. We reinforced this with young maize which grew everywhere in the valley and had wonderful soup and corn on the cob, boiled in tinned milk and then fried. Then too the Vet. and I had a wonderful afternoon's wild bull hunting with revolvers. We filled the wretched animal with lead before getting near enough to give the *coup de grace* beside a little stream. The Vet. whipped off his tunic, turned up his sleeves and with a long trench knife conducted a masterly post mortem which resulted in about forty pounds of filet mignon. The next morning before dawn the carcase was brought in in the cook's cart and the Headquarters Staff lived on the fat of the land and invited all the battery commanders to the discussion of that excellent bull.

10.

From our point of view it wasn't at all a bad sort

of war. We hadn't had a single casualty. The few rounds which ever came anywhere near the batteries were greeted with ironic cheers and the only troubles with telephone lines were brought about by our own infantry who removed lengths of five hundred yards or so to mend their bivvies with.

But about the second week of December indications were not wanting of hostile activity. Visibility was very bad owing to early morning fogs, but odd rounds began to fall in the valley behind us in the neighbourhood of the advancing wagon lines, and we fired on infantry concentrations and once even an S.O.S. Rifle fire began to increase and stray bullets hummed like bees on the mountain paths.

In the middle of this I became ill with a temperature which remained for four days in the neighbourhood of 104°. The doctor talked of hospital but I'd never seen the inside of one and didn't want to.

However on the fourth day it was the Colonel's order that I should go. It transpired afterwards that the doctor diagnosed enteric. So away I went labelled and wrapped up in a four-mule ambulance wagon. The cold was intense, the road appalling, the pip-squeaks not too far away until we got out of the valley, and the agony unprintable. That night was spent in a Casualty Clearing Station in the company of half a dozen infantry subalterns all splashed with blood.

At dawn next morning when we were in a hospital train on our way to Salonica, the attack began. The unconsidered right flank was the trouble. Afterwards I heard about a dozen versions of the show, all much the same in substance. The Bulgars poured over the right in thousands, threatening to surround us. Some of the infantry put up a wonderful fight. Others — didn't. Our two advanced batteries fired over open sights into the brown until they had exhausted their ammunition, then removed breech blocks and dial sights, destroyed the pieces and got out, arming themselves with rifles and ammunition picked up ad lib. on the way down. "Don" and "AC" went out of one end of the village of Valandovo while the enemy were held up at the other by the Gunners of the other two batteries. Then two armies, the French and English, got tangled up in the only road of retreat, engineers hastening the stragglers and then blowing up bridges. "Don" and "AC" filled up with ammunition and came into action in support of the other brigades at Causli which now opened fire while "Beer" and "C" got mounted and chased those of our infantry who "didn't", rounded them up, and marched them back to face the enemy. Meanwhile I was tucked away in a hospital bed in a huge marquee, trying to get news from every wounded officer who was brought in. The wildest rumours were going about but no one knew anything officially. I heard that the infantry were wiped out, that the gunners had all been killed or captured to a man, that the remnants of the French were fighting desperately and that the whole thing was a *débacle*.

There we all were helpless in bed, with nurses looking after us, splendid English girls, and all the time those infernal guns coming nearer and nearer. —

UBIQUE 125

At night, sleepless and in a fever, one could almost hear the rumble of their wheels, and from the next tent where the wounded Tommies lay in rows, one or two would suddenly scream in their agony and try and stifle their sobs, calling on Jesus Christ to kill them and put them out of their pain. —

11.

The brigade, when I rejoined, was in camp east of Salonica, under the lee of Hortiac, knee-deep in mud and somewhat short of kit. It was mighty good to get back and see them in the flesh again, after all those rumours which had made one sick with apprehension.

Having pushed us out of Serbia into Greece the Bulgar contented himself with sitting on the frontier and making rude remarks. The Allies, however, silently dug themselves in and prepared for the defence of Salonica in case he should decide to attack again. The Serbs retired to Corfu to reform, and although Tino did a considerable amount of spluttering at this time, the only sign of interest the Greeks showed was to be more insolent in the streets.

We drew tents and moved up into the hills and Woodbine joined us again, no longer a shipwrecked mariner in clothes off the peg, but in all the glory of new uniform and breeches out from home, a most awful duke. Pot-face and the commander of "C" battery went to hospital shortly afterwards and were sent home. Some of the Brass Hats also changed rounds. One, riding forth from a headquarters with cherry brandy and a fire in each room, looked upon our harness immediately on our return from the retreat and said genially that he'd heard that we were a "rabble." When however the commander of "Don" battery asked him for the name and regiment of his informant, the Brass Hat rode away muttering uncomfortably. Things were a little strained!

However Christmas was upon us, so we descended upon the town with cook's carts and visited the base cashier. Salonica was a modern Babel. The cobbles of the Rue Venizelos rang with every tongue in the world, — Turkish, Russian, Yiddish, Serbian, Spanish, Levantine, Arabic, English, French, Italian, Greek and even German. Little tin swords clattered everywhere and the place was a riot of colour, the Jew women with green pearl-sewn headdresses, the Greek peasants in their floppy-seated trousers elbowing enormous Russian soldiers in loose blouses and jack boots who in turn elbowed small-waisted Greek highlanders in kilts with puffballs on their curly-toed shoes. There were black-robed priests with long beards and high hats, young men in red fezzes, civilians in bowlers, old hags who gobbled like turkeys and snatched cigarette ends, all mixed up in a kaleidoscopic jumble with officers of every country and exuding a smell of garlic, fried fish, decaying vegetable matter, and those aromatic eastern dishes which fall into no known category of perfume. Fling into this chaos numbers of street urchins of untold dirt chasing turkeys and chickens between one's legs and you get a slight idea of what sort of place we came to to do our Christmas shopping.

The best known language among the shopkeepers

was Spanish, but French was useful and after hours of struggling one forced a passage out of the crowd with barrels of beer, turkey, geese, pigs, fruit and cigarettes for the men, and cigars and chocolates, whisky, Grand Marnier and Cointreau for the mess. Some fund or other had decided that every man was to have a plum pudding, and these we had drawn from the A.S.C. on Christmas Eve.

In Egypt letters had taken thirteen days to arrive. Here they took from fifteen to seventeen, sometimes twenty-one. Christmas Day however was one of the occasions when nothing came at all and we cursed the unfortunate post office in chorus. I suppose it's the streak of childhood in every man of us that makes us want our letters *on* the day. So the morning was a little chilly and lonely until we went round to see that the men's dinner was all right. It was, with lashings of beer.

This second Christmas on active service was a tremendous contrast to the first. Then there was the service in the barn followed by that depressing lonely day in the fog and flat filth of Flanders. Now there was a clear sunny air and a gorgeous view of purple mountains with a glimpse of sea far off below.

In place of Mass in the barn Woodbine and I went for a walk and climbed up to the white Greek church above the village, surrounded by cloisters in which shot up cypress trees, the whole picked out in relief against the brown hill. We went in. The church was empty but for three priests, one on the altar behind the screen, one in a pulpit on each side in the body of the church. For a long time we stood there listening as they flung prayers and responses from one to another in a high shrill nasal minor key that had the wail of lost souls in it. It was most un-Christmassy and we came out with a shiver into the sun.

Our guest at dinner that night was a Serbian liaison officer from Divisional Headquarters. We stuffed him with the usual British food and regaled him with many songs to the accompaniment of the banjo and broke up still singing in the small hours but not having quite cured the ache in our hearts caused by "absent friends."

12.

The second phase of the campaign was one of endless boredom, filthy weather and the nuisance of changing camp every other month. The boredom was only slightly relieved by a few promotions, two or three full lieutenants becoming captains and taking command of the newly arranged sections of D.A.C., and a few second lieutenants getting their second pip. I was one. The weather was characteristic of the country, unexpected, violent. About once a week the heavens opened themselves. Thunder crashed round in circles in a black sky at midday, great tongues of lightning lit the whole world in shuddering flashes. The rain made every nullah a roaring waterfall with three or four feet of muddy water racing down it and washing away everything in its path. The trenches round our bell tents were of little avail against such violence. The trench sides dissolved and the water poured in. These storms lasted an hour or two and then the sky cleared almost as quickly as it had darkened and the mountain peaks gradually appeared again, clean and fresh. On one such occasion, but much later in the year, the Adjutant was caught riding up from Salonica on his horse and a thunderbolt crashed to earth about thirty yards away from him. The horse stood trembling for full two minutes and then galloped home in a panic.

The changing of camps seemed to spring from only one reason, — the desire for "spit and polish" which covers a multitude of sins. It doesn't matter if your gunners are not smart at gun drill or your subalterns in utter ignorance of how to lay out lines of fire and make a fighting map. So long as your gun park is aligned to the centimetre, your horse lines supplied conspicuously with the type of incinerator fancied by your Brigadier General, and the whole camp liberally and tastefully decorated with white stones, — then you are a crack brigade, and Brass Hats ride round you with oily smiles and pleasant remarks and recommend each other for decorations.

But adopt your own incinerator (infinitely more practical as a rule than the Brigadier General's) and let yourself be caught with an untidy gun park and your life becomes a hell on earth. We learnt it bitterly, until at last the Adjutant used to ride ahead with the R.S.M., a large fatigue party and several miles of string and mark the position of every gun muzzle and wagon wheel in the brigade. And when the storms broke and washed away the white stones the Adjutant would dash out of his tent immediately the rain ceased, calling upon God piteously, the R.S.M. irritably, and every man in the brigade would collect other stones for dear life.

Time hung very heavy. The monotony of week after week of brigade fatigues, standing gun drill, exercising and walking horses, inspecting the men's dinners, with nothing to do afterwards except play cards, read, write letters and curse the weather and the war and all Brass Hats. Hot baths in camp were as usual as diamonds in oysters. Salonica was about twelve miles away for a bath, a long weary ride mostly at a walk on account of the going. But it was good to ride in past the village we used to call Peacockville, for obvious reasons, put the horses up in a Turkish stable in a back street in Salonica, and bathe and feed at the Tour Blanche and watch the crowd. It was a change at least from the eternal sameness of camp and the cramped discomfort of bell tents and there was always a touch of mystery and charm in the ride back in the moonlight.

The whole thing seemed so useless, such an utter waste of life. There one sat in the mud doing nothing. The war went on and we weren't helping. All our civil ambitions and hopes were withering under our very eyes. One hopeless dawn succeeded another. I tried to write but my brain was like a sponge dipped into khaki dye. One yearned for France where at least there was fighting and leave, or if not leave then the hourly chance of a "blighty" wound.

About April there came a welcome interlude.

The infantry had also chopped and changed and been moved about and in the intervals had been kept warm and busy in digging a chain of defences in a giant hundred-mile half-circle around Salonica, the hub of our existence. The weather still didn't seem to know quite what it wanted to do. There was a hint of spring but it varied between blinding snowstorms, bursts of warm sun and torrents of rain.

"Don" battery had been moved to Stavros in the defensive chain and the Colonel was to go down and do Group Commander. The Adjutant was left to look after the rest of the brigade. I went with the Colonel to do Adjutant in the new group. So we collected a handful of signallers, a cart with our kits and servants and set out on a two-day trek due east along the line of lakes to the other coast.

The journey started badly in a howling snow-storm. To reach the lake level there was a one-way pass that took an hour to go down, and an hour and a half to climb on the return trip. The Colonel went on ahead to see the General. I stayed with the cart and fought my way through the blizzard. At the top of the pass was a mass of Indian transport. We all waited for two hours, standing still in the storm, the mud belly-deep because some unfortunate wagon had got stuck in the ascent. I remember having words with a Captain who sat hunched on his horse like a sack the whole two hours and refused to give an order or lend a hand when every one of his teams jibbed, when at last the pass was declared open. God knows how he ever got promoted.

However we got down at last and the sun came out and dried us. I reported to the Colonel and we went on in a warm golden afternoon along the lake shore, with ducks getting up out of the rushes in hundreds and, later, woodcock flashing over our heads on their way to water. As far as I remember the western lake is some eight miles long and about three wide at its widest part, with fairy villages nestling against the purple mountain background, the sun glistening on the minarets and the faint sound of bells coming across the water. We spent the night as guests of a battery which we found encamped on the shore and on the following morning trekked along the second lake which is about ten miles in length, ending at a jagged mass of rock and thick undergrowth which had split open into a wild wooded ravine with a river winding its way through the narrow neck to the sea about five miles farther on.

We camped in the narrow neck on a sandy bay by the river, rock shooting up sheer from the back of the tents, the horses hidden under the trees. The Colonel's command consisted of one 60-pounder — brought round by sea and thrown into the shallows by the Navy who said to us, "Here you are, George. She's on terra firma. It's up to you now" — two naval 6-inch, one eighteen-pounder battery, "Don", one 4.5 howitzer battery, and a mountain battery whose commander rode about on a beautiful white mule with a tail trimmed like an hotel bell pull. "AC" battery of ours came along a day or two later to join the merry party because, to use the vulgar but expressive phrase, the Staff "got the wind up" and saw Bulgars behind every tree.

13.

In truth it was a comedy, — though there were elements of tragedy in the utter inefficiency displayed. We rode round to see the line of our zone. It took two days because, of course, the General had to get back to lunch. Wherever it was possible to cut tracks, tracks had been cut, beautiful wide ones, making an enemy advance easy. They were guarded by isolated machine-gun posts at certain strategic points, and in the nullahs was a little barbed wire driven in on wooden stakes. Against the barbed wire however were piled masses of dried thorn, — utterly impassable but about as inflammable as gunpowder. This was all up and down the wildest country. If a massacre had gone on fifty yards to our right or left at any time we shouldn't have been able to see it. And the line of infantry was so placed that it was impossible to put guns anywhere to assist them.

It is to be remembered that although I have two eyes, two ears, and a habit of looking and listening, I was only a lieutenant with two pips in those days and therefore my opinion is not of course worth the paper it is written on. Ask any Brass Hat!

An incident comes back to me of the action before the retreat. I had only one pip then. Two General Staffs wished to make a reconnaissance. I went off at 3 A.M. to explore a short way, got back at eight o'clock after five hours on a cold and empty stomach, met the Staffs glittering in the winter sun and led them up a goat track, rideable of course. They left the horses eventually and I brought them to the foot of the crest from which the reconnaissance was desired. The party was some twenty strong and walked up on to the summit and produced many white maps. I was glad to sit down and did so under the crest against a rock. Searching the opposite sky line with my glasses I saw several parties of Bulgars watching us, — only recognisable as Bulgars because the little of them that I could see moved from time to time. The Colonel was near me and I told him. He took a look and went up the crest and told the Staffs. The Senior Brass Hat said, "Good God! What are you all doing up here on the crest? Get under cover at once,"— and he and they all hurried down. The reconnaissance was over!

On leading them a short way back to the horses (it saved quite twenty minutes' walk) it became necessary to pass through a wet boggy patch about four yards across. The same Senior Brass Hat stopped at the edge of it and said to me, "What the devil did you bring us this way for? You don't expect me to get my boots dirty, do you? — Good God!"

I murmured something about active service,— but as I say I had only one pip then. —

It isn't that one objects to being cursed. The thing that rankles is to have to bend the knee to a system whose slogan is efficiency, but which retains the doddering and the effete in high commands simply because they have a quarter of a century of service to their records. The misguided efforts of these dodderers are counteracted to a certain extent by the young keen men under them. But it is the dodderers who get the credit, while the real men lick their boots and have to kowtow in the most servile manner. Furthermore it is no secret. We know it and yet we let it go on: and if to-day there are twenty thousand unnecessary corpses among our million dead, after all, what are they among so many? The dodderers have still got enough life to parade at Buckingham Palace and receive another decoration and we stand in the crowd and clap our hands and say, "Look at old So-and-so! Isn't he a grand old man? Must be seventy-six if he's a day!"

So went the comedy at Stavros. One Brass Hat dug a defence line at infinite expense and labour. Along came another, just a pip senior, looked round and said, "Good God! You've dug in the wrong place. — Must be scrapped." And at more expense and more labour a new line was dug. And then a third Brass Hat came along and it was all to do over again. Men filled the base hospitals and died of dysentery; the national debt added a few more insignificant millions, — and the Brass Hats went on leave to Alexandria for a well-earned rest.

Not only at Stavros did this happen but all round the half circle in the increasingly hot weather as the year became older and disease more rampant.

After we'd been down there a week and just got the hang of the country another Colonel came and took over the command of the group, so we packed up our traps and having bagged many woodcock and duck, went away, followed after a few days by "AC" and "Don."

About that time, to our lasting grief, we lost our Colonel, who went home. It was a black day for the brigade. His thoughtfulness for every officer under him, his loyalty and unfailing cheeriness, had made him much loved. I, who had ridden with him daily, trekked the snowy hills in his excellent company, played chess with him, strummed the banjo while he chanted half-remembered songs, shared the same tent with him on occasions and appreciated to the full his unfailing kindness, mourned him as my greatest friend. The day he went I took my last ride with him down to the rest-camp just outside Salonica, a wild threatening afternoon with a storm which burst on me in all its fury as I rode back miserably, alone.

In due course his successor came and we moved to Yailajik — well called by the men Yellow-Jack — and the hot weather was occupied with training schemes at dawn, officers' rides and drills, examinations A and B (unofficial of course), horse shows and an eternity of unnecessary work while one gasped in shirt sleeves and stupid felt hats after the Anzac pattern; long, long weeks of appalling heat and petty worries, until it became a toss-up between suicide or murder. The whole spirit of the brigade changed. From having been a happy family working together like a perfect team the spirit of discontent spread like a canker. The men looked sullen and did their work grudgingly, going gladly to hospital at the first signs of dysentery. Subalterns put in applications for the Flying Corps, — I was one of their number, — and ceased to take an interest in their sections. Battery Commanders raised sarcasm to a fine art and cursed the day that ever sent them to this ghastly backwater.

I left the headquarters and sought relief in "C" battery where, encouraged by the sympathetic commanding officer, I got nearer to the solution of the mysterious triangle T.O.B. than I'd ever been before. He had a way of talking about it that the least intelligent couldn't fail to grasp.

At last I fell ill and with an extraordinary gladness went down to the 5th Canadian hospital on the eastern outskirts of Salonica on the seashore. The trouble was an ear. Even the intensest pain, dulled by frequent injections of morphia, did not affect my relief in getting away from that brigade where, up to the departure of the Colonel, I had spent such a happy time. The pity of it was that everybody envied me.

They talked of an operation. Nothing would have induced me to let them operate in that country where the least scratch turned septic. After several weeks I was sent to Malta where I was treated for twenty-one days. At the end of that time the specialist asked me if my career would be interfered with if he sent me home for consultation as to an operation. One reason he could not do it was that it was a long business, six weeks in bed at least, and they were already overfull. The prison door was about to open! I assured him that on the contrary my career would benefit largely by a sight of home, and to my eternal joy he then and there, in rubber gloves, wrote a recommendation to send me to England. His name stands out in my memory in golden letters.

Within twenty-four hours I was on board.

The fact that all my kit was still with the battery was a matter of complete indifference. I would have left a thousand kits. At home all the leaves were turning, blue smoke was filtering out of red chimneys against the copper background of the beech woods — and they would be waiting for me in the drive.

PART III

THE WESTERN FRONT

III. THE WESTERN FRONT

1.

ENGLAND had changed in the eighteen months since we put out so joyously from Avonmouth. Munition factories were in full blast, food restrictions in force, women in all kinds of uniforms, London in utter darkness at night, the country dotted with hutted training camps. Everything was quiet. We had taken a nasty knock or two and washed some of our dirty linen in public, not too clean at that. My own lucky star was in the ascendant. The voyage completely cured me and within a week I was given a month's sick leave by the Medical Board, — a month of heaven more nearly describes it, for I passed my days in a state of bliss which nothing could mar, except perhaps the realisation, towards the end, of the fact that I had to go back and settle into the collar again.

My mental attitude towards the war had changed. Whatever romance and glamour there may have been had worn off. It was just one long bitter waste of time, — our youth killed like flies by "dugouts" at the front so that old men and sick might carry on the race, while profiteers drew bloated profits and politicians exuded noxious gas in the House. Not a comforting point of view to take back into harness. I was told on good authority that to go out to France in a field battery was a certain way of finding death. They were being flung away in the open to take another thousand yards of trench, so as to make a headline in the daily papers which would stir the drooping spirits of the old, the sick, and the profiteer over their breakfast egg. The *embusqué* was enjoying those headlines too. The combing-out process had not yet begun. The young men who had never been out of England were Majors and Colonels in training camps. It was the officers who returned to duty from hospital, more or less cured of wounds or sickness, who were the first to be sent out again. The others knew a thing or two.

That was how it struck me when I was posted to a reserve brigade just outside London.

Not having the least desire to be "flung away in the open" I did my best to get transferred to a six-inch battery. The Colonel of the reserve brigade did his best but it was queered at once, without argument or appeal, by the nearest Brass Hat, in the following manner. The Colonel having signed and recommended the formal application, spoke to the General personally on my behalf.

"What sort of a fellow is he?" asked the General.

"Seems a pretty useful man," said the Colonel.

"Then we'll keep him," said the General.

"The pity of it is," said the Colonel to me later, "that if I'd said you were a hopeless damned fool he would have signed it."

THE WESTERN FRONT

On many subsequent occasions the Colonel flung precisely that expression at me, so he might just as well have said it then.

However, as it seemed that I was destined for a short life I determined to make it as merry as possible and in the company of a kindred spirit who was posted from hospital a couple of days after I was, and who is now a Bimbashi in the Soudan, I went up to town about three nights a week, danced and did a course of theatres. By day there was no work to do as the brigade already had far too many officers, none of whom had been out. The battery to which we were both posted was composed of category C1 men, — flat-footed unfortunates, unfit to fight on medical grounds, not even strong enough to groom horses properly.

A futile existence in paths of unintelligence and unendeavour worshipping perforce at the altar of destruction, creating nothing, a slave to dishonesty and jobbery, — a waste of life that made one mad with rage in that everything beautiful in the world was snapped in half and flung away because the social fabric which we ourselves had made through the centuries had at last become rotten to the core and broken into flaming slaughter, and was being fanned by yellow press hypocrisy. Every ideal cried out against it. The sins of the fathers upon the wilfully blind children. The Kaiser was only the most pitch-covered torch chosen by Nemesis to set the bonfire of civilisation ablaze. But for one branch in the family tree he would have been England's monarch, and then —?

There have been moments when I have regretted not having sailed to New York in August, 1914, — bitter moments when all the dishonesty has beaten upon one's brain and one has envied the pluck of the honest conscientious objector who has stood out against the ridicule of the civilised world.

The only thought that kept me going was "suppose the Huns had landed in England and I not been fighting?" It was unanswerable, — as I thought then.

Now I wish that the Hun had landed in England in force and laid waste the East coast as he has devastated Belgium and the north of France. There would have been English refugees with perambulators and babies, profiteers crying Kamerad! politicians fleeing the House. There would have been some hope of England's understanding. But she doesn't even now. There were in 1918 before the armistice men — MEN ! — who, because their valets failed to put their cuff links in their shirts one morning, were sarcastic to their war-working wives and talked of the sacrifices they had made for their country.

How *dared* they have valets while we were lousy and unshaved, with rotting corpses round our gun wheels? How *dared* they have wives while we "unmarried and without ties" were either driven in our weakness to licensed women, or clung to our chastity because of the one woman with us every hour in our hearts whom we meant to marry if ever we came whole out of that hell?

Christmas came. They would not let me go down to that little house among the pines and beeches

THE WESTERN FRONT 145

which has ever been "home" to me. But the day was spent quietly in London with my best pal. Seven days later I was on my way to Ireland as one of the advance representatives of the Division. The destination of my brigade was Limerick, that place of pigs and smells and pretty girls and schoolboy rebels who chalked on every barrack wall "Long live the Kaiser! Down with the King!" Have you ever been driven to the depths of despair, seen your work go to pieces before your eyes, and spent the dreadful days in dishonest idleness on the barrack square, hating it all the while but unable to move hand or foot to get out of the mental morass? That is what grew up in Limerick. Even now my mind shivers in agony at the thought of it.

Reinforcements had poured into the battery of cripples and the order came that from it a fighting battery should be formed. As senior subaltern, who had been promised a captaincy, I was given charge of them. The only other officer with me was the loyalest pal a man ever had. He had been promoted on the field for gallantry, having served ten years in the ranks as trumpeter, gunner, corporal and sergeant. Needless to say he knew the game backwards and was the possessor of amazing energy and efficiency. He really ought to have had the command, for my gunnery was almost nil, but I had one pip more than he and so the system put him under my orders. So we paraded the first men, and told them off into sections and were given a horse or two, gradually building up a battery as more reinforcements arrived.

How we worked! The enthusiasm of a first command! For a fortnight we never left the barracks, — drilling, marching, clothing and feeding the fighting unit of which we hoped such great things. All our hearts and souls were in it and the men themselves were keen and worked cheerily and well. One shook off depressing philosophies and got down to the solid reality of two hundred men. The early enthusiasm returned and Pip Don — as my pal was called — and I were out for glory and killing Huns.

The Colonel looked us over and was pleased. Life wasn't too bad, after all.

And then the blight set in. An officer was posted to the command of the little fighting unit.

In a week all the fight had gone out of it. In another week Pip Don and I declared ourselves beaten. All our interest was killed. The sergeant major, for whom I have a lasting respect, was like Bruce's spider. Every time he fell, he at once started re-climbing. He alone was responsible for whatever discipline remained. The captaincy which I had been promised on certain conditions was filled by some one else the very day I carried out the conditions. It didn't matter. Everything was so hopeless that the only thing left was to get out, — and that was the one thing we couldn't do because we were more or less under orders for France. It reached such a pitch that even the thought of being flung away in the open was welcome. At least it would end it all. There was no secret about it. The Colonel knew. Didn't he come to my room one night and say, "Look here, Gibbs, what is the matter with your battery?" And didn't we have another try, and another?

So for a time Pip Don and I smoked cigarettes on the barrack square, strolling listlessly from parade to parade, cursing the fate that should have brought us to such dishonour. We went to every dance in Limerick, organised concerts, patronised the theatre and filled our lives as much as we could with outside interests until such time as we should go to France. And then. — It would be different when shells began to burst!

2.

In the ranks I first discovered that it was a struggle to keep one's soul alive. That struggle had proved far more difficult as an officer in the later days of Salonica. The bitterness of Limerick, together with the reason, as I saw it, of the wholesale slaughter, made one's whole firmament tremble. Rough hands seemed to tear down one's ideals and fling them in the mud. One's picture of God and religion faded under the red light of war. One's brain flickered in the turmoil, seeking something to cling to. What was there? Truth? There was none. Duty? It was a farce. Honour? It was dead. There was only one thing left, one thing which might give them all back again, — Love.

If there was not that in one's heart to keep fragrant, to cherish, to run to for help, to look forward to as the sunshine at the end of a long and awful tunnel then one's soul would have perished and a bullet been a merciful thing.

I was all unconscious that it had been my salvation in the ranks, in Salonica. Now on the eve of going out to the Western Front I recognised it for the first time to the full. The effect of it was odd, — a passionate longing to tear off one's khaki and leave all this uncleanness, and at the same time the certain knowledge that one must go on to the very end, otherwise one would lose it. If I had been offered a war job in New York how could I have taken it, unwounded, the game unfinished, much as New York called me? So its third effect was a fierce impatience to get to France, making at least one more battery to help to end the war.

The days dragged by, the longer from the new knowledge within me. From time to time the Sinn Fein gave signs of renewed activity and either we were all confined to barracks in consequence, presumably to avoid street fighting, or else we hooked into the guns and did route marches through and round about the town. From time to time arrests were made but no open conflict recurred. Apart from our own presence there was no sign of war in Ireland. Food of all kinds was plentiful and cheap, restrictions nil. The streets were well lit at night. Gaiety was the keynote. No aeroplanes dropped bombs on that brilliant target. The Hun and pro-Hun had spent too much money there.

Finally our training was considered complete. The Colonel had laboured personally with all the subalterns and we had benefited by his caustic method of imparting knowledge. And so once more we sat stiffly to attention while Generals rode round us, metaphorically poking our ribs to see if we were fat enough for the slaughter. Apparently we were, for the fighting units said good-bye to their parent batteries — how gladly! — and shipped across to England to do our firing practice.

The camp was at Heytesbury on the other side of the vast plain which I had learnt so well as a trooper. We were a curious medley, several brigades being represented, each battery a little distrustful of the next, a little inclined to turn up its nose. Instead of being "AC", "Beer", "C" and "Don" as before we were given consecutive numbers, well into the hundreds, and after a week or so of dislocation were formed into brigades, and each put under the command of a Colonel. Then the stiffness wore off in friendly competition of trying to pick the best horses from the remounts. Our men challenged each other to football, sergeant majors exchanged notes. Subalterns swapped lies about the war and Battery Commanders stood each other drinks in the mess. Within a fortnight we were all certain we'd got the best Colonel in England and congratulated ourselves accordingly.

Meanwhile Pip Don and I were still outcasts in our own battery, up against a policy of continual distrust, suspicion, and scarcely veiled antagonism. It was at the beginning of April, 1917, that we first got to Heytesbury and snow was thick upon the ground. Every day we had the guns out behind the stables and jumped the men about at quick short series, getting them smart and handy, keeping their interest and keeping them warm. When the snow disappeared we took the battery out mounted, taking turns in bringing it into action, shooting over the sights on moving targets — other batteries at work in the distance — or laying out lines for indirect targets. We took the staff out on cross-country rides, scouring the country for miles and chasing hares — it shook them down into the saddle — carrying out little signalling schemes. In short we had a final polish up of all the knowledge we had so eagerly begun to teach them when he and I had been in sole command. I don't think either of us can remember any single occasion on which the commanding officer took a parade.

Embarkation leave was in full swing, four days for all ranks, and the brigade next to us was ordered to shoot. Two range officers were appointed from our brigade. I was one. It was good fun and extremely useful. We took a party of signallers and all the rations we could lay hands on and occupied an old red farmhouse tucked away in a fold of the plain in the middle of all the targets. An old man and his wife lived there, a quaint old couple, toothless and irritable, well versed in the ways of the army and expert in putting in claims for fictious damages. Our job was to observe and register each round from splinter proofs, send in a signed report of each series, stop the firing by signalling if any stray shepherd or wanderer were seen on the range, and to see that the targets for the following day's shoot had not been blown down or in any other way rendered useless. It was a four-day affair, firing ending daily between three and four P.M. This left us ample time to canter to all the battery positions and work out ranges, angle of sight and compass bearings for every target, — information which would have been invaluable when our turn to fire arrived. Unfortunately, however, several slight alterations were intentionally made and all our labour was wasted. Still it was a good four days of bracing weather with little clouds scudding across a blue sky, never quite certain whether in ten minutes' time the whole world would be blotted out in a blizzard. The turf was springy, miles upon endless miles, and we had some most wonderful gallops and practised revolver shooting on hares and rooks, going back to a huge tea and a blazing wood fire in the old draughty farmhouse.

The practice over, we packed up and marched back to our respective batteries. Events of a most cataclysmic nature piled themselves one upon the other, — friction between the commanding officer and myself, orders to fire on a certain day, orders to proceed overseas on a certain later day, and my dismissal from the battery, owing to the aforesaid friction, on the opening day of the firing. Pip Don was furious, the commanding officer wasn't, and I "pursued a policy of masterly inactivity." The outcome of the firing was not without humour and certainly altered the whole future career of at least two of us. The Captain and the third subaltern left the battery and became "details." The commanding officer became second in command under a new Major who dropped out of the blue and I was posted back to the battery, together with a new third subaltern who had just recovered from wounds.

The business of getting ready was speeded up. The Ordnance Department, hitherto of miserly reluctance, gave us lavishly of their best. Gas masks were dished out and every man marched into a gas chamber, — there either to get gassed or come out with the assurance that the mask had no defects! Final issues of clothing and equipment kept the Q.M.S. sweating from dawn to dusk and the Major signed countless pay books, indents and documents generally.

Thus we were ready and eager to go and strafe the Hun in the merry month of May, 1917.

3.

The personnel of the battery was odd but extremely interesting. Pip Don and myself knew every man, bombardier, corporal and sergeant, what he had done, tried to do, or could do. In a word we knew the battery inside out and exactly what it was worth. Not a man of them had ever been on active service but we felt quite confident that the test of shell fire would not find them wanting. The great majority of them were Scots and they were all as hard as nails.

The third subaltern was an unknown quantity but all of us had been out. The Captain hadn't.

The Major had been in every battle in France since 1914, but he didn't know us or the battery, and if we felt supremely confident in him, it was, to say the least of it, impossible for him to return the compliment. He himself will tell you that he didn't win the confidence of the battery until after a bold and rapidly-decided move in full light of day which put us on the flank of a perfectly hellish bombardment. That may be true of some of the men, but as far as Pip Don and myself went we had adopted him after the first five minutes and never swerved, — having, incidentally, some wonderful arguments about him in the sleeping quarters at Heytesbury with the subalterns of other batteries.

It is extraordinary how the man at the head of a little show like that remains steadily in the limelight. Everything he does, says or looks is noted, commented on and placed to either his credit or debit until the men have finally decided that he's all right or — not. If they come to the first decision, then the Major's life is not more of a burden to him than Divisional and Corps Staffs and the Hun can make it. The battery will do anything he asks of it at any hour of day or night and will go on shooting till the last man is knocked out. If on the other hand they decide that he is not all right, God help him. He gives orders. They are not carried out. Why? An infinite variety of super-excellent excuses. It is a sort of passive resistance, and he has got to be a mighty clever man to unearth the root of it and kill it before it kills him.

We went from Southampton to Havre — it looked exactly the same as when I'd landed there three years previously — and from Havre by train to Merville. There a guide met us in the chilly dawn and we marched up to Estaires, the guide halting us at a mud patch looking like the abomination of desolation, which he said was our wagon line. It was only about seven miles from the place where I'd been in the cavalry and just as muddy, but somehow I was glad to be back. None of those side shows at the other end of the map had meant anything. France was obviously where the issue would ultimately be decided and, apart from the Dardanelles, where the only real fighting was, or ever had been. Let us therefore get on with the war with all speed. Every year had brought talk of peace before Christmas, soon dwindling into columns about preparations for another winter campaign. Even our own men just landed discussed the chances of being back in Scotland for the New Year!

We were an Army brigade, — one of a series of illegitimate children working under Corps orders and lent to Divisions who didn't evince any friendliness when it came to leave allotments, or withdrawn from our Divisional area to be hurried to some other part of the line and flung in in heaps to stiffen the barrage in some big show. Nobody loved us. Divisions saved their own people at our expense, — it was always an Army brigade which hooked in at zero hour and advanced at zero + 15, until after the Cambrai show. Ordnance wanted to know who the hell we were and why our indents had a Divisional signature and not a Corps one, or why they hadn't both, or neither; A.S.C. explained with a straight face how we *always* got the best fresh meat ration; Corps couldn't be bothered with us, until there was a show brewing; Army were polite but incredulous.

THE WESTERN FRONT

The immortal Pyecroft recommends the purchase of a ham as a sure means of seeing life. As an alternative I suggest joining an Army brigade.

4.

In the old days of trench warfare the Armentières front was known as the peace sector. The town itself, not more than three thousand yards from the Hun, was full of happy money-grubbing civilians who served you an excellent dinner and an equally excellent bottle of wine, or, if it was clothes you sought, directed you to Burberry's, almost as well installed as in the Haymarket. Divisional infantry used it as a rest billet. Many cook's carts ambled peacefully along the cobbled streets laden with eggs, vegetables and drinks for officers' messes. Now and then a rifle was fired in the front line, resulting, almost, in a Court of Enquiry. Three shells in three days was considered a good average, a trench mortar a gross impertinence.

Such was the delightful picture drawn for us by veterans who heard we were going there.

The first step was the attaching of so many officers and N.C.O.'s to a Divisional battery in the line for "instruction." The Captain and Pip Don went up first and had a merry week. The Major and I went up next and heard the tale of their exploits. The battery to which we were attached, in command of a shell-shocked Major, was in a row of houses, in front of a smashed church on the fringe of the town, and I learnt to take cover or stand still at the blast of a whistle which meant aeroplanes; saw a fighting map for the first time; an S.O.S. board in a gun pit and the explanation of retaliation targets; read the Divisional Defence Scheme through all its countless pages and remained in *statu quo;* went round the front-line trench and learned that a liaison officer didn't take his pyjamas on raid nights; learned also that a trench mortar bombardment was a messy, unpleasant business; climbed rung by rung up a dark and sooty chimney, or was hauled up in a coffin-like box, to a wooden deck fitted with seats and director heads and telescopes and gazed down for the first time on No Man's Land and the Hun trench system and as far as the eye could reach in his back areas, learning somewhat of the difficulties of flank observation. Every day of that week added depths to the conviction of my exceeding ignorance. Serbia had been nothing like this. It was elementary, child's play. The Major too uttered strange words like calibration, meteor corrections, charge corrections. A memory of Salonica came back to me of a huge marquee in which we had all sat and listened to a gilded staff officer who had drawn diagrams on a blackboard and juggled with just such expressions while we tried hard not to go to sleep in the heat; and afterwards the Battery Commanders had argued it and decided almost unanimously that it was "all right for schools of gunnery but not a damn bit o' use in the field." To the Major, however, these things seemed as ordinary as whisky and pickles.

I came to the conclusion that the sooner I began to learn something the better. It wasn't easy because young Pip Don had the hang of it all, so he and the Major checked each other's figures while I looked on, vainly endeavouring to follow. There was never any question as to which of us ought to have had the second pip. However it worked itself out all right because, owing to the Major, he got his captaincy before I did, which was the best possible thing that could have happened, for I then became the Major's right-hand man and felt the responsibility of it.

At the end of our week of instruction the brigade went into action, two batteries going to the right group, two to the left. The group consisted of the Divisional batteries, trench mortar batteries, the 60-pounders and heavy guns attached like ourselves. We were on the left, the position being just in front of a 4.5 howitzer battery and near the Lunatic Asylum.

It was an old one, four gun pits built up under a row of huge elms, two being in a row of houses. The men slept in bunks in the pits and houses; for a mess we cleaned out a room in the château at the corner which had been sadly knocked about, and slept in the houses near the guns. The château garden was full of lilac and roses, the beds all overgrown with weeds and the grass a jungle, but still very beautiful. Our zone had been allotted and our own private chimney O.P. — the name of which I have forgotten — and we had a copy of that marvellous defence scheme.

Then for a little we found ourselves in the routine of trench warfare, — tours of duty at the O.P. on alternate days and keeping a detailed log book in its swaying deck, taking our turn weekly to supply a liaison officer with the infantry who went up at dark, dined in their excellent mess, slept all night in the signalling officer's bunk, and returned for a shave and a wash after breakfast next morning; firing retaliation salvos at the call of either the O.P. or the infantry; getting up rations and ammunition and letters at a regular hour every night; sending off the countless "returns" which are the curse of soldiering; and quietly feeling our feet.

The O.P. was in an eastern suburb called Houplines, some twenty minutes' walk along the tram lines. At dawn one had reached it with two signallers and was looking out from the upper deck upon an apparently peaceful countryside of green fields splashed yellow with mustard patches, dotted with sleepy cottages from whose chimneys smoke never issued, woods and spinneys in all the glory of their spring budding running up on to the ridge, the Aubers ridge. The trenches were an intricate series of gashes hidden by Nature with poppies and weeds. Then came a grim brown space unmarked by any trench, tangled with barbed wire, and then began the repetition of it all except for the ridge at our own trenches. The early hours were chilly and misty and one entered in the log book, "6 A.M. Visibility nil."

But with the sun the mist rolled up like a blind at one's window and the larks rocketed into the clear blue as though those trenches were indeed deserted. Away on the left was a town, rising from the curling river in terraces of battered ruins, an inexpressible desolation, silent, empty, dead. Terrible to see that gaping skeleton of a town in the flowering countryside. Far in the distance, peeping above the ridge and visible only through glasses, was a faint pencil against the sky — the great factory chimney outside Lille.

Peace seemed the keynote of it all in the soft perfumed heat of that early summer. Yet eyes looked steadily out from every chimney and other eyes from the opposite ridge; and with just a word down the wire trenches went in smoking heaps, houses fell like packs of cards touched by a child's finger, noise beat upon the brain and Death was the master whom we worshipped, upon whose altar we made bloody sacrifice.

We hadn't been there much more than a week when we had our first hint of the hourly reality of it. The third subaltern, who hadn't properly recovered from the effect of his wound, was on his way up to the O.P. one morning and had a misadventure with a shell. He heard it coming, a big one, and sought refuge in the nearest house. The shell unfortunately selected the same house.

When the dust had subsided and the ruins had assumed their final shape the subaltern emerged, unwounded, but unlike his former self. — The doctor diagnosed shell shock and the work went on without him.

It seemed as though that were the turning point in the career of the peace sector.

The Hun began a leisurely but persistent destruction of chimneys with five-nines. One heard the gun in the distance, not much more than the popping of a champagne cork at the other end of the Carlton Grill. Some seconds later you thought you heard the inner circle train come in at Baker Street. Dust choked you, the chimney rocked in the frightful rush of wind, followed a soul-shaking explosion, — and you looked through the back aperture of the chimney to see a pillar of smoke and falling earth spattering down in the sunshine. And from the lower deck immediately beneath you came the voice of the signaller, "They ought to give us sailor suits up 'ere, sir!"

And passing a finger round the inside of your sticky collar, which seemed suddenly a little tight, you sat down firmly again and said, "Yes. — Is the steward about?"

Within sixty seconds another champagne cork popped. Curse the Carlton Grill!

In addition to the delights of the O.P. the Hun "found" the battery. It happened during the week that the Captain came up to have a look round and in the middle of the night. I was sleeping blissfully at liaison and returned next morning to find a most unpleasant smell of cordite hanging about, several houses lying on the pavement, including the one Pip Don and I shared, great branches all over the road and one gun pit looking somewhat bent. It appeared that Pip Don had spent the remainder of the night rounding up gunners in his pyjamas. No one was hurt. The Captain returned to the wagon line during the course of the morning.

Having found us, the Hun put in a few hundred rounds whenever he felt bored, — during the 9 A.M. parade, at lunch time, before tea and at the crack of dawn. The old red garden wall began to look like a Gruyère cheese, the road was all pockmarked, the gun pits caught fire and had to be put out, the houses began to fall even when there was no shelling and it became a very unhealthy corner. Through it all the Major was a tower of strength. So long as he was there the shelling didn't seem to matter, but if he were absent one didn't *quite* know whether to give the order to clear for the time being or stick it out. The Huns' attentions were not by any means confined to our position. The systematic bombardment of the town had begun and it became the usual thing to hear a horrible crackling at night and see the whole sky red. The Major of one of our batteries was killed, the senior subaltern badly wounded and several of their guns knocked out by direct hits. We were lucky.

5.

Meanwhile the Right Group, who had been watching this without envy from the undisturbed calm of the countryside, decided to make a daylight raid by way of counter-attraction and borrowed us for the occasion. The Major and I went down to reconnoitre a battery position and found a delightful spot behind a hedge, under a row of spreading elms. Between the two, camouflage was unnecessary and, as a cobbled road ran immediately in front of the hedge, there was no danger of making any tracks.

It was a delightful position with a farmhouse two hundred yards along the road. The relief of getting out of the burning city, of not having to dodge shells at unexpected moments, of knowing that the rations and ammunition could come up without taking a twenty to one chance of being scuppered!

The raid was just like any other raid, except that it happened to be the first barrage we fired, the first barrage table we worked out, the first time we used the 106 fuze, and the first time that at the eleventh hour we were given the task, in which some one else had failed, of cutting the wire. I had been down with the Major when he shot the battery in, — and hadn't liked it. In places there was no communication trench at all and we had to crawl on our bellies over a chaos of tumbled earth and revetments in full few of any sniper, and having to make frequent stops because the infernal signaller would lag behind and turn off. And a few hours before the show the Major was called upon to go down there and cut the wire at all costs. Pip Don was signalling officer. He and every available signaller, stacks of wire and lamps, spread themselves in a living chain between the Major in the front-line trench and me at the battery. Before going the Major asked me if I had the barrage at my finger tips. I had. Then if he didn't get back in time, he said, I could carry out the show all right? I could, — and watched him go with a mouth full of bitter curses against the Battery Commander who had failed to cut that wire. My brain drew lurid pictures of stick-bombs, minnies, pineapples, pip squeaks and five-nines being the reason why the Major wouldn't get back "in time." And I sat down by the telephonist, praying for the call that would indicate at least his safe arrival in the front-line trench.

Beside every gun lay a pile of 106 fuzes ready. Orders were to go on firing if every German plane in the entire Vaterland came over. — Still they weren't through on the 'phone!

I went along from gun to gun, making sure that everything was all right and insisting on the necessity of the most careful laying, stopping from time to time to yell to the telephonist "Through yet?" and getting a "No, sir" every time that almost made me hear those cursed minnies dropping on the Major. At last he called up. The tension was over. We had to add a little for the 106 fuze but each gun was registered on the wire within four rounds. The Major was a marvel at that. Then the shoot began.

Aeroplanes came winging over, regardless of our Archies. But we, regardless of the aeroplanes, were doing "battery fire 3 secs." as steadily as if we were on Salisbury Plain, getting from time to time the order, "Five minutes more right." We had three hundred rounds to do the job with and only about three per gun were left when the order "Stop" arrived. I stopped and hung on to the 'phone. The Major's voice, coming as though from a million miles away, said, "Napoo wire. How many more rounds?"

"Three per gun, sir."

"Right. — All guns five degrees more right for

the onlooker, add two hundred, three rounds gun fire."

I made it so, received the order to stand down, put the fitter and the limber gunners on to sponging out, — and tried to convince myself that all the noise down in front was miles away from the Major and Pip Don. — It seemed years before they strolled in, a little muddy but as happy as lambs.

It occurred to me then that I knew something at least of what our women endured at home every day and all day, — just one long suspense, without even the compensation of *doing* anything.

The raid came off an hour or so later like clockwork, without incident. Not a round came back at us and we stood down eventually with the feeling of having put in a good day's work.

We were a very happy family in those days. The awful discouragement of Limerick had lifted. Bombardments and discomforts were subjects for humour, work became a joy, "crime" in the gun line disappeared and when the time arrived for sending the gunners down to the wagon line for a spell there wasn't one who didn't ask if he might be allowed to stay on. It was due entirely to the Major. For myself I can never be thankful enough for having served under him. He came at a time when one didn't care a damn whether one were court-martialled and publicly disgraced. One was "through" with the Army and cared not a curse for discipline or appearances. With his arrival all that was swept away without a word being said. Unconsciously he set a standard to which one did one's utmost to

THE WESTERN FRONT 165

live, and that from the very moment of his arrival. One found that there was honour in the world and loyalty, that duty was not a farce. In some extraordinary way he embodied them all, forcing upon one the desire for greater self-respect; and the only method of acquiring it was effcrt, physical and mental, in order to get somewhere near his high standard. I gave him the best that was in me. When he left the brigade, broken in health by the ceaseless call upon his own effort, he wrote me a letter. Of all that I shall take back with me to civil life from the Army that letter is what I value most.

6.

We had all cherished the hope that we had seen the last of the town; that Right Group, commanded by our own Colonel, would keep us in our present position.

There was a distinct drop in the mental temperature when, the raid over, we received the order to report back to Left Group. But we still clung to the hope that we might be allowed to choose a different gun position. That avenue of trees was far too accurately pin-pointed by the Hun. Given, indeed, that there were many other places from which one could bring just as accurate and concentrated fire to bear on our part of the zone, it was criminal folly to order us back to the avenue. That, however, was the order. It needed a big effort to find any humour in it.

We hooked in and pulled out of that peaceful raid position with a sigh of regret and bumped our way back over the cobbles through the burning town, keeping a discreet distance between vehicles. The two houses which had been the emplacements of the left section were unrecognisable as gun pits, so we used the other four pits and put the left section forward in front of the Asylum under camouflage. Not less than ten balloons looked straight down on the gun muzzles. The detachment lived in a cellar under the Asylum baths.

Then Pip Don got his captaincy and went to another battery, to the safety and delights of the wagon line. One missed him horribly. We got a new subaltern who had never been out before but who was as stout as a lion. Within a few days our Captain was sent back ill and I followed Pip Don to the wagon lines as Captain in my own battery, a most amazing stroke of luck. We foregathered in a restaurant at Estaires and held a celebration dinner together, swearing that between us we would show the finest teams and the best harness in France, discussing the roads we meant to build through the mud, the improvements we were instantly going to start in the horse standings.

Great dreams that lasted just three days! Then his Major went on leave and he returned to command the battery, within five hundred yards of ours. The following day I was hurriedly sent for to find the whole world reeking with gas, mustard gas. Everybody had streaming eyes and noses. Within three minutes I was as bad as the rest.

How anybody got through the next days I don't know. Four days and nights it lasted, one curious hissing rain of shells which didn't burst with a crash but just uttered a little pop, upon which the ground became spattered with yellow liquid and a greyish fog spread round about. Five-nines, seventeen-inch, high explosive and incendiary shells were mixed in with the gas. Communications went wholesale. Fires roared in every quarter of the town. Hell was let loose and always the gas choked and blinded. Hundreds of civilians died of it, although they had previously been warned repeatedly to clear out. The conviction was so strong that Armentières was the peace sector that the warnings were disregarded.

The howitzer battery behind us had been reinforced with ninety men and two officers the day before the show started. After that first night one officer was left. He had been up a chimney O.P. all night. The rest went away again in ambulance wagons. It was a holocaust, a shambles. A colossal attack was anticipated, and as all communications had gone the signallers were out in gas masks all over the town, endeavouring to repair lines broken in a hundred places, and a constant look-out was kept for S.O.S. signals from the infantry.

Except when shooting, all our men were kept underground in gas masks, beating the gas away with "flappers." The shelling was so ceaseless and violent round about the position that when men were sent from one section to another with messages they went in couples, their departure being telephoned to the section. If their arrival was not reported within ten minutes a search party was sent to find them. To put one's head above ground at any moment of day or night was to take one's life in one's hands. Ammunition went up, and gun pits caught fire and the rain of shells never ceased. To get to the O.P. one had to fling oneself flat in a ditch, countless times always with an ear stretched for the next shell. From minute to minute it was a toss-up, and blackened corpses and screaming, mangled wounded left a bloody trail in the stinking, cobbled streets. The peace sector!

Was it just a Boche measure to prevent us from using the town as billets any more? Or was it a retaliation for the taking of the Messines Ridge which we had watched from our chimney not many weeks before, watched in awe and wonder, thanking God we were not taking part in that carnage? The unhealthy life and the unceasing strain told even on the Major. We were forced to live by the light of candles in a filthy cellar beneath the chateau, snatching uneasy periods of rest when one lay on a bunk with goggles on one's smarting eyes, breathing with labour, listening to the heavy thud of shells up above and the wheezing and sneezing of the unfortunate signallers, getting up and going about one's work in a sort of stupor, dodging shells rather by instinct than reason and tying up wounded with a dull sickness at the pit of one's stomach.

But through it all one's thoughts of home intertwined with the reek of death like honeysuckle with deadly nightshade, as though one's body were imprisoned in that foul underground hole while one's mind soared away and refused to come back.

It was all a strange dream, a clammy nightmare. Letters came, filled with all the delicious everyday doings of another world, filling one's brain with a scent of verbena and briar rose, like the cool touch of a woman's hands on the forehead of a man in delirium.

7.

On the morning of the fifth day the gas shelling ceased and the big stuff became spasmodic, — concentrations of twenty minutes' duration.

One emerged into the sun, sniffing carefully. The place was even more unrecognisable than one had imagined possible. The chateau still stood but many direct hits had filled the garden with blocks of stone. The Asylum was a mass of ruins, the grounds pitted with shell holes. The town itself was no longer a place to dine and shop. A few draggled inhabitants slunk timidly about like rats, probing the debris of what had once been their homes. The cobbled streets were great pits where seventeen-inch shells had landed, half filled again with the houses which had toppled over on either side. The hotels, church and shops in the big square were gutted by fire, great beams and house fronts blocking the roadway. Cellars were blown in and every house yawned open to the sky. In place of the infantry units and transports clattering about the streets was a desolate silent emptiness punctuated by further bombardments and the echoing crash of falling walls. And, over all, that sickly smell of mustard.

It was then that the Left Group Commander had

a brain wave and ordered a trial barrage on the river Lys in front of Frelinghein. It was about as mad a thing as making rude noises at a wounded rhinoceros, given that every time a battery fired the Boche opened a concentration.

Pip Don had had three seventeen-inch in the middle of his position. Nothing much was found of one gun and its detachment except a head, and a boot containing a human foot.

The Group Commander had given the order, however, and there was nothing to do but to get on with it. —

The barrage was duly worked out. It was to last eighteen minutes with a certain number of lifts and switches. The Group Commander was going to observe it from one of the chimneys.

My job was to look after the left section in the open in front of the Asylum. Ten minutes before zero I dived into the cellar under the baths breathless, having dodged three five-nines. There I collected the men and gathered them under cover of the doorway. There we waited for a minute to see where the next would burst. It hit a building twenty-five yards away.

"Now!" said I, "double!" and we ran, jumping shell holes and flinging ourselves flat for one more five-nine. The guns were reached all right, the camouflage pulled back and everything made ready for action. Five Hun balloons gazed down at us straight in front, and three of his aeroplanes came and circled low over our heads, and about every minute the deafening crash of that most

THE WESTERN FRONT 171

demoralising five-nine burst just behind us. I lay down on the grass between the two guns and gazed steadfastly at my wrist watch.

"Stand by!"

The hands of the Numbers 3 stole out to the handles of the firing lever.

"Fire!"

The whole of Armentières seemed to fire at once. The Group Commander up in his chimney ought to have been rather pleased. Four rounds per gun per minute was the rate. Then at zero plus one I heard that distant pop of Hun artillery and with the usual noise the ground heaved skyward between the two guns just in front. It wasn't more than twelve and a half yards away. The temptation to run made me itch all over.

Pop! it went again. My forehead sank on to my wrist watch.

A good bracket, twelve and a half yards behind, and again lumps of earth spattered on to my back. The itch became a disease. The next round, according to all the laws of gunnery, ought to fall between my collar and my waist. —

I gave the order to lift, straining my ears.

There came no pop. I held my breath so that I might hear better, — and only heard the thumping of my heart. We lifted again and again. —

I kept them firing for three full seconds after the allotted time before I gave the order to cease fire. The eighteen minutes — lifetimes — were over and that third pop didn't come till we had stopped. Then having covered the guns we ran helter-skelter, each man finding his own way to the cellar through the most juicy bombardment we'd heard for quite twenty-four hours.

Every man answered to his name in the cellar darkness and there was much laughter and tobacco smoke while we got back our breath.

Half an hour later their bombardment ceased. The sergeant and I went back to have a look at the guns. Number 5 was all right. Number 6, however, had had a direct hit, one wheel had burnt away and she lay on her side, looking very tired.

I don't know how many other guns had been knocked out in the batteries taking part, but, over and above the value of the ammunition, that trial barrage cost at least one eighteen-pounder! And but for a bit of luck would have cost the lives of the detachment.

8.

The Major decided to move the battery and gained the reluctant consent of the Group Commander who refused to believe that there had been any shelling there till he saw the gun lying burnt and smashed and the pits burnt and battered. The Hun seemed to take a permanent dislike to the Asylum and its neighbourhood. It may have been coincidence but any time a man showed there a rain of shells chivvied him away. It took the fitter and the detachment about seven trips before they got a new wheel on, and at any hour of day or night you could bet on at least a handful of four-twos. The gas was intermittent.

At four o'clock in the morning after a worrying night when I had gone out twice to extinguish gun pits reported on fire, the Major announced that he was going to get the gun out and disappeared out of the cellar into the shell-lit darkness.

Two hours later he called up from Group Headquarters and told me to get the other out and take her to Archie Square, a square near the station, so called because a couple of anti-aircraft guns had used it as an emplacement in the peace days. With one detachment on each drag rope we ran the gantlet in full daylight of a four-two bombardment, rushing shell holes and what had once been flower beds, keeping at a steady trot, the sweat pouring off us.

The Major met us in Archie Square and we went back to our cellar for breakfast together.

Of the alternative positions one section was in Chapelle d'Armentières. We hoped great things of it. It looked all right, pits being built in the back yards of a row of small houses, with plenty of trees for cover and lots of fruit for the men, — raspberries, plums, and red currants. Furthermore the shell holes were all old. The only crab about it was getting there. Between us and it were two much-shelled spots called Sandbag Corner and Snow Corner. Transports used to canter past them at night and the Hun had an offensive habit of dropping barrages on both of them any time after dark. But there was a place called Crown Prince House at Sandbag Corner and I fancy he used this as a datum point. While the left section went straight on to the Chapelle the other two turned to the right at Snow Corner and were to occupy some houses just along the road and a garden next to them under camouflage.

I shall not forget the night of that move in a hurry. In the afternoon the Major returned to the battery at tea time. There was no shelling save our own anti-aircraft, and perfect sunshine.

"The teams are due at ten o'clock," said he. "The Hun will start shelling precisely at that time. We will therefore move *now*. Let us function." We functioned!

The battery was called together and the nature of the business explained. Each detachment pulled down the parados in the rear of the gun pits and such part of the pit itself as was necessary to allow the gun to come out,—no light task, because the pits had been built to admit the gun from the front. As soon as each reported ready double detachments were told off to the drag ropes and the gun, camouflaged with branches, was run out and along the lane and round the corner of the chateau. There they were all parked, one by one. Then the ammunition was brought, piles of it. Then all the gun stores and kits.

At ten o'clock the teams were heard at the other end of the cobbled street. A moment later shells began to burst on the position, gun fire. From the cover afforded by the chateau and the wall we loaded up without casualty and hooked in, bits of shell and wall flying over our heads viciously.

I took charge of the left section in Archie Square.

The vehicles were packed, dixies tied on underneath. The Major was to follow with the four guns and the other subaltern at ten minutes' interval.

Keeping fifty yards between vehicles I set off, walking in front of the leading gun team. We clattered along the cobbled streets, rattling and banging. The station was being bombarded. We had to go over the level crossing a hundred yards or so in rear of it. I gave the order to trot. A piece of shell sent up a shower of sparks in front of the rear gun team. The horses bucked violently and various dixies fell off, but I kept on until some distance to a flank under the houses. The dixies were rescued and re-tied. There was Sandbag Corner to navigate yet, *and* Snow Corner. It was horribly dark, impossible to see shell holes until you were into them, and all the time shells were bursting in every direction. The road up to the two Corners ran straight towards the Hun, directly enfiladed by him. We turned into it at a walk and were half-way along when a salvo fell round Crown Prince House just ahead. I halted immediately, wondering where in heaven's name the next would fall, the horses snorting and prancing at my back. For a couple of minutes there was a ragged burst of gun fire while we stood with the bits missing us. Then I gave the order to trot. The horses needed no encouragement. I could only just keep in front, carrying maps and a torch and with most of my equipment on. We carried on past Crown Prince House, past Sandbag Corner and walked again, blown and tottering, towards Snow Corner, and only just got past it when a barrage dropped right on the cross-roads. It was there that the Major would have to turn to the right with his four guns presently. Please God it would stop before he came along.

We weren't very far behind the support lines now and the pop-pop-pop, pop-pop-pop of machine guns was followed by the whistling patter of bullets. I kept the teams as close under the houses as I dared. There was every kind of devilment to bring a horse down, open drains, coils of tangled wire, loose debris. Eventually we reached the Chapelle and the teams went off at the trot as soon as the ammunition was dumped and the kits were off.

Then in the black night we heaved and hauled the guns into their respective pits and got them on to their aiming posts and S.O.S. lines.

It was 3 A.M. before I got back to the new headquarters, a house in an orchard, and found the Major safe and sound.

A couple of days later the Major was ordered to a rest camp, and at a moment's notice I found myself in command of the battery. It was one of the biggest moments of my life. Although I had gone down to take the Captain's place my promotion hadn't actually gone through and I was still a subaltern, faced with the handling of six guns at an extremely difficult moment and with the lives of some fifty men in my hands, to say nothing of the perpetual responsibility to the infantry in the front line.

It was only when the Major had said good-bye

and I was left that I began to realise just how greatly one had depended on him. All the internal arrangements which he had handled so easily that they seemed no trouble loomed up as insurmountable difficulties — returns, ammunition, rations, relieving the personnel — all over and above the constant worry of gun detachments being shelled out, lines being cut, casualties being got away. It was only then that I realised what a frightful strain he must have endured during those days of continual gas and bombardment, the feeling of personal responsibility towards every single man, the vital necessity through it all of absolute accuracy of every angle and range lest by being flustered or careless one should shoot one's own infantry, the nights spent with one ear eternally on the telephone and the added strain of sleeplessness. — A lonely job, Battery Commander.

I realised too what little use I had been to him, carrying out orders, yes, but not really taking any of the weight off his shoulders.

The insignificance of self was never so evident as that first night with my ear to the 'phone, all the night noises accentuated in the darkness, the increasing machine-gun fire which might mean an attack, the crashing of shells which might get my supply wagons on their way back, the jump when the 'phone buzzed suddenly, making my heart leap against my ribs, only to put me through to Group for an order to send over thirty rounds on a minnie firing in C 16 d o 4. — It was good to see the blackness turn to grey and recognise objects once more in the room, to know that at last the infantry were standing down and to sink at last into deep sleep as the grey became rose and the sun awoke.

Do the men ever realise, I wonder, that the Major who snaps out orders, who curses so freely, who gives them extra guards and docks their pay, can be a human being like themselves whose one idea is *their* comfort and safety, that they may strafe the Hun and not get strafed?

It was my first experience in handling subalterns too and I came to see them from a new point of view. Hitherto one's estimation of them had been limited by their being good fellows or not. The question of their knowledge or ignorance hadn't mattered. One could always give them a hand or do the thing oneself. Now it was reversed. Their knowledge, working capabilities and stout-heartedness came first. Their being good fellows was secondary, but helpful. The most ignorant will learn more in a week in the line than in ten weeks in a gunnery school.

9.

The first few days in the new position were calm. It gave one time to settle down. We did a lot of shooting and apart from a spare round or two in our direction nothing came back in return. The Hun was still plastering the Asylum and the avenue at all times of day, to our intense joy. The more he shelled it the more we chuckled. One felt that the Major had done Fritz in the eye. So we gathered plums and raspberries in the warm sun, rejoicing that the horrible smell of mustard gas was no more.

There was a fly in the ointment of course. It consisted of several thousand rounds of ammunition in the Asylum which we were ordered to salvage. The battery clerk, a corporal of astounding stoutheartedness who had had countless escapes by an inch already in the handling of it, and who subsequently became one of the best sergeants in the battery, undertook to go and see what could be done. He took with him the fitter, a lean Scot, who was broken-hearted because he had left a file there and who wanted to go and scratch about the ruins to try and recover it. These two disappeared into the Asylum during a momentary lull. Before they returned the Hun must have sent in about another fifteen hundred rounds, all big stuff. They came in hot and covered with brick dust. The fitter had got his file and showed it with joy and affection. The corporal had made a rough count of the rounds and estimated that at least a couple of hundred had "gone up" or were otherwise rendered useless.

To my way of thinking it would have been manslaughter to have sent teams to get the stuff away, so I decided to let time solve the problem and leave well alone. Eventually it did solve itself. Many weeks later another battery occupied the position (Poor devils. It still reeked of gas) and I had the pleasure of showing the Battery Commander where the ammunition was and handing it over.

Meanwhile the Boche had "found" the left and centre sections. In addition to that the Group Commander conceived a passion to experiment with guns in the front-line trenches, to enfilade the enemy over open sights at night and generally to put the fear of God into him. Who more suitable than the Army brigade battery commanded by that subaltern?

I was sent for and told all about it and sent to reconnoitre suitable positions. Seeing that the enemy had all the observation and a vast preponderance of artillery I did all in my power to dissuade the Commander. He had been on active service, however, before I was born — he told me so — and had forgotten more things than I should ever know. He had indeed forgotten them.

The long and short of it was that I took a subaltern with me and armed with compasses and trench maps we studied the whole zone at distances varying from three to five hundred yards from the enemy front-line trench. The best place of all happened to be near Battalion Headquarters. Needless to say the Colonel ordered me off.

"You keep your damn things away. There's quite enough shelling here without your planting a gun. Come and have a drink."

Eventually, however, we got two guns "planted" with cover for the detachments. It was an absolute waste of guns. The orders were to fire only if the enemy came over the top by day and on special targets by night. The difficulty of rationing them was extreme, it made control impossible from battery headquarters because the lines went half a dozen times a day and left me only two sections to do all the work with.

The only thing they ever fired at was a very near balloon one afternoon. Who gave the order to fire

THE WESTERN FRONT

remains a mystery. The sergeant swore the infantry Colonel gave it.

My own belief is that it was a joy shoot on the sergeant's part. He was heartily cursed for his pains, didn't hit the balloon, and within twenty-four hours the gun was knocked out. The area was liberally shelled, to the discomfort of the infantry, so if the Colonel did give the order, he had only himself to thank for the result.

The headquarters during this time was an odd round brick building like a pagoda in the middle of a narrow orchard. A high red brick wall surrounded the orchard which ran down to the road. At the road edge were two houses completely annihilated. Plums, greengages, raspberries and red currants were in abundance. The signallers and servants were in dugouts outside the wall. Curiously enough, this place was not marked on the map. Nor did the Hun seem to have it on his aeroplane photographs. In any case, although he shelled round about I can only remember one which actually burst inside the walls.

Up at Chapelle d'Armentières the left section was almost unrecognisable. Five-nines had thumped it out of all shape, smashed down the trees, ploughed up the garden and scattered the houses into the street. The detachment spent its time day and night in clearing out into neighbouring ditches and dugouts and coming back again. They shot between whiles, neither of the guns having been touched and I don't think they slept at all. None of them had shaved for days.

As regards casualties we were extraordinarily lucky. Since leaving the town not a man had been hit or gassed. For the transport at night I had reconnoitred a road which avoided the town entirely and those dangerous crossroads and took them right through the support line, within a quarter of a mile of the Boche. The road was unshelled and only a few machine-gun bullets spat on it from time to time. So they used it nightly and not a horse or driver was touched.

Then the Right Group had another raid and borrowed us again. The white house and the orchard which we had used before were unoccupied. I decided to squeeze up a bit and get all six guns in. The night of the move was a colossal undertaking. The teams were late and the Hun chose to drop a gas barrage round us. More than that, in the afternoon I had judged my time and dodged in between two bombardments to visit the left section. They were absolutely done in, so tired that they could hardly keep their eyes open. The others were little better, having been doing all the shooting for days. However I ordered them to vacate the left section and come along to me at Battery Headquarters for a rest before the night's work. They dragged themselves there and fell asleep in heaps in the orchard in the wet. The subaltern and the sergeant came into the building, drank a cup of tea each and filled the place with their snores. So I sent for another sergeant and suggested that he and his men who had had a brief rest that day should go and get the left section guns out while these people handled his as

THE WESTERN FRONT 183

best they could. He jumped at it and swore he'd get the guns out, begging me to keep my teams well to the side of the road. If he had to canter they were coming out and he was going to ride the lead horse himself, — splendid fellow.

Then I collected the subalterns and detailed them for the plan of campaign. The left section man said he was going with his guns. So I detailed the junior to see the guns into the new positions and send me back the ammunition wagons as he emptied them. The third I kept with the centre section. The corporal clerk was to look after the headquarters. I was to function between the lot.

The teams should have been up at 9 P.M. They didn't arrive till ten, by which time the gas hung about thick and people were sneezing right and left. Then they hung up again because of a heavy shelling at the corner on the way to the left section. However they got through at last and after an endless wait that excellent sergeant came trotting back with both guns intact. We had meanwhile yanked out the centre section and sent them back. The forward guns came back all right from the trenches, but no ammunition wagons or G.S. returned from the position, although filled by us ages before and sent off.

So I got on a bicycle and rode along to see what the trouble was. It was a poisonous road, pitch dark, very wet and full of shell holes. I got there to find a column of vehicles standing waiting all mixed up, jerked the bicycle into a hedge and went downstairs to find the subaltern.

There was the Major! Was I pleased? — I felt years younger. However this was his night off. I was running the show. "Carry on, Old Thing," said he.

So I went out into the chaotic darkness and began sorting things out. Putting the subaltern in charge of the ammunition I took the guns. It was a herculean task to get those six bundooks through the wet and spongy orchard with men who were fresh. With these men it was asking the impossible. But they did it, at the trot.

You know the sort of thing — "Take the strain — together — heave! Together — heave! Now keep her going! Once more — heave! Together — heave! and again — heave! Easy all! Have a blow — Now look here, you fellows, you *must* wait for the word and put your weight on *together*. Heels into the mud and lean on it, but lean together, all at the same moment, and she'll go like a baby's pram. Now then, come on and I'll bet you a bottle of bass all round that you get her going at a canter if only you'll heave together. — Take the strain — *together* — heave! Ter-rot! Canter! Come on now, like that — splendid, — and you owe me a bottle of bass all round."

Sounds easy, doesn't it? but oh, my God, to see those poor devils, dropping with fatigue, putting their last grunting ounce on to it, with always just one more heave left! Magnificent fellows who worked till they dropped and then staggered up again, in the face of gas and five-nines, and went on shooting till they were dead, — *they've* won this war

THE WESTERN FRONT

for us if anybody has, these Tommies who don't know when they're beaten, these "simple soldiers" as the French call them, who grouse like hell but go on working whether the rations come up or whether they don't, until they're senseless from gas or stop a shell and get dropped into a hole in an army blanket. These are the men who have saved England and the world, these, — and not the gentlemen at home who make fortunes out of munitions and "war work" and strike for more pay, not the *embusqué* who cannot leave England because he's "indispensable" to his job, not the politicians and vote-seekers who bolster up their parties with comfortable lies more dangerous than mustard gas, not the M.L.O.'s and R.T.O.'s and the rest of the alphabetic fraternity and Brass Hats who live in comfort in back areas doing a lot of brain work and filling the Staff leave boat, — not any of these, but the cursing, spitting, lousy Tommy, God save him!

10.

The last of the guns was in by three o'clock in the morning but there wasn't a stitch of camouflage in the battery. However I sent every last man to bed, having my own ideas on the question of camouflage. The subaltern and I went back to the house. The ammunition was also unloaded and the last wagon just about to depart. The servants had tea and sandwiches waiting, a perfect godsend.

"What about tracks?" The Major cocked an eye in my direction. He was fully dressed, lying on his valise. I stifled a million yawns and spoke round a sandwich. "Old Thing and I are looking after that when it gets light."

"Old Thing" was the centre section commander, blinking like a tired owl, a far-away expression on his face.

"And camouflage?" said the Major.

"Ditto," said I.

The servants were told to call us in an hour's time. I was asleep before I'd put my empty tea-cup on the ground. A thin grey light was creeping up when I was roughly shaken. I put out a boot and woke Old Thing. Speechless, we got up shivering, and went out. The tracks through the orchard were feet deep.

We planted irregular branches and broke up the wheel tracks. Over the guns was a roof of wire netting which I'd had put up a day previously. Into these we stuck trailing vine branches one by one, wet and cold. The Major appeared in the middle of the operation and silently joined forces. By half-past four the camouflage was complete. Then the Major broke the silence.

"I'm going up to shoot 'em in," he said.

Old Thing dosing on a gun seat woke with a start and stared. He hadn't been with the Major as long as I had.

"D'you mind if one detachment does the whole thing?" said I. "They're all just about dead but C's got a kick left."

The Major nodded. Old Thing staggered away, collected two signallers who looked like nothing human and woke up C sub-section. They came one by one like silent ghosts through the orchard, tripping over stumps and branches, sightless with sleep denied.

The Major took a signaller and went away. Old Thing and I checked aiming posts over the compass.

Fifteen minutes later the O.P. rang through and I reported ready.

The sun came out warm and bright and at nine o'clock we "stood down." Old Thing and I supported each other into the house and fell on our valises with a laugh. Some one pulled off our gum boots. It must have been a servant but I don't know. I was asleep before they were off.

The raid came off at one o'clock that night in a pouring rain. The gunners had been carrying ammunition all day after about four hours' sleep. Old Thing and I had one. The Major didn't have any. The barrage lasted an hour and a half, during which one sub-section made a ghastly mistake and shot for five full minutes on a wrong switch.

A raid of any size is not just a matter of saying, "Let's go over the top to-night, and nobble a few of 'em! Shall us?"

And the other fellow in the orthodox manner says, "Let's" — and over they go with a lot of doughty bombers and do a lot of dirty work. I wish it were.

What really happens is this. First the Brigade Major, quite a long way back, undergoes a brainstorm which sends showers of typewritten sheets to all sorts of Adjutants who immediately talk of transferring to the Anti-Aircraft. Other sheets follow in due course, contradicting the first and giving also a long list of code words of a domestic nature usually, with their key. These are hotly pursued by maps on tracing paper, looking as though drawn by an imaginative child.

At this point Group Commanders, Battalion Commanders, and Battery Commanders join in the game, taking sides. Battery Commanders walk miles and miles daily along duck boards, and shoot wire in all sorts of odd places on the enemy front trench and work out an exhaustive barrage.

Then comes a booklet, which is a sort of revision of all that has gone before and alters the task of every battery. A new barrage table is worked out. Follows a single sheet giving zero day.

The raiders begin cutting off their buttons and blacking their faces and putting oil drums in position.

Battery wagon lines toil all night bringing up countless extra rounds. The trench mortar people then try to cut the real bit of wire at which the raiders will enter the enemy front line. As a rule they are unsuccessful and only provoke a furious retaliatory bombardment along the whole sector.

Then Division begins to get excited and talks rudely to Group. Group passes it on. Next a field battery is ordered to cut that adjective wire and does.

A Gunner officer is detailed to go over the top with the raid commander. He writes last letters to his family, drinks a last whisky, puts on all his Christmas-tree and says "Cheero" as though going to his own funeral. It may be.

THE WESTERN FRONT

Then telephones buzz furiously in every brigade and everybody says "Carrots" in a whisper.

You look up "Carrots" in the code book and find it means "raid postponed 24 hours." Everybody sits down and curses.

Another paper comes round saying that the infantry have changed the colours of all the signal rockets to be used. All gunners go on cursing.

Then comes the night! Come up to the O.P. and have a dekko with me, but don't forget to bring your gas mask.

Single file we zigzag down the communication trenches. The O.P. is a farmhouse, or was, in which the sappers have built a brick chamber just under the roof. You climb up a ladder to get to it and find room for just the signaller and ourselves with a long slit through which you can watch Germany. The Hun knows it's an O.P. He's got a similar one facing you, only built of concrete, and if you don't shell him he won't shell you. But if you do shell him with a futile 18-pounder H.E. or so, he turns on a section of five-nines and the best thing you can do is to report that it's "snowing", clear out quick and look for a new O.P. The chances are you won't find one that's any good.

It's frightfully dark; can't see a yard. If you want to smoke for any sake don't strike matches. Use a tinder. See that sort of extra dark lump, just behind those two trees — all right, poles if you like. They *were* trees! — Well, that's where they're going over.

Not a sound anywhere except the rumble of a battle away up north. Hell of a strafe apparently.

Hullo! What's the light behind that bank of trees? — Fritz started a fire in his own lines? Doesn't look like a fire. — It's the moon coming up, moon, moon, so brightly shining. Pity old Pelissier turned up his toes. — Ever heard the second verse of "Au Clair de la Lune"?

(Singing)

> Au clair de la lune
> Pierrot répondit,
> "Je n'ai pas de plume,
> Je suis dans mon lit."
>
> "Si tu es donc couché,"
> Chuchotta Pierrette,
> "Ouvre moi ta porte
> Pour que je m'y mette."

'*Tis* the moon all right, a corker too. — What do you make the time? — A minute to go, eh? Got your gas mask at the alert?

The moon came out above the trees and shed a cold white light on the countryside. On our side at least the ground was alive with men, although there wasn't a sound or a movement. Tree stumps, blasted by shell fire, stood out stark naked. The woods on the opposite ridge threw a deep belt of black shadow. The trenches were vague uneven lines, camouflaging themselves naturally with the torn ground.

Then a mighty roar that rocked the O.P. made the ground tremble and set one's heart thumping and the peaceful moonlight was defiled. Bursts of flame and a thick cloud of smoke broke out on the enemy trenches. Great red flares shot up, the oil drums, staining all the sky the colour of blood. Rifle and machine-gun fire pattered like the chattering of a thousand monkeys as an accompaniment to the roaring of lions. Things zipped past or struck the O.P. The smoke out there was so thick that the pin-points of red fire made by the bursting shells could hardly be seen. The raiders were entirely invisible.

Then the noise increased steadily as the German sky was splashed with all-coloured rockets and Verey lights and star shells, and their S.O.S. was answered. There's a gun flash! What's the bearing? Quick. — There she goes again! — Nine-two magnetic, that's eighty true. Signaller! Group. — There's another! By God, that's some gun. Get it while I bung this through. — Hullo! Hullo, Group! O.P. speaking. Flash of enemy gun eight — 0 degrees true. Another flash, a hell of a big one, what is it? — One, one, two degrees. — Yes, that's correct. Good-bye.

Then a mighty crash sent earth and duckboards spattering on to the roof of the O.P., most unpleasantly near. The signaller put his mouth to my ear and shouted "Brigade reports gas, sir." Curse the gas. You can't see anything in a mask. — Don't smell it yet, anyhow.

Crash again, and the O.P. rocked. Damn that five-nine. Was he shooting us or just searching? Anyhow, the line of the two bursts doesn't look *quite* right for us, do you think? If it hits the place, there's not an earthly. Tiles begin rattling down off the roof most suggestively. It's a good twenty-foot drop down that miserable ladder. Do you think his line.... Look out! She's coming. — Crash!

God, not more than twenty yards away! However we're all right. He's searching to the left of us. Where *is* the blighter? Can you see his flash? Wonder how our battery's getting on? —

Our people were on the protective barrage now, much slower. The infantry had either done their job or not. Anyhow they were getting back. The noise was distinctly tailing off. The five-nine was searching farther and farther behind to our left. The smell of gas was very faint. The smoke was clearing. Not a sign of life in the trenches. Our people had ceased fire.

The Hun was still doing a ragged gun fire. Then he stopped.

A Verey light or two went sailing over in a big arc.

The moon was just a little higher, still smiling inscrutably. Silence, but for that sustained rumble up north. How many men were lying crumpled in that cold white light?

Division reported "Enemy front line was found to be unoccupied. On penetrating his second line slight resistance was encountered. One prisoner taken. Five of the enemy were killed in trying to escape. Our casualties slight."

At the end of our barrage I called that detachment up, reduced three of them to tears, and in awful gloom of spirit reported the catastrophe to the Major. He passed it on to Brigade who said they would investigate.

A day later Division sent round a report of the "highly successful raid which from the adverse weather conditions owed its success to the brilliance of the artillery barrage. . . ."

That same morning the Colonel went to Division, the General was on leave. The Major was sent for to command the Group, and my secret hopes of the wagon line were dashed to the ground. I was a Battery Commander again in deed if not in rank.

11.

The wagon line all this while had, in the charge of the sergeant major, been cursed most bitterly by horse masters and A.D.V.S.'s who could not understand how a sergeant major aged perhaps thirty-nine could possibly know as much about horse management as a new-fledged subaltern anywhere between nineteen and twenty-one.

From time to time I pottered down on a bicycle for the purpose of strafing criminals and came away each time with a prayer of thanks that there was no new-fledged infant to interfere with the sergeant major's methods.

On one occasion he begged me to wait and see an A.D.V.S. of sorts who was due at two o'clock that afternoon and who on his previous tour of inspection had been just about as nasty as he could be. I waited.

Let it be granted, as our old enemy Euclid says, that the horse standings were the worst in France — the Division of course had the decent ones — and that every effort was being made to repair them. The number of shelled houses removed bodily from the firing line to make brick standings and pathways through the mud would have built a model village. The horses were doing this work in addition to ammunition fatigues, brigade fatigues and every other sort of affliction. Assuming too that a sergeant major doesn't carry as much weight as a Captain (I'd got my third pip) in confronting an A.S.C. forage merchant with his iniquities, and I think every knowledgeable person admitted that our wagon line was as good as, if not better than, shall we say, any Divisional battery. Yet the veterinary expert (?) crabbed my very loyal supporter, the sergeant major, who worked his head and his hands off day in, day out. It was displeasing, — more, childish.

In due course he arrived, — in a motor car. True it wasn't a Rolls Royce, but then he was only a Colonel. But he wore a fur coat just as if it had been a Rolls Royce. He stepped delicately into the mud and left his temper in the car. To the man who travels in motors a splash of mud on the boots is as offensive as the sight of a man smoking a pipe in Bond Street at eleven o'clock in the morning. It isn't done.

I saluted and gave him good morning. He grunted and flicked a finger. Amicable relations were established.

"Are you in charge of these wagon lines?" said he.

"In theory, yes, sir."

He didn't quite understand and cocked a doubtful eye at me.

I explained. "You see, sir, the B.C. and I are carrying on the war. He's commanding Group and I'm commanding the battery. But we've got the fullest confidence in the sergeant maj. —"

Was it an oath he swallowed? Anyhow, it went down like an oyster.

The Colonel moved, thus expressing his desire to look round.

I fell into step.

"Have you got a hay sieve?" said he.

"Sergeant Major, where's the hay sieve?" said I.

"This way, sir," said the sergeant major.

Two drivers were busily passing hay through it. The Colonel told them how to do it.

"Have you got wire hay racks above the horses?"

"Sergeant Major," said I, "have we got wire hay racks?"

"This way, sir," said the sergeant major.

Two drivers were stretching pieces of bale wire from pole to pole.

The Colonel asked them if they knew how to do it.

"How many horses have you got for casting?" said the Colonel.

"Do we want to cast any horses, Sergeant Major?" said I.

"Yes, sir," said the sergeant major. "We've got six."

It was a delightful morning. Every question that the Colonel asked I passed on to the sergeant major, whose answer was ever ready. Wherever the Colonel wished to explore, there were men working.

Could a new-fledged infant unversed in the ways of the Army have accomplished it?

One of the sections was down the road quite five minutes away. During the walk we exchanged views about the war. He confided to me that the ideal was to have in each wagon line an officer who knew no more about gunnery than that turnip but who knew enough about horses to take advice from veterinary officers.

In return I told him that there ought not to be any wagon lines, that the horse was effete in a war of this nature, that over half the man-power of the country was employed in grooming and cleaning harness, half the tonnage of the shipping taken up in fetching forage and that there was more strafing over a bad turn-out than if a battery had shot its own infantry for four days running.

The outcome of it all was pure farce. He inspected the remaining section and then told me he was immensely pleased with the marked improvement in the condition of the animals and the horse management generally (nothing had been altered) and that if I found myself short of labour when it came to building a new wagon line he thought he knew where he could put his hand on a dozen useful men. Furthermore he was going to write and tell my Colonel how pleased he was.

The sergeant major's face was a study!

The psychology of it is presumably the same that brings promotion to the officer who, smartly and with well polished buttons, in reply to a question from the General, "What colour is black?" whips out like a flash, "White, sir!"

And the General nods and says, "Of course! — Smart young officer that! What's his name?"

Infallible!

12.

It is difficult to mark the exact beginnings of mental attitudes when time out there is one long action of nights and days without names. One keeps the date, because of the orders issued. For the rest it is all one. One can only trace points of view, feelings, call them what you will, as dating before or after certain outstanding events. Thus I had no idea of war until the gas bombardment in Armentières, no idea that human nature could go through such experiences and emotions and remain sane. So once in action I had not bothered to find the reason of it all, contenting myself merely with the profound conviction that the world was mad, that it was against human nature, — but that tomorrow we should want a full echelon of ammunition. Even the times when one had seen death only gave one a momentary shock. One such incident will never leave me but I cannot feel now anything of the horror I experienced at the moment.

It was at lunch one day before we had left the chateau. A trickle of sun filtered down into the cellar where the Major, one other subaltern and myself were lunching off bully beef and ration pickles. Every now and again an H.E. shell exploded outside in the road along which infantry were constantly passing. One burst was followed by piercing screams. My heart gave a leap and I sprang for the stairs and out. Across the way lay three bodies, a great purple stain on the pavement, the mark of a direct hit on the wall against which one was huddled. I ran across. Their eyes were glassy, their faces black. Grey fingers curled upwards from a hand that lay back down. Then the screams came again from the corner house. I dashed in. Our corporal signaller was trying to bandage a man whose right leg was smashed and torn open, blood and loose flesh everywhere. He lay on his back, screaming. Other screams came from round the corner. I went out again and down the passage saw a man, his hands to his face, swaying backwards and forwards.

I ran to him. "Are you hit?"

He fell on to me. "My foot! Oh, my foot! Christ!"

Another officer, from the howitzer battery, came running. We formed a bandy chair and began to carry him up towards the road.

"Don't take me up there," he blubbered. "Don't take me there!"

We had to. It was the only way, to step over those three black-faced corpses and into that house where there was water and bandages. There was a padre there now and another man. I left them and returned to the cellar to telephone for an ambulance. I was cold, sick. But they weren't *our* dead. They weren't our gunners with whose faces one was familiar, who were part of our daily life. The feeling passed and I was able to go on with the bully beef and pickles and the war.

During the weeks that followed the last raid I was to learn differently. They were harassing weeks with guns dotted all over the zone. The luck seemed to have turned and it was next to impossible to find a place for a gun which the Hun didn't immediately shell violently. Every gun had of course a different pin-point and map work became a labour, map work and the difficulty of battery control and rationing. One's brain was keyed incessantly up to concert pitch.

Various changes had taken place. We had been taken into Right Group and headquarters was established in a practically unshelled farm with one section beside it. Another section was right forward in the Brickstack. The third was away on the other side of the zone, an enfilade section which I handed over, lock, stock and barrel, to the section commander who had his own O.P. in Moat Farm and took on his own targets. We were all extremely happy, doing a lot of shooting.

One morning, hot and sunny, I had to meet the Major to reconnoitre an alternative gun position. So I sent for the enfilade section commander to come and take charge and set out in shorts and shirt sleeves on a bicycle. The Major, another Headquarters officer and myself had finished reconnoitring and were eating plums, when a heavy bombardment began in the direction of the battery farm. Five-nines they were in section salvos and the earth went up in spouts, not on the farm but mighty close. I didn't feel anxious at first, for that subaltern had been in charge of the Chapelle section and knew all about clearing out. But the bombardment went on. The Major and the other left me, advising me to "give it a chance" before I went back.

So I rode along to an O.P. and tried to get through to the battery on the 'phone. The line was gone.

Through glasses I could see no signs of life round about the farm. They must have cleared, I thought. However, I had to get back some time or other, so I rode slowly back along the road. A track led between open fields to the farm. I walked the bicycle along this until bits of shell began flying. I lay flat. Then the bombardment slackened. I got up and walked on. Again they opened, so I lay flat again.

For perhaps half an hour bits came zooming like great stagbeetles all round, while I lay and watched.

They were on the gun position, not the farm, but somehow my anxiety wouldn't go. After all I was in charge of the battery and here I was, while God knew what might have happened in the farm. So I decided to make a dash for it and timed the bursts. At the end of five minutes they slackened and I thought I could do it. Two more crashed. I jumped on the bike, pedalled hard down the track until it was blotted out by an enormous shell hole into which I went, left the bike lying and ran to the farm gate just as two pip-squeaks burst in the yard.

I fell into the door, covered with brick dust and tiles but unhurt.

The sound of singing came from the cellar. I called down "Who's there?" The servants and the corporal clerk were there. And the officer? Oh, he'd gone over to the guns to see if everybody had cleared the position. He'd given the order as soon as the bombardment began. But over at the guns the place was being chewed up.

Had he gone alone? No. One of the servants had gone with him. How long ago? Perhaps twenty minutes. Meanwhile during question and answer four more pip-squeaks had landed, two at the farm gate, one in the yard, one just over.

It was getting altogether too hot. I decided to clear the farm first. Two at a time, taking the word from me, they made a dash for it through the garden and the hedge to a flank, till only the corporal clerk and myself were left. We gathered the secret papers, the "wind gadget", my compass and the telephone and ran for it in our turn.

We caught the others who were waiting round the corner well to a flank. I handed the things we'd brought to the mess cook and asked the corporal clerk if he'd come with me to make sure that the subaltern and the gunners had got away all right.

We went wide and got round to the rear of the position. Not a sign of any of the detachments in any houses round about. Then we worked our way up a hedge which led to the rear of the guns, dropping flat for shells to burst. They were more on the farm now than the guns. We reached the signal pit, — a sort of dugout with a roof of pit props and earth and a trench dug to the entrance.

The corporal went along the trench. "Christ!" he said and came blindly back.

For an instant the world spun. Without seeing I saw. Then I climbed along the broken trench. A five-nine had landed on the roof of the pit and crashed everything in.

A pair of boots was sticking out of the earth. —

He had been in charge of the battery for *me*. From the safety of the cellar he had gone out to see if the men were all right. He had done *my* job!

Gunners came with shovels. In five minutes we had him out. He was still warm. The doctor was on his way. We carried him out of the shelling on a duck board. Some of the gunners went on digging for the other boy. The doctor was there by the time we'd carried him to the road. He was dead.

13.

A pair of boots sticking out of the earth.

For days I saw nothing else. That jolly fellow whom I'd left laughing, sitting down to write a letter to his wife, — a pair of boots sticking out. Why? Why?

We had laid him in a cottage. The sergeant and I went back and by the light of a candle which flickered horribly, emptied his pockets and took off his ring. How cold Death was. It made him look ten years younger.

Then we put him into an army blanket with his

boots on and all his clothes. The only string we had was knotted. It took a long time to untie it. At last it was done.

A cigarette holder, a penknife, a handkerchief, the ring. I took them out with me into the moonlight, all that King and country had left of him.

What had this youngster been born for, sent to a Public School, earned his own living and married the pretty girl whose photo I had seen in the dugout? To die like a rat in a trap, to have his name one day in the Roll of Honour and so break two hearts, and then be forgotten by his country because he was no more use to it. What was the worth of Public School education if it gave the country no higher ideal than war? — to kill or be killed. Were there no brains in England big enough to avert it? He hadn't wanted it. He was a representative specimen. What had he joined for? Because all his pals had. He didn't want them to call him coward. For that he had left his wife and his home, and to-morrow he would be dropped into a hole in the ground and a parson would utter words about God and eternal life.

What did it all mean? Why, because it was the "thing to do", did we all join up like sheep in a Chicago packing yard? What right had our country — the "free country" — to compel us to live this life of filth and agony?

The men who made the law that sent us out, they didn't come too. They were the "rudder of the nation", steering the "Ship of State." They'd never seen a pair of boots sticking out of the earth.

Why did we bow the neck and obey other men's wills?

Surely these conscientious objectors had a greater courage in withstanding our ridicule than we in wishing to prove our possession of courage by coming out. What was the root of this war, — honour? How can honour be at the root of dishonour, and wholesale manslaughter? What kind of honour was it that smashed up homesteads, raped women, crucified soldiers, bombed hospitals, bayoneted wounded? What idealism was ours if we took an eye for an eye? What was our civilisation, twenty centuries of it, if we hadn't reached even to the barbaric standards, — for no barbarian could have invented these atrocities. What was the festering pit on which our social system was built?

And the parson who talked of God, — is there more than one God, then, for the Germans quoted him as being on their side with as much fervour and sincerity as the parson? How reconcile any God with this devastation and deliberate killing? This war was the proof of the failure of Christ, the proof of our own failure, the failure of the civilised world. For twenty centuries the world had turned a blind eye to the foulness stirring inside it, insinuating itself into the main arteries; and now the lid was wrenched off and all the foul stench of a humbug Christian civilisation floated over the poisoned world.

One man had said he was too proud to fight. We, filled with the lust of slaughter, jeered him as we had jeered the conscientious objectors. But wasn't there in our hearts, in saner moments, a respect which we were ashamed to admit, — because we in our turn would have been jeered at? Therein lay our cowardice. Death we faced daily, hourly, with a laugh. But the ridicule of our fellow cowards, that was worse than death. And yet in our knowledge we cried aloud for Peace, who in our ignorance had cried for War. Children of impulse satiated with new toys and calling for the old ones! We would set back the clock and in our helplessness called upon the Christ whom we had crucified.

And back at home the law-makers and the old men shouted patriotically from their club fenders, "We will fight to the last man!"

The utter waste of the brown-blanketed bundle in the cottage room!

What would I not have given for the one woman to put her arms round me and hide my face against her breast and let me sob out all the bitterness in my heart?

14.

From that moment I became a conscientious objector, a pacifist, a most bitter hater of the Boche whose hand it was that had wrenched the lid off the European cesspit. Illogical? If you like, but what is logic? Logically the war was justified. We crucified Christ logically and would do so again.

From that moment my mind turned and twisted like a compass needle that had lost its sense of the north. The days were an endless burden blackened by the shadow of death, filled with emptiness, bitterness and despair.

The day's work went on as if nothing had happened. A new face took his place at the mess table, the routine was exactly the same. Only a rough wooden cross showed that he had ever been with us. And all the time we went on shooting, killing just as good fellows as he, perhaps, doing our best to do so at least. Was it honest, thinking as I did? Is it honest for a convict who doesn't believe in prisons to go on serving his time? There was nothing to be done but go on shooting and try to forget.

But war isn't like that. It doesn't let you forget. It gives you a few days, or weeks, and then takes some one else. "Old Thing" was the next, in the middle of a shoot in a front line O.P.

I was lying on my bed playing with a tiny kitten while the third subaltern at the 'phone passed on the corrections to the battery. Suddenly, instead of saying "Five minutes more right," he said, "*What's* that? — Badly wounded?" and the line went.

I was on the 'phone in a flash, calling up battalion for stretcher bearers and doctors.

They brought me his small change and pencil-ends and pocketbook, — and the kitten came climbing up my leg.

The Major came back from leave — which he had got on the Colonel's return — in time to attend Old Thing's funeral with the Colonel and myself. Outside the cemetery a football match was going on all the time. They didn't stop their game. Why should they? They were too used to funerals, — and it might be their turn in a day or two.

THE WESTERN FRONT

Thanks to the Major my leave came through within a week. It was like the answer to a prayer. At any price I wanted to get away from the responsibility, away from the sight of khaki, away from everything to do with war.

London was too full of it, of immaculate men and filmy girls who giggled. I couldn't face that.

I went straight down to the little house among the beeches and pines, — an uneasy guest of long silences, staring into the fire, of bursts of violent argument, of rebellion against all existing institutions.

But it was good to watch the river flowing by, to hear it lapping against the white yacht, to hear the echo of rowlocks, flung back by the beech woods, and the wonderful whir! whir! whir! of swans as they flew down and down and away; to see little cottages with wisps of blue smoke against the brown and purple of the distant woods, not lonely ruins and sticks; to see the feathery green moss and the watery rays of a furtive sun through the pines, not smashed and torn by shells; at night to watch the friendly lights in the curtained windows and hear the owls hooting to each other unafraid and let the rest and peace sink into one's soul; to shirk even the responsibility of deciding whether one should go for a walk or out in the dingy, or stay indoors, but just to agree to anything that was suggested.

To decide anything was for out there, not here where war did not enter in.

Fifteen dream days, like a sudden strong whiff of verbena or honeysuckle coming out of an envelope.

For the moment one shuts one's eyes, — and opens them again to find it isn't true. The sound of guns is everywhere.

So with that leave. I found myself in France again, trotting up in the mud and rain to report my arrival as though I'd never been away. It was all just a dream to try and call back.

15.

Everything was well with the battery. My job was to function with all speed at the building of the new horse lines. Before going on leave I had drawn a map to scale of the field in which they were to be. This had been submitted to Corps and approved and work had started on it during my leave.

My kit followed me and I installed myself in a small canvas hut with the acting-Captain of another of our batteries whose lines were belly deep in the next field. He had succeeded Pip Don who went home gassed after the Armentières shelling and who, on recovering, had been sent out to Mesopotamia.

The work was being handled under rather adverse conditions. Some of the men were from our own battery, others from the Brigade Ammunition Column, more from a Labour Company, and there was a full-blown Sapper private doing the scientific part. They were all at loggerheads; none of the N.C.O.'s would take orders from the Sapper private, and the Labour Company worked Trades Union hours, although dressed in khaki and calling themselves soldiers. The subaltern in charge was on the verge of putting every one of them under arrest, — not a bad idea, but what about the standings?

By the time I'd had a look round tea was ready. At least there seemed to be plenty of material.

At seven next morning I was out. No one else was. So I took another look round, did a little thinking, and came and had breakfast. By nine o'clock there seemed to be a lot of cigarette smoke in the direction of the works.

I began functioning. My servant summoned all the heads of departments and they appeared before me in a sullen row. At my suggestion tongues wagged freely for about half an hour. I addressed them in their own language and then, metaphorically speaking, we shook hands all round, sang hymn number 44, and standings suddenly began to spring up like mushrooms.

It was really extraordinary how those fellows worked once they'd got the hang of the thing. It left me free to go joy-riding with my stable companion in the afternoons. We carried mackintoshes on the saddle and scoured the country, splashing into Bailleul — it was odd to revisit the scene of my trooper days after three years — for gramophone records, smokes, stomachic delicacies and books. We also sunk a lot of francs in a series of highly artistic picture post cards which, pinned all round the hut at eye level, were a constant source of admiration and delight to the servants and furnished us with a splash of colour which at least broke the monotony of khaki canvas. These were — it goes without saying — supplemented from time to time with the more reticent efforts of *La Vie Parisienne*.

All things being equal we were extremely comfortable, and, although the stove was full of surprises, quite sufficiently frowzy during the long evenings, which were filled with argument, invention, music and much tobacco. The invention part of the programme was supplied by my stable companion who had his own theories concerning acetylene lamps, and who, with the aid of a couple of shell cases and a little carbide nearly wrecked the happy home. Inventions were therefore suppressed.

They were tranquil days in which we built not only book shelves, stoves and horse standings but a great friendship, — ended only by his death on the battlefield. He was all for the gun line and its greater strenuousness.

As for me, then at least, I was content to lie fallow. I had seen too much of the guns, thanked God for the opportunity of doing something utterly different for a time and tried to conduct a mental spring-clean and rearrangement. As a means to this I found myself putting ideas on paper in verse — a thing I'd never done in all my life — bad stuff but horribly real. One's mind was tied to war, like a horse on a picketing rope, and could only go round and round in a narrow circle. To break away was impossible. One was saturated with it as the country was with blood. Every cog in the machinery of war was like a magnet which held one in spite of all one's struggles, giddy with the noise, dazed by its enormity, nauseated by its results.

THE WESTERN FRONT

The work provided one with a certain amount of comic relief. Timber ran short and it seemed as if the standings would be denied completion. Stones, gravel and cinders had been already a difficulty, settled only by much importuning. Bricks had been brought from the gun line. But asking for timber was like trying to steal the chair from under the General. I went to Division and was promptly referred to Corps who were handling the job. Corps said, "You've had all that's allowed in the R.E. handbook. Good morning." I explained that I wanted it for wind screens. They smiled politely and suggested my getting some ladies' fans from any deserted village. On returning to Division they said, "If Corps can't help you, how the devil can you expect us to?"

I went to Army. They looked me over and asked me where I came from and who I was, and what I was doing, and what for and on what authority, and why I came to them instead of going to Division and Corps? To all of which I replied patiently. Their ultimate answer was a smile of regret. There wasn't any in the country, they said.

So I prevailed upon my brother who, as War Correspondent, ran a big car and no questions asked about petrol, to come over and lunch with me. To him I put the case and was immediately whisked off to O.C. Forests, the Timber King. At the lift of his little finger down came thousands of great oaks. Surely a few branches were going begging?

He heard my story with interest. His answer

threw beams of light. "Why the devil don't Division and Corps and all the rest of them *ask* for it if they want it? I've got tons of stuff here. How much do you want?"

I told him the cubic stature of the standings.

He jotted abstruse calculations for a moment. "Twenty tons," said he. "Are you anywhere near the river?"

The river flowed at the bottom of the lines.

"Right. I'll send you a barge. To-day's Monday. Should be with you by Wednesday. Name? Unit?"

He ought to have been commanding an army, that man.

We lunched most triumphantly in Hazebrouck, had tea and dinner at Cassel and I was dropped on my own doorstep well before midnight.

It was not unpleasing to let drop, quite casually of course, to Division and Corps and Army, that twenty tons of timber were being delivered at my lines in three days and that there was more where that came from. If they wanted any, they had only to come and ask *me* about it.

16.

During this period the Major had handed over the eighteen-pounders, receiving 4.5 howitzers in exchange, nice little cannons, but apparently in perpetual need of calibration. None of the gunners had ever handled them before but they picked up the new drill with extraordinary aptitude, taking the most unholy delight in firing gas shells. They hadn't forgotten Armentières either.

THE WESTERN FRONT 213

My wagon line repose was roughly broken into by an order one afternoon to come up immediately. The Colonel was elsewhere and the Major had taken his place once more.

Furthermore, a raid was to take place the same night and I hadn't the foggiest idea of the numberless 4.5 differences. However we did our share in the raid and at the end of a couple of days I began to hope we should stick to howitzers. The reasons were many, — a bigger shell with more satisfactory results, gas as well as H.E., four guns to control instead of six, far greater ease in finding positions and a longer range. This was in October, '17. Things have changed since then. The air recuperator with the new range drum and fuze indicator have made the 18-pounder a new thing.

Two days after my going up the Hun found us. Between 11 A.M. and 4 P.M. he sent over three hundred five-nines, but as they fell between two of the guns and the billet, and he didn't bother to switch, we were perfectly happy. To my way of thinking his lack of imagination in gunnery is one of the factors which has helped him to lose the war. He is consistent, amazingly thorough and amazingly accurate. We have those qualities too, not quite so marked perhaps, but it is the added touch of imagination, of sportingness, which has beaten him. What English subaltern for instance up in that Hun O.P. wouldn't have given her five minutes more right for luck, — and got the farm and the gun and the ammunition? But because the Boche had been allotted a definite target and a definite number of rounds he just went on according to orders and never thought of budging off his line. We all knew it and remained in the farm although the M.P.I. was only fifty yards to a flank.

The morning after the raid I went the round of the guns. One of them had a loose breechblock. When fired the back flash was right across the gun pit. I put the gun out of action, the chances being that very soon she would blow out her breech and kill every man in the detachment.

As my knowledge was limited to eighteen-pounders, however, I sent for the brigade artificer. His opinion confirmed mine.

That night she went down on the tail of a wagon. The next night she came back again, the breech just as loose. Nothing had been done. The Ordnance workshop sent a chit with her to say she'd got to fire so many hundred more rounds at 4th charge before she could be condemned.

What was the idea? Surely to God the Hun killed enough gunners without our trying to kill them ourselves? Assuming that a 4.5 cost fifteen hundred pounds in round figures, four gunners and a sergeant at an average of two shillings a day were worth economising, to say nothing of the fact that they were all trained men and experienced soldiers, or to mention that they were human beings with wives and families. It cannot have been the difficulty of getting another gun. The country was stiff with guns and it only takes a busy day to fire four hundred rounds.

It was just the good old system again! I left the gun out of action.

Within a couple of days we had to hand over again. We were leaving that front to go up into the salient, Ypres. But I didn't forget to tell the in-coming Battery Commander all about that particular gun.

Ypres! One mentions it quite casually but I don't think there was an officer or man who didn't draw a deep breath when the order came. It was a death trap.

There was a month's course of gunnery in England about to take place, — the Overseas Course for Battery Commanders. My name had been sent in. It was at once cancelled so that the Ypres move was a double disappointment.

So the battery went down to the wagon line and prepared for the worst. For a couple of days we hung about uneasily. Then the Major departed for the north in a motor lorry to take over positions. Having seen him off we foregathered with the officers of the Brigade Ammunition Column, cursed with uneasy laughter and turned the rum-specialist on to brewing flaming toddy.

The next day brought a telegram from the Major of which two words at least will never die: "Move cancelled."

We had dinner in Estaires that night!

But the brigade was going to move, although none of us knew where. The day before they took the road I left for England in a hurry to attend the Overseas Course. How little did I guess what changes were destined to take place before I saw them again!

17.

The course was a godsend in that it broke the back of the winter. A month in England, sleeping between sheets, with a hot bath every day and brief week-ends with one's people was a distinct improvement on France, although the first half of the course was dull to desperation. The chief interest, in fact, of the whole course was to see the fight between the two schools of gunners, — the theoretical and the practical. Shoebury was the home of the theoretical. We filled all the Westcliff hotels and went in daily by train to the school of gunnery, there to imbibe drafts of statistics — not excluding our old friend T.O.B. — and to relearn all the stuff we had been doing every day in France in face of the Hun, a sort of revised up-to-date version, including witty remarks at the expense of Salisbury which left one with the idea, "Well, if this is the last word of *the* School of Gunnery, I'm a damned sight better gunner than I thought I was."

Many of the officers had brought their wives down. Apart from them the hotels were filled with indescribable people, — dear old ladies in eighteenth-century garments who knitted and talked scandal and allowed their giggling daughters to flirt and dance with all and sundry. One or two of the more advanced damsels had left their parents behind and were staying there with "uncles", — rather lascivious-looking old men, rapidly going bald. Where they all came from is a mystery. One didn't think England contained such people, and the thought that one was fighting for them was intolerable.

After a written examination which was somewhat of a farce at the end of the first fortnight, we all trooped down to Salisbury to see the proof of the pudding in the shooting. Shoebury was routed. A couple of hundred bursting shells duly corrected for temperature, barometer, wind and the various other disabilities attaching to exterior ballistics will disprove the most likely-sounding theory.

Salisbury said, "Of course they will tell you *this* at Shoebury. They may be perfectly right. I don't deny it for a moment, but I'll show you what the ruddy bundook says about it." And at the end of half an hour's shooting the "ruddy bundook" behind us had entirely disposed of the argument. We had calibrated that unfortunate battery to within half a foot a second, fired it with a field clinometer, put it through its paces in snowstorms and every kind of filthy weather and went away impressed. The gun does not lie. Salisbury won hands down.

The verdict of the respective schools upon my work was amusing and showed that at least they had fathomed the psychology of me.

Shoebury said, "Fair. A good second in command." Salisbury said, "Sound, practical work. A good Battery Commander."

Meanwhile the papers every day had been ringing with the Cambrai show. November, '17, was a memorable month for many others besides the Brigade. Of course I didn't know for certain that we were in it, but it wasn't a very difficult guess. The news became more and more anxious reading, especially when I received a letter from the Major who said laconically that he had lost all his kit; would I please collect some more that he had ordered and bring it out with me?

This was countermanded by a telegram saying he was coming home on leave. I met him in London and in the luxury of the Carlton Grill he told me the amazing story of Cambrai.

The net result to the Brigade was the loss of the guns and many officers and men, and the acquiring of one D.S.O. which should have been a V.C., and a handful of M.C.'s, Military Medals, and Croix de Guerre.

I found them sitting down, very merry and bright, at a place called Poix in the Lines of Communication, and there I listened to stories of Huns shot with rifles at one yard, of days in trenches fighting as infantry, of barrages that passed conception, of the amazing feats of my own Major who was the only officer who got nothing out of it, — through some gross miscarriage of justice and to my helpless fury.

There was a new Captain commanding my battery in the absence of the Major. But I was informed that I had been promoted Major and was taking over another battery whose commander had been wounded in the recent show. Somehow it had happened that that battery and ours had always worked together, had almost always played each other in the finals of brigade football matches and there was as a result a strong liking between the two. It was good therefore to have the luck to go to them instead of one of the others. It completed the entente between the two of us.

Only the Brigade Headquarters was in Poix. The batteries and the Ammunition Column had a village each in the neighbourhood. My new battery, my first command, was at Bergicourt, some three miles away, and thither I went in the brigade trap, a little shy and overwhelmed at this entirely unexpected promotion, not quite sure of my reception. The Captain was an older man than I and he and some of the subalterns had all been lieutenants together with me in the Heytesbury days.

From the moment of getting out of the trap, as midday stables was being dismissed, the Captain's loyalty to me was of the most exceptional kind. He did everything in his power to help me the whole time I remained in command and I owe him more gratitude and thanks than I can ever hope to repay. The subalterns too worked like niggers, and I was immensely proud of being in command of such a splendid fighting battery.

Bergicourt was a picturesque little place that had sprung up in a hillside cup. A tiny river ran at the bottom of the hill, the cottages were dotted with charming irregularity up and down its flank and the surrounding woody hills protected it a little from the biting winter winds. The men and horses were billeted among the cottages. The battery office was in the Mairie, and the mess was in the presbytery. The Abbé was a diminutive, round-faced, blue-chinned little man with a black skull cap, whose simplicity was altogether exceptional. He had once been on a Cook's tour to Greece, Egypt and Italy but for all the knowledge of the world he got from it he might as well have remained in Bergicourt. He shaved on Sundays and insinuated himself humbly into the mess room — his best parlour — with an invariable "*Bonjour, mon commandant!*" and a "*je vous remerc — ie,*" that became the passwords of the battery. The S sound in *remercie* lasted a full minute to a sort of splashing accompaniment emerging from the teeth. We used to invite him in to coffee and liqueurs after dinner and his round-eyed amazement when the Captain and one of the subalterns did elementary conjuring tricks, producing cards from the least expected portions of his anatomy and so on as he sat there in front of the fire with a drink in his hand and a cigarette smouldering in his fingers, used to send us into helpless shrieks of laughter.

He bestowed on me in official moments the most wonderful title that even Haig might have been proud of. He called me "*Monsieur le Commandant des armées anglaises à Bergicourt,*" — a First Command indeed!

Christmas Day was a foot deep in snow, wonderfully beautiful and silent with an almost uncanny stillness. The Colonel and the Intelligence Officer came and had dinner with us in the middle of the day, after the Colonel had made a little speech to

THE WESTERN FRONT 221

the men, who were sitting down to theirs, and been cheered to the echo.

At night there was a concert and the battery got royally tight. It was the first time they'd been out of action for eight months and it probably did them a power of good.

Four Christmases back I had been in Florida splashing about in the sea, revelling in being care free, deep in the writing of a novel. It was amazing how much water had flowed under the bridges since then, — one in Fontainehouck, one in Salonica, one in London, and now this one at Bergicourt with six guns and a couple of hundred men under me. I wondered where the next would be and thought of New York with a sigh. If any one had told me in Florida that I should ever be a Major in the British Army I should have thought he'd gone mad.

18.

The time was spent in Poix in completing ourselves with all the things of which the batteries were short — technical stores — in making rings in the snow and exercising the horses, in trying to get frost nails without success, in a comic *chasse au sanglier* organised by a local sportsman in which we saw nothing but a big red fox and a hare and bagged neither, in endeavouring to camouflage the fuel stolen by the men, in wondering what 1918 would bring forth.

The bitter cold lasted day after day without any sign of a break and in the middle of it came the order to move. We were wanted back in the line again.

I suppose there is always one second of apprehension on receiving that order, of looking round with the thought, "Whose turn this time?" There seemed to be no hope or sign of peace. The very idea was so remote as to be stillborn. Almost it seemed as if one would have to go on and on for ever. The machine had run away with us and there was no stopping it. Every calendar that ran out was another year of one's youth burnt on the altar of war. There was no future. How could there be when men were falling like leaves in autumn?

One put up a notice board on the edge of the future. It said, "Trespassers will be pip-squeaked." The present was the antithesis of everything one had ever dreamed, a ghastly slavery to be borne as best one could. One sought distractions to stop one's thinking. Work was insufficient. One developed a literary gluttony, devouring cannibalistically all the fiction writers, the war poets, everything that one could lay hands on, developing unconsciously a higher criticism, judging by the new standards set by three years of war — that school of post-impressionism that rubs out so ruthlessly the essential, leaving the unessential crowing on its dunghill. It only left one the past as a mental playground and even there the values had altered. One looked back with a very different eye from that with which one had looked forward only four years ago. One had seen Death now and heard Fear whispering, and felt the pulse of a world upheaved by passions.

The war itself had taken on a different aspect.

THE WESTERN FRONT

The period of peace sectors was over. Russia had had enough. Any day now would see the released German divisions back on the western front. It seemed that the new year must inevitably be one of cataclysmic events. It was not so much "can we attack?" as "will they break through?" And yet trench warfare had been a stalemate for so long that it didn't seem possible that they could. But whatever happened it was not going to be a joy-ride.

We were going to another army. That at least was a point of interest. The batteries, being scattered over half a dozen miles of country, were to march independently to their destinations. So upon the appointed day we packed up and said good-bye to the little priest and interviewed the mayor and haggled over exorbitant claims for damages and impossible thefts of wood and potatoes, wondering all the while how the horses would ever stand up on the frozen roads without a single frost nail in the battery. It was like a vast skating rink and the farrier had been tearing his hair for days.

But finally the last team had slithered down to the gun park, hooked in and everything was reported ready. Billeting parties had gone on ahead.

It is difficult to convey just what that march meant. It lasted four days, once the blizzard being so thick and blinding that the march was abandoned, the whole brigade remaining in temporary billets. The pace was a crawl. The team horses slid into each other and fell, the leads bringing the centres down, at every twenty yards or so. The least rise had to be navigated by improvising means of foothold — scattering a near manure heap, getting gunners up with picks and shovels and hacking at the road surface, assisting the horses with drag-ropes — and all the time the wind was like a razor on one's face and the drivers up on the staggering horses beat their chests with both arms and changed over with the gunners when all feeling had gone from their limbs. Hour after hour one trekked through the blinding white, silent country, stamping up and down at the halts with an anxious eye on the teams, chewing bully beef and biscuits and thanking God for coffee piping hot out of a thermos in the middle of the day. Then on again in the afternoon while the light grew less and dropped finally to an inky grey and the wind grew colder, — hoping that the G.S. wagons, long since miles behind, would catch up. Hour after hour stiff in the saddle with icy hands and feet, one's neck cricked to dodge the wind, or sliding off stiffly to walk and get some warmth into one's aching limbs, the straps and weight of one's equipment becoming more and more irksome and heavy with every step forward that slipped two back. To reach the destination at all was lucky. To get there by ten o'clock at night was a godsend, although watering the horses and feeding them in the darkness with frozen fingers that burned on straps and buckles drew strange Scotch oaths. For the men, shelter of sorts, something at least with a roof where a fire was lit at risk of burning the whole place down. For the officers sometimes a peasant's bed, or valises spread on the floor, unpacking as little as possible for the early start in the morning, the servants cooking some sort of a meal, either on the peasant's stove or over a fire of sticks.

The snow came again and one went on next day, blinded by the feathery touch of flakes that closed one's eyes so gently, crept down one's neck and pockets, lodged heavily in one's lap when mounted, clung in a frozen garment to one's coat when walking, hissed softly on one's pipe and made one giddy with the silent, whirling, endless pattern which blotted out the landscape, great flakes like white butterflies, soft, velvety, beautiful but also like little hands that sought to stop one persistently, insidiously. "Go back," said their owner, "go back. We have hidden the road and the ditches and all the country. We have closed your eyelids and you cannot see. Go back before you reach that mad place where we have covered over silent things that once were men, trying to give back beauty to the ugliness that you have made. Why do you march on in spite of us? Do you seek to become as they? — Go back. Go back," they whispered.

But we pushed blindly through, stumbling to another billet to hear that the snow had stalled the motor lorries and therefore there were no rations for the men and that the next day's march was twenty miles.

During the night a thaw set in. Snowflakes turned to cold rain and in the dawn the men splashed, shivering, and harnessed the shivering horses. One or two may have drunk a cup of coffee given them by the villagers. The rest knew empty stomachs as well as shivering. The village had once been in the war zone and only old women and children clung precariously to life. They had no food to give or sell. The parade was ordered for six o'clock. Some of the rear wagons, in difficulties with teams, had not come in till the dawn, the Captain and all of them having shared a biscuit or two since breakfast. But at six the battery was reported ready and not a man was late or sick. The horses had been in the open all night.

So on we went again with pools of water on the icy crust of the road, the rain dripping off our caps. Would there be food at the other end? Our stomachs cried out for it.

And back in England full-fed fathers hearing the rain splashing against the windows put an extra coal on the fire, crying again, "We will fight to the last man!"; railway men and munitioners yelled, "Down tools! We need more pay!" and the Government flung our purses to them and said, "Help yourselves — of course we shall count on you to keep us in power at the next election."

19.

The village of Chuignolles, ice-bound, desolate, wood-patched, was our destination. The battles of the Somme had passed that way, wiping everything out. Old shell holes were softened with growing vegetation. Farm cottages were held together by bits of corrugated iron. The wind whistled through them, playing ghostly tunes on splintered trunks that once had been a wood.

Two prison camps full of Germans, who in some

mysterious way knew that we had been in the Cambrai push and commented about it as we marched in, were the only human beings, save the village schoolmaster and his wife and child, in whose cottage we shared a billet with a Canadian forester. The schoolmaster was minus one arm, the wife had survived the German occupation and the child was a golden-haired boy full of laughter, with tiny teeth, blue eyes and chubby fingers that curled round his mother's heart. The men were lodged under bits of brick wall and felting that constituted at least shelter, and warmed themselves with the timber that the Canadian let them remove from his Deccaville train which screamed past the horse lines about four or five times a day. They had stood the march in some marvellous way that filled me with speechless admiration. Never a grouse about the lack of rations, or the awful cold and wet, always with a song on their lips they had paraded to time daily, looked after the horses with a care that was almost brotherly, put up with filthy billets and the extremes of discomfort with a readiness that made me proud. What kept them going? Was it that vague thing patriotism, the more vague because the war wasn't in their own country? Was it the ultimate hope of getting back to their Flos and Lucys, although leave, for them, was practically non-existent? What had they to look forward to but endless work in filth and danger, heaving guns, grooming horses, cleaning harness eternally? And yet their obedience and readiness and courage were limitless, wonderful.

We settled down to training and football and did our best to acquire the methods of the new army. My Major, who had been in command of the brigade, had fallen ill on the march and had been sent to England. The doctor was of opinion that he wouldn't be coming out again. He was worn out. How characteristic of the wilfully blind system which insists that square pegs shall be made to fit round holes! There was a man who should have been commanding an army, wasted in the command of a battery, while old men without a millionth part of his personality, magnetism or knowledge recklessly flung away lives in the endeavour to justify their positions. In the Boer War, if a General lost three hundred men there was an enquiry into the circumstances. Now if he didn't lose three hundred thousand he was a bad General. There were very few bad ones apparently!

At least one could thank God that the Major was out of it with a whole skin, although physically a wreck.

The guns we drew from Ordnance at Poix and Chuignolles were not calibrated, but there was a range half a day's march distant and we were ordered to fire there in readiness for going back into the line. So one morning before dawn we set out to find the pin-point given us on the map. Dawn found us on a road which led through a worse hell than even Dante visited. Endless desolation spread away on every side, empty, flat, filled with an infinite melancholy. No part of the earth's surface remained intact. One shell hole merged into another in an endless pattern of pockmarks, unexploded duds lying in hundreds in every direction. Bits of wreckage lay scattered, shell baskets, vague shapes of iron and metal which bespoke the onetime presence of man. Here and there steam rollers, broken and riddled, stuck up like the bones of camels in the desert. A few wooden crosses marked the wayside graves, very few. For the most part the dead had lain where they fell, trodden into the earth. Everywhere one almost saw a hand sticking up, a foot that had worked up to the surface again. A few bricks half overgrown marked where once maidens had been courted by their lovers. The quiet lane ringing with the songs of birds where they had met in the summer evenings at the stroke of the Angelus was now one jagged stump, knee-high, from which the birds had long since fled. The spirits of a million dead wailed over that ghastly graveyard, unconsecrated by the priests of God. In the grey light one could nearly see the corpses sit up in their countless hundreds at the noise of the horses' feet and point with long fingers, screaming bitter ridicule through their shapeless gaping jaws. And when at last we found the range and the guns broke the eerie stillness the echo in the hills was like bursts of horrible laughter.

And on the edge of all this death was that little sturdy boy with the golden hair, bubbling with life, who played with the empty sleeve of his young father spewed out of the carnage, mutilated, broken in this game of fools.

20.

February found us far from Chuignolles. Our road south had taken us through a country of optimism where filled-in trenches were being cultivated once more by old women and boys, barbed wire had been gathered in like an iron harvest and life was trying to creep back again like sap up the stem of a bruised flower. Their homes were made of empty petrol tins, bits of corrugated iron, the wreckage of the battlefield, — these strange persistent old people clinging desperately to their clod of earth, bent by the storm but far from being broken, ploughing round the lonely graves of the unknown dead, sparing a moment to drop a bunch of green stuff on them. Perhaps some one was doing the same to their son's grave.

We came to Jussy and Flavy-le-Martel, an undulating country of once-wooded hillsides now stamped under the Hun's heel and where even then the spiteful long-range shell came raking in the neatly swept muck heaps that once had been villages. The French were there those blue-clad, unshaven poilus who, having seen their land laid waste, turned their eyes steadily towards Germany with the gleam of faith in them that moves mountains, officered by men who called them "*mes enfants*" and addressed each one as "thou."

We had reached the southern end of the British line and were to take over the extra bit down to Barisis. Our own zone was between Essigny and Benay and in a morning of thick fog the Divisional

Battery Commanders and ourselves went up to the gun positions held by the slim French 75's. They welcomed us politely, bowing us into scratches in the earth and offering sausages and red wine and cigarettes of Caporal. It appeared that peace reigned on that front. Not a shell fell, hardly was a round ever fired. Then followed maps and technical details of pin-points and zero lines and O.P.'s and the colour of S.O.S. rockets. We visited the guns and watched them fire a round or two and discussed the differences between them and our eighteen-pounders, and at last after much shaking of hands bade them au revoir and left them in the fog.

The relief took place under cover of night without a hitch, in a silence unbroken by any gun, and finally, after having journeyed to the O.P. with the French Battery Commander, up to our thighs in mud, fired on the zero point to check the line, reported ourselves ready to take on an S.O.S., and watched the French officer disappear in the direction of his wagon line, we found ourselves masters of the position.

The fog did eventually lift, revealing the least hopeful of any gun positions it has ever been my lot to occupy. The whole country was green, a sort of turf. In this were three great white gashes of upturned chalk visible to the meanest intelligence as being the three battery positions. True, they were under the crest from any Hun O.P., but that didn't minimise the absurdity. There were such things as balloons and aeroplanes. Further inspection revealed shell holes neatly bracketing the guns, not many, but quite sufficient to prove that Fritz had done his job well. Beside each gun pit was a good deep dugout for the detachment and we had sleeping quarters that would stop at least a four-two. The mess was a quaint little hut of hooped iron above ground, camouflaged with chalky earth, big enough to hold a table and four officers, if arranged carefully. We rigged up shelves and hung new fighting maps and Kirchners and got the stove to burn and declared ourselves ready for the war again. We spent long mornings exploring the trenches, calling on a rather peevish infantry whose manners left much to be desired, and found that as usual the enemy had all the observation on the opposite ridge. Behind the trench system we came upon old gun positions shelled out of all recognition, and looked back over an empty countryside with rather a gloomy eye. It was distinctly unprepossessing. If there were ever a show —

So we played the gramophone by night and invented a knife-throwing game in the door of the hut and waited for whatever Fate might have in store for us. The Captain had gone on leave from Chuignolles. The night after his return he came up to the guns as my own leave was due again. So having initiated him into the defence scheme and the S.O.S. rules I packed up my traps and departed, — as it turned out for good.

Fate decreed that my fighting was to be done with the battery which I had helped to make and whose dead I had buried.

On my return from leave fourteen days later, towards the end of February, I was posted back to them. The end of February, — a curious period of mental tightening up, of expectation of some colossal push received with a certain incredulity. He'd push all right, but not here. And yet, in the depths of one's being, there formed a vague apprehension that made one restless and took the taste out of everything. The work seemed unsatisfactory in the new battle positions to which we were moved, a side-step north, seven thousand yards from the front line, just behind Essigny which peeped over a million trenches to St. Quentin. The men didn't seem to have their hearts in it and one found fault in everything. The new mess, a wooden hut under trees on a hilltop with a deep dugout in it, was very nice, allowing us to bask in the sun whenever it shone and giving a wonderful view over the whole zone, but seemed to lack privacy. One yearned to be alone sometimes and always there was some one there. The subalterns were practically new to me, and although one laughed and talked one couldn't settle down as in the old days with the Major and Pip Don. The Scotch Captain was also occupying the hilltop. It was good to go off on long reconnaissances with him and argue violently on all the known philosophies and literatures, to challenge him to revolver shooting competitions and try and escape the eternal obsession that clouded one's brain, an uneasiness that one couldn't place, like the feeling that makes one cold in the pit of the stomach before going down to get ready for a boxing competition, magnified a million times.

The weather was warm and sunny after misty dawns and the whole country was white with floating cobwebs. The last touches were being put to the gun position and a narrow deep trench ran behind the guns which were a quarter of a mile beyond the hilltop, down beyond the railway line under camouflage in the open. Word came round that "The Attack" was for this day, then that, then the other, and the heavy guns behind us made the night tremble with their counter-preparation work, until at last one said, "Please God, they'll get on with it, and let's get it over!" The constant cry of "Wolf! Wolf!" was trying.

Everybody knew about it and all arrangements were made, extra ammunition, and extra gunners at the positions, details notified as to manning O.P.'s, the probable time at which we should have to open fire being given as ten o'clock at night at extreme range.

My Captain, a bloodthirsty Canadian, had gone on leave to the south of France, which meant leaving a subaltern in the wagon line while I had three with me.

The days became an endless tension, the nights a jumpy stretch of darkness, listening for the unknown. Matters were not helped by my brother's rolling up one day and giving out the date definitely as the twenty-first. It was on the ninth that he arrived and took me for a joy-ride to Barisis to have a look at the Hun in the Forêt de St. Gobain, so deeply wooded that the car could run to within a hundred yards of the front-line trench. We dined at the charming old town of Noyon on the way back and bought English books in a shop there and stayed the night in a little inn just off the market square. The next morning he dropped me at the battery and I watched him roll away in the car, feeling an accentuated loneliness, a yearning to go with him and get out of the damned firing line, to escape the responsibility that rode one like an Old Man of the Sea.

In war there is only one escape.

The nights of the eighteenth and nineteenth were a continuous roll of heavy guns, lasting till just before the dawn, the days comparatively quiet. Raids had taken place all along the front on both sides and identifications made which admitted of no argument.

On the night of the twentieth we turned in as usual about midnight with the blackness punctuated by flashes and the deep-voiced rumble of big guns a sort of comfort in the background. If Brother Fritz was massing anywhere for the attack at least he was having an unpleasant time. We were unable to join in because we were in battle positions seven thousand yards behind the front line. The other eighteen-pounders in front of us were busy, however, and if the show didn't come off we were going up to relieve them in a week's time. So we played our good-night tune on the gramophone, the junior subaltern waiting in his pyjamas while the last notes were sung. Then he flicked out the light and hopped into bed and presently the hut was filled by his ungentle snores. Then one rang through a final message to the signaller on duty at the guns and closed one's eyes.

21.

The twenty-first of March, 1918, has passed into history now, a page of disaster, blood and prisoners, a turning point in the biggest war in history, a day which broke more hearts than any other day in the whole four and a half years; and yet to some of us it brought an infinite relief. The tension was released. The fight was on to the death.

We were jerked awake in the darkness by a noise which beat upon the brain, made the hill tremble and shiver, which seemed to fill the world and all time with its awful threat.

I looked at my watch, — 4 A.M.

The subaltern who lay on the bed beside mine said, "She's off!" and lit a candle with a laugh. He was dead within six hours. We put coats over our pyjamas and went out of the hut. Through the fog there seemed to be a sort of glow along the whole front right and left like one continuous gun flash. The Scots Captain came round with his subalterns and joined us, and two "Archie" gunners who shared a tent under the trees and messed with us. We stood in a group, talking loudly to make ourselves heard. There was nothing to be done but to stand by. According to plan we should not come into action until about 10 P.M. that night to cover the retreat, if necessary, of the gunners and infantry in

THE WESTERN FRONT

the line. Our range to start with would be six thousand yards.

So we dressed and talked to Brigade, who had no information. At six o'clock Brigade issued an order, "Man O.P.'s at once." The fog still hung like a blanket and no news had come through from the front line. The barrage was reported thick in front of and in Essigny with gas.

The signallers were ready, three of them. The subaltern detailed had only to fill his pockets with food.

The subaltern detailed! It sounds easy, doesn't it? But it isn't any fun detailing a man to go out into a gas barrage in any sort of a show, and this was bigger than the wildest imagination could conceive. I wondered, while giving him instructions, whether I should ever see him again. I never did. He was taken prisoner, and the signallers too.

They went out into the fog while the servants lit the fire and bustled about, getting us an early breakfast. The Anti-Aircraft discussed the advisability of withdrawing immediately or waiting to see what the barrage would do. They waited till about 9 A.M. and then got out. The Scots Captain and I wished them luck and looked at each other silently and refilled pipes.

There was a hint of sun behind the fog now, but visibility only carried about two hundred yards. The Guns reported that the barrage was coming towards them. The Orderly Officer had been down and found all things in readiness for any emergency. None of the O.P.'s answered. Somewhere in that mist they were dodging the barrage while we sat and waited, an eye on the weather, an eye on the time, an ear always for the buzz of the telephone; box respirators in the alert position, the guns laid on the S.O.S. loaded with H.E.

Does one think in times like that? I don't know. Only little details stand out in the brain like odd features revealed in a flash of lightning during a storm. I remember putting a drawing-pin into the corner of a Kirchner picture and seeing the headlines of the next day's paper at home; I saw the faces of my people as they read them. I saw them just coming down to breakfast at the precise moment that I was sticking in the drawing-pin, the door open on to the lawn — in America, still asleep, as they were six hours behind, or possibly only just turning in after a dance — in Etaples, where perhaps the noise had already reached one of them. When would they hear from me again? They would be worrying horribly.

The 'phone buzzed. "Brigade, sir!"

"Right. Yes? — S.O.S. 3000! *Three* thousand? — Right! Battery! Drop to *three* thousand, S.O.S. — Three rounds per gun per minute till I come down."

It was 10 A.M. and that was the range, when according to plan it shouldn't have come till 10 P.M. at double the range.

The subalterns were already out, running down to the guns as I snatched the map and followed after, to hear the battery open fire as I left the hut.

The greater significance of this S.O.S. came to me

before I'd left the hut. At that range our shells would fall just the other side of Essigny, still a vague blur in the mist. What had happened to the infantry three thousand yards beyond? What had become of the gunners? There were no signs of our people coming back. The country, as far as one could see in the fog, was empty save for the bursting shells which were spread about between Essigny and the railway, with the battery in the barrage. The noise was still so universal that it was impossible to know if any of our guns farther forward were still in action. They couldn't be if we were firing. It meant — God knew what it meant!

The subalterns went on to the guns while I stopped in the control dug into the side of the railway and shed my coat, sweating after the quarter-mile run. Five-nines and pip-squeaks were bursting on the railway and it seemed as if they had the battery taped.

To get off my coat was a matter of less than half a minute. It had only just dropped to the ground when the signaller held me the instrument. "Will you speak here, sir?"

I took it.

"Is that the Major?"

"Yes."

"Will you come, sir? Mr. B.'s badly wounded. Sergeant —— has lost an eye and there's no one here to —"

"Go on firing. I'm coming over." Badly wounded?

I leaped up out of the dugout and ran. There

was no shell with my name on it that morning. The ground went up a yard away from me half a dozen times but I reached the guns and dived under the camouflage into the trench almost on top of poor old B. who was lying motionless, one arm almost smashed off, blood everywhere. It was he who had said "She's off!" and lit the candle with a laugh. A man was endeavouring to tie him up. Behind him knelt a sergeant with his face in his hands. As I jumped down into the trench he raised it. "I'm blind, sir," he said. His right eye was shot away.

The others were all right. I went from gun to gun and found them firing steadily.

Somehow or other we tied up the subaltern and carried him along the narrow trench. Mercifully he was unconscious. We got him out at last on to a stretcher. Four men went away with it, the sergeant stumbling after. The subaltern was dead before they reached a dressing station. He left a wife and child.

There were only the junior subaltern and myself left to fight the battery. He was twenty last birthday and young at that. If I stopped anything there was only that boy between King and country and the Hun. Is *any* reward big enough for these babes of ours?

Perhaps God will give it. King and country won't.

Vague forms of moving groups of men could be seen through my glasses in the neighbourhood of

THE WESTERN FRONT 241

Essigny, impossible to say whether British or German. The sun was struggling to pierce the mist. The distance was about a thousand yards. We were still firing on the S.O.S. range as ordered.

I became aware of a strange subaltern grinning up at me out of the trench.

"Where the devil do you spring from?" said I.

He climbed out and joined me on the top, hatless, minus box respirator, cheery. Another babe.

"I'm from the six-inch section straight in front, sir," he said. "They've captured my guns. Do you think you could take 'em on?"

They *were* Germans, then, those moving forms!

I swept the glasses round once more anxiously. There were six, seven, ten, creeping up the railway embankment on the left flank *behind* the battery. Where the hell were our infantry reinforcements? My Babe sent the news back to Brigade while I got a gun on top and fired at the six-inch battery in front over open sights at a thousand yards with fuze 4. The Hun was there all right. He ran at the third round. Then we switched and took on individual groups as they appeared.

The party on the railway worried me. It was improper to have the enemy behind one's battery. So I got on the 'phone to the Scots Captain and explained the position. It looked as if the Hun had established himself with machine guns in the signal box. The skipper took it on over open sights with H.E. At the fourth round there was only a settling mass of red brick dust. I felt easier in my mind and continued sniping groups of two or three with an added zest and most satisfactory results. The Hun didn't seem to want to advance beyond Essigny. He hung about the outskirts and, when he showed, ran, crouching low. From his appearance it looked as if he had come to stay. Each of them had a complete pack strapped on to his back with a new pair of boots attached. The rest of the battery dropped their range and searched and swept from the pits. The Skipper joined in the sniping.

A half platoon of infantry came marching at a snail's pace along the railway behind me, — on the top of course, in full view! I wanted to make sure of those Huns on the embankment, so I whistled to the infantry officer and began semaphoring, a method of signalling at which I rather fancied myself.

It seemed to frighten that infantry lad. At the first waggle he stopped his men and turned them about. In twenty leaps I covered the hundred yards or so between us, screaming curses, and brought him to a halt. He wore glasses and looked like a sucking curate. He may have been in private life but I gave tongue at high pressure, regardless of his feelings, and it was a very red-faced platoon that presently doubled along the other side of the railway under cover towards the embankment, thirsting for blood, mine for choice, Fritz's from *embarras de richesse*.

I returned to my sniping, feeling distinctly better, as the little groups were no longer advancing but going back, — and there was that ferocious platoon chivvying them in the rear!

Things might have been much worse.

A megaphone's all right, but scream down it for three hours and see what happens to your voice. Mine sounded much like a key in a rusty lock. Hunger too was no longer to be denied about three o'clock in the afternoon after breakfast at cockcrow. The six-inch subaltern had tried unsuccessfully to get back to his guns. The Hun, however, had established a machine-gun well the other side of them and approach single-handed was useless. Lord knew where his gunners were! Prisoners probably. So he returned and asked if I had any use for him. Stout lads of his kidney are not met with every day. So I sent him up the hill to get food and a box respirator. He returned, grinning more cheerily than before, so I left him and the Babe to fight the good fight and went to get a fresh point of view from the tree O.P. up the hill. They seemed to be doing useful work between them by the time I got up the tree, so I left them to it and went to the mess to get some food.

It seemed curiously empty. Kits, half-packed, lay about the floor. The breakfast plates, dirty, were still on the table. I called each servant by name. No answer.

The other battery's servants were round the corner. I interviewed them. They had seen nothing of my people for hours. They thought that they had gone down to the wagon line. In other words it meant that while we were stopping the Hun, with poor old B. killed and the sergeant with an eye blown out, those dirty servants had run away!

It came over me with something of a shock that

if I put them under arrest the inevitable sentence was death.

I had already sent one officer and three men to their death, or worse, at the O.P. and seen another killed at the guns. Now these four! Who would be a Battery Commander?

However, food was the immediate requirement. The other battery helped and I fed largely, eased my raw throat with pints of water and drank a tot of rum for luck. Those precious servants had left my even more precious cigars unpacked. If the Hun was coming I'd see him elsewhere before he got those smokes. So I lit one and filled my pockets with the rest, and laden with food and a flask of rum went back to the guns and fed my subaltern. The men's rations had been carried over from the cook house.

A few more infantry went forward on the right and started a bit of a counter-attack but there was no weight behind it. They did retake Essigny or some parts of it, but as the light began to fail they came back again, and the Hun infantry hung about the village without advancing.

With the darkness we received the order to retire to Flavy as soon as the teams came up. The barrage had long since dropped to desultory fire on the Hun side, and as we were running short of ammunition, we only fired as targets offered. On returning up the hill I found it strongly held by our infantry, some of whom incidentally stole my trench coat.

The question of teams became an acute worry as time went on. The Hun wasn't too remote and one never knew what he might be up to in the dark, and our infantry were no use because the line they held was a quarter of a mile behind the nearest battery. The skipper and I sent off men on bicycles to hurry the teams, while the gunners got the guns out of the pits in the darkness ready to hook in and move off at a moment's notice.

Meanwhile we ate again and smoked and summoned what patience we could, endeavouring to snatch a sleep. It wasn't till ten o'clock that at last we heard wheels,—the gun limbers, cook's cart and a G.S. wagon came up with the wagon line officer who had brought the servants back with him. There was no time to deal with them. The officer went down to hook in to the guns and I saw to the secret papers, money, maps and office documents which are the curse of all batteries. The whole business of packing up had to be done in pitch darkness, in all the confusion of the other battery's vehicles and personnel, to say nothing of the infantry. We didn't bother about the Hun. Silence reigned.

It was not till midnight that the last of the guns was up and the last of the vehicles packed and then I heard the voice of the Babe calling for me. He crashed up on a white horse in the darkness and said with a sob, "Dickie's wounded!"

"Dickie" was the wagon line subaltern, a second lieutenant who had got the D.S.O. in the Cambrai show, one of the stoutest lads God ever made. In my mind I had been relying on him enormously for the morrow.

"Is he bad? Where is he?"

"Just behind, sir," said the Babe. "I don't know how bad it is."

Dickie came up on a horse. There was blood down the horse's shoulder and he went lame slightly.

"Where is it, Dickie, Old Thing?"

His voice came from between his teeth. "A shrapnel bullet through the foot," he said. "I'm damn sorry, Major."

"Let's have a look." I flashed a torch on it. The spur was bent into his foot just behind the ankle, broken, the point sticking in.

There was no doctor, no stretcher, no means of getting the spur out.

"Can you stick it? The wagon is piled mountains high. I can't shove you on that. Do you think you can hang on till we get down to Flavy?"

"I think so," he said.

He had a drink of rum and lit a cigarette and the battery got mounted. I kept him in front with me and we moved off in the dark, the poor little horse, wounded also, stumbling now and again. What that boy must have suffered I don't know. It was nearly three hours later before the battery got near its destination and all that time he remained in the saddle, lighting one cigarette from another and telling me he was "damn sorry." I expected him to faint every moment and stood by to grab him as he fell.

At last we came to a crossroads at which the battery had to turn off to reach the rendezvous. There was a large casualty clearing station about half a mile on.

So I left the battery in charge of the Babe and took Dickie straight on, praying for a sight of lights.

The place was in utter darkness when we reached it, the hut doors yawning open, everything empty. They had cleared out!

Then round a corner I heard a motor lorry starting up. They told me they were going to Ham. There was a hospital there.

So Dickie slid off his horse and was lifted into the lorry.

As my trench coat had been stolen by one of the infantry he insisted that I should take his British warm, as within an hour he would be between blankets in a hospital.

I accepted his offer gladly, — little knowing that I was not to take it off again for another nine days or so!

Dickie went off and I mounted my horse again, cursing the war and everything to do with it, and led his horse, dead lame now, in search of the battery. It took me an hour to find them, parked in a field, the gunners rolled up in blankets under the wagons.

The 21st of March was over. The battery had lost three subalterns, a sergeant, three signallers and a gunner.

France lost her temper with England.

Germany, if she only knew it, had lost the war.

22.

The new line of defence was to be the canal at Flavy.

After two hours' sleep in boots, spurs and Dickie's

coat, a servant called me with tea and bacon. Washing or shaving was out of the question. The horses were waiting — poor brutes, how they were worked those days — and the Quartermaster sergeant and I got mounted and rode away into the unknown dark, flickering a torch from time to time on to the map and finding our way by it.

With the Captain on leave, one subaltern dead, another left behind in Germany, a third wounded, one good sergeant and my corporal signaller away on a course, it didn't look like a very hopeful start for fighting an indefinite rearguard action.

I was left with the Babe, keen but not very knowledgeable, and one other subaltern who became a stand-by. They two were coming with me and the guns; the sergeant major would be left with the wagon line. Furthermore I had absolutely no voice and couldn't speak above a whisper.

Of what had happened on the flanks of our army and along the whole front, there was absolutely no news. The Divisional infantry and gunners were mostly killed or captured in the mist. We never saw anything of them again but heard amazing tales of German officers walking into the backs of batteries in the fog and saying, "Will you cease fire, please? You are my prisoners," as polite as you please.

What infantry were holding the canal, I don't know, — presumably those who had held our hilltop overnight. All we knew was that our immediate job was to meet the Colonel in Flavy and get a position in the Riez de Cugny just behind and pump shells into the Germans as they advanced on the canal. The Babe and the Stand-by were to bring the battery to a given rendezvous. Meanwhile the Colonel and all of us foregathered in a wrecked cottage in Flavy and studied maps while the Colonel swallowed a hasty cup of tea. He was ill and a few hours later was sent back in an ambulance.

By eight o'clock we had found positions and the guns were coming in. Camouflage was elementary. Gun platforms were made from the nearest cottage wall or barn doors. Ammunition was dumped beside the gun wheels.

While that was being done I climbed trees for an O.P., finding one eventually in a farm on a hill but the mist hid everything. The Huns seemed to get their guns up as if by magic and already shells were smashing what remained of Flavy. It was impossible to shoot the guns in properly. The bursts couldn't be seen, so the line was checked and rechecked with compass and director, and we opened fire on targets ordered by Brigade, shooting off the map.

Riez de Cugny was a collection of cottages with a street running through and woods and fields all around and behind. The inhabitants had fled in what they stood up in. We found a chicken clucking hungrily in a coop and had it for dinner that night. We installed ourselves in a cottage and made new fighting maps, the Scots Captain and I — his battery was shooting not a hundred yards from mine — and had the stove lit with anything burnable that came handy, old chairs, meat rolling boards, boxes, drawers and shelves.

It seemed that the attack on the canal was more or less half-hearted. The bridges had been blown up by our sappers and the machine gunners made it too hot for the Hun. Meanwhile we had the gun limbers hidden near the guns, the teams harnessed. The wagon line itself was a couple of miles away, endeavouring to collect rations, forage and ammunition. The sergeant major was a wonder. During the whole show he functioned alone and never at any time did he fail to come up to the scratch.

Even when I lost the wagon line for two days I knew that he was all right and would bring them through safely. Meanwhile aeroplanes soared over and drew smoke trails above the battery and after a significant pause five-nines began searching the fields for us. Our own planes didn't seem to exist and the Hun explored at will. On the whole things seemed pretty quiet. Communication was maintained all the time with Brigade; we were quietly getting rid of a lot of ammunition on targets indicated by the infantry and the five-nines weren't near enough to worry about. So the Scot and I went off in the afternoon and reconnoitred a way back by a cross-country trail to the wagon line,— a curious walk that, across sunny fields where birds darted in and out of hedges in utter disregard of nations which were stamping each other into the earth only a few hedges away. Tiny buds were on the trees, tingling in the warmth of the early sun.

THE WESTERN FRONT

All nature was beginning the new year of life while we fools in our blind rage and folly dealt openhandedly with death, heeding not the promise of spring in our veins, with its colour and tenderness and infinite hope.

Just a brief pause it was, like a fleecy cloud disappearing from view, and then we were in the wagon lines, soldiers again, in a tight position, with detail trickling from our lips, and orders and arrangements. Dickie was well on his way to England now, lucky Dickie! And yet there was a fascination about it, an exhilaration that made one "fill the unforgiving minute with sixty seconds' worth of distance run." It was the real thing this, red war in a moving battle, and it took all one's brain to compete with it. I wouldn't have changed places with Dickie. A "Blighty" wound was the last thing that seemed desirable. Let us see the show through to the bitter end.

We got back to the guns and the cottage and in front of us Flavy was a perfect hell. Fires in all directions and shells spreading all round and over the area. Our wagons returned, having snatched ammunition from blazing dumps, like a new version of snapdragon, and with the falling darkness the sky flared up and down fitfully. That night we dished out rum all round to the gunners and turned half of them in to sleep beside the guns while the other half fought. Have you ever considered sleeping beside a firing eighteen-pounder? It's easy — when you've fought it and carried shells for forty-eight hours.

We had dinner off that neglected fowl, both batteries in the cottage, and made absurd remarks about the photos left on the mantelpiece and fell asleep, laughing, on our chairs, or two of us on a bed, booted and spurred still, taking turns to wake and dash out and fire a target called by the liaison officer down there with the infantry, while the others never moved when the salvos rocked the cottage to its foundations, or five-nines dropped in the garden and splashed it into the street.

The Hun hadn't crossed the canal. That was what mattered. The breakfast was very nearly cooked next morning about seven and we were shooting gun fire and salvos when the order came over the 'phone to retire immediately and rendezvous on the Villeselve-Beaumont crossroads. Fritz was over the canal in the fog. The Babe dashed round to warn the teams to hook in. They had been in cottages about two hundred yards from the guns, the horses harnessed but on a line, the drivers sleeping with them. The Stand-by doubled over to the guns and speeded up the rate of fire. No good leaving ammunition behind. The signallers disconnected telephones and packed them on gun limbers. Both gunners and drivers had breakfasted. We ate ours half cooked in our fingers while they were packing up.

The mist was like a wet blanket. At twenty yards objects lost their shape and within about twenty minutes of receiving the order the battery was ready. We had the other battery licked by five good minutes and pulled out of the field on to the road at a good walk. In the fog the whole country looked different. Direction was impossible. One prayed that one wasn't marching towards Germany — and went on. At last I recognised the cross-country track with a sigh of relief. It was stiff going for the horses, but they did it and cut off a mile of road echoing with shouts and traffic in confusion, coming out eventually on an empty main road. We thought we were well ahead, but all the wagon lines were well in front of us. We caught up their tail-ends just as we reached Beaumont, which was blocked with every kind of infantry, artillery and R.A.M.C. transport, mules, horses, and motors. However there was a Headquarters in Beaumont, with Generals buzzing about and signallers, so I told the Stand-by to take the battery along with the traffic to the crossroads and wait for me.

Our own General was in that room. I cleaved a passage to him and asked for orders. He told me that it was reported that the Hun was in Ham, — right round our left flank. I was therefore to get into position at the crossroads and "Cover Ham."

"Am I to open fire, sir?"

"No. Not till you see the enemy."

I'd had enough of "seeing the enemy" on the first day. It seemed to me that if the Hun was in Ham the whole of our little world was bound to be captured. There wasn't any time to throw away, so I leaped on to my horse and cantered after the battery, followed by the groom. At the crossroads the block was double and treble while an officer yelled disentangling orders and pushed horses in the nose.

The map showed Ham to be due north of the crossroads. There proved to be an open field, turfed, just off the road with a dozen young trees planted at intervals. What lay between them and Ham it was impossible to guess. The map looked all right. So I claimed the traffic officer's attention, explained that a battery of guns was coming into action just the other side and somehow squeezed through, while the other vehicles waited. We dropped into action under the trees. The teams scattered about a hundred yards to a flank and we laid the line due north.

At that moment a Staff subaltern came up at the canter. "The General says that the Hun is pretty near, sir. Will you send out an officer's patrol."

He disappeared again, while I collected the Stand-by, a man of considerable stomach.

The orders were simply, "Get hold of servants, cooks, spare signallers and clerks. Arm them with rifles and go off straight into the fog. Spread out and if you meet a Hun fire a salvo and double back immediately to a flank."

While that was being done the Babe went round and had a dozen shells set at fuze 4 at each gun. It gives a lovely burst at a thousand yards. The Stand-by and his little army went silently forth. The corner house seemed to indicate an O.P. I took a signaller with me and we climbed up-stairs into the roof, knocked a hole in the tiles and installed a telephone which eventually connected with Brigade.

I began to get the fidgets about the Stand-by. This cursed fog was too much of a good thing. It

THE WESTERN FRONT

looked as if the God the Huns talked so much about was distinctly on their side. However, after an agonising wait, with an ear strained for that salvo of rifle fire, the fog rolled up. Like dots in the distant fields I saw the Stand-by with two rows of infantry farther on. The Stand-by saw them too and turned about. More than that, through glasses I could see troops and horse transports advancing quickly over the skyline in every direction. Columns of them, Germans, far out of range of an eighteen-pounder. As near as I could I located them on the map and worried Brigade for the next hour with pin-points.

Ham lay straight in front of my guns. The Germans were still shelling it and several waves of our own infantry were lying in position in series waiting for their infantry to emerge round the town. It was good to see our men out there, although the line looked dangerously bulgy.

After a bit I climbed down from the roof. The road had cleared of traffic and there was a subaltern of the Scot's battery at the corner with the neck of a bottle of champagne sticking out of his pocket. A thoughtful fellow.

So was I! A little later one of the Brigade Headquarters officers came staggering along on a horse, done to the world, staying in the saddle more by the grace of God than his own efforts. Poor old thing, he was all in, mentally and physically. We talked for a while but that didn't improve matters and then I remembered that bottle of fizz. In the name of humanity and necessity I commandeered it from the reluctant subaltern and handed it up to the man in the saddle. Most of it went down his unshaven chin and inside his collar, but it did the trick all right.

What was left was mine by right of conquest, and I lapped it down, a good half bottle of it. There were dry biscuits forthcoming too, just as if one were in town, and I was able to cap it with a fat cigar. Happy days!

Then the Scot arrived upon his stout little mare followed by his battery, which came into position on the same crossroads a hundred yards away, shooting at right angles to me, due east, back into Cugny from where we had come. Infantry were going up, rumours of cavalry were about and the bloodstained Tommies who came back were not very numerous. There seemed to be a number of batteries tucked away behind all the hedges and things looked much more hopeful. Apart from giving pin-points of the far distant enemy there was nothing to be done, except talk to all and sundry and try and get news. Some French machine-gunner officers appeared who told us that the entire French army was moving by forced marches to assist in stopping the advance and were due to arrive about six o'clock that night. They were late.

Then, too, we found that the cellar of the O.P. house was stored with apples. There weren't many left by the time the two batteries had helped themselves. As many horses as the farmyard would hold were cleared off the position and put under cover. The remainder and the guns were forced to remain slap in the open. It was bad luck because the Hun sent out about a dozen low-flying machines that morning and instead of going over Ham, which would have been far more interesting for them, they spotted us and opened with machine guns.

The feeling of helplessness with a dozen great roaring machines spitting at you just overhead is perfectly exasperating. You can't cock an eighteen-pounder up like an Archie and have a bang at them, and usually, as happened then, your own machine gun jams. It was a comic twenty minutes but trying for the nerves. The gunners dived under the gun shields and fired rifles through the wheels. The drivers stood very close to the horses and hoped for the best. The signallers struggled with the machine gun, uttering a stream of blasphemies. And all the time the Hun circled and emptied drum after drum from a height of about a hundred feet. I joined in the barrage with my revolver.

Two horses went down with a crash and a scream. A man toppled over in the road. Bullets spat on the ground like little puffs of smoke. Two went through my map, spread out at my feet, and at last away they roared, — presumably under the impression that they had put us out of action. The horses were dead!

The man was my servant, who had run away on the first morning. Three through his left leg. Better than being shot at dawn, anyhow.

Curiously enough, the mess cook had already become a casualty. He was another of the faint-hearted and had fallen under a wagon in the fog and been run over. A rib or two went. Poetic justice was rampant that morning. It left me two to deal with. I decided to let it go for the time and see if fate would relieve me of the job. As a matter of fact it didn't, and many many lifetimes later, when we were out of action, I had the two of them up, in a room with a ceiling and a cloth on the table, and the Babe stood at my elbow as a witness.

One was a man of about thirty-eight or forty, a long-nosed, lazy, unintelligent blighter. The other was a short, scrubby, Dago-looking, bullet-headed person, — poor devils both, cannon fodder. My face may have looked like a bit of rock but I was immensely sorry for them. Given a moment of awful panic, what kind of intelligence could they summon to fight it, what sort of breeding and heredity was at the back of them? None. You might as well shoot two horses for stampeding at a bursting shell. They were gripped by blind fear and ran for it. They didn't want to. It was not a reasoned thing. It was a momentary lack of control.

But to shoot them for it was absurd, a ridiculous parody of justice. Supposing I had lost my nerve and cleared out? The chances are that being a senior officer I should have been sent down to the base as R.T.O. or M.L.O. and after a few months received the D.S.O. It has been done. They, as Tommies, had only earned the right to a firing party.

It seemed to me therefore that my job was to prevent any recurrence, so in order to uproot the

THE WESTERN FRONT

fear of death I implanted the fear of God in them both. Sweat and tears ran down their faces at the end of the interview, — and I made the Dago my servant forthwith.

He has redeemed himself many times under worse shell fire than that barrage of the 21st of March.

23.

Headquarters gave me another subaltern during the day. He had been with the battery in the early days at Armentières but for various reasons had drifted to another unit.

He joined us just before the order was received to take up another position farther back and lay out a line on the Riez de Cugny. The enemy was apparently coming on. So we hooked in once more about 4.30 in the afternoon and trekked up the road on to a ridge behind which was the village of Villeselve. The Hun seemed to have taken a dislike to it. Five-nines went winging over our heads as we came into action and bumped into the village about two hundred yards behind. The Babe rode back to Brigade to report and ask for orders. There was no means of knowing where our infantry were except through Brigade, who were at infantry headquarters, and obviously one couldn't shoot blind.

Meanwhile the Dago servant collected bread and bully and a Tommy's water bottle, which stank of rum but contained only water, and the Stand-by, the new lad and myself sat under a tree watching the Hun barrage splash in all directions and made a meal.

The Babe didn't return as soon as he ought to have done. With all that shooting going on I was a little uneasy. So the new lad was told to go to Brigade and collect both the orders and the Babe.

It was getting dark when the Scot brought up his battery and wheeled them to drop into action beside us. As he was doing so the Babe and the new lad returned together. Their news was uncomforting. Brigade Headquarters had retired into the blue, and the other two batteries which had been on the road had also gone. There was no one there at all.

So the Scotsman and I held a council of war, while the Stand-by went off on a horse to reconnoitre a passable way round the shelled village. The light had gone and the sky behind us was a red glare. The village was ablaze and at the back of it on the next ridge some aeroplane hangars were like a beacon to guide storm-tossed mariners. The crackling could be heard for miles.

There was no one to give us the line or a target, no means of finding where the headquarters were or any likelihood of their finding us as we hadn't been able to report our position. We were useless.

At the back of my brain was the word Guivry. I had heard the Adjutant mention it as a rendezvous. On the map it seemed miles away, but there was always the chance of meeting some one on the way who would know. So while the other people snatched a mouthful of ration biscuit we brought the teams up and hooked in.

The Scotsman led as his battery was nearest the

track that the Stand-by reported passable. The only light was from the burning hangars and we ran into mud that was axle deep. Incidentally we ran into the barrage. A subaltern of the other battery was blown off his feet and deposited in a sitting position in a mud hole. He was fished out, spluttering oaths, and both batteries went off at a trot that would have made an inspecting General scream unintelligible things in Hindustani. Mercifully they don't inspect when one is trying to hurry out of a barrage, so we let it rip up the slope until we had got past the hangars in whose glow we showed up most uncomfortably on the top of the ridge. As soon as we had got into darkness again we halted and took stock of ourselves. No one was hurt or missing, but all the dismounted men were puffing and using their sleeves to wipe the sweat off their faces. I was one.

It was from this point that the second phase of the retreat began. It was like nothing so much as being in that half dead condition on the operating table when the fumes of ether fill one's brain with phantasies and flapping birds and wild flights of imagination just before one loses consciousness, knowing at the time that one hasn't quite "gone." Overfatigue, strain, lack of food, and above all was a craving to stop everything, lie down, and sleep and sleep and sleep. One's eyes were glued open and burnt in the back of one's head, the skin of one's face and hands tightened and stretched, one's feet were long since past shape and feeling; wherever the clothes touched one's body they irritated, —

not that one could realise each individual ache then. The effect was one ceaseless dolour from which the brain flung out and away into the no man's land of semi-consciousness, full of thunder and vast fires, only to swing back at intervals to find the body marching, marching endlessly, staggering almost drunkenly, along the interminable roads of France in the rain and cold. Hour after hour one rode side by side with the Scot, silent, swaying in the saddle, staring hollow-eyed into the dark ahead, or sliding with a stiff crash to the ground and blundering blindly from rut to rut, every muscle bruised and torn. Unconsciously every hour one gave a ten-minute halt. The horses stood drooping, the men lay down on the side of the road, motionless bundles like the dead, or sprawled over the vehicles, limp and exhausted, not smoking, not talking, content to remain inert until the next word of command should set them in motion again; wonderful in their recognition of authority, their instant unquestioning obedience, their power of summoning back all their faculties for just one more effort, and then another after that.

The country was unknown. Torches had given out their last flicker. Road junctions were unmarked. We struck matches and wrestled with maps that refused to fold in the right place, and every time Guivry seemed a million miles away. The noise of shelling dropped gradually behind until it became a mere soothing lullaby like the breaking of waves upon a pebble beach while we rolled with crunching wheels down the long incline into Buchoire, a village of the dead, without lights, doors creaking open at the touch of the wind.

We halted there to water the horses and give them what forage could be scraped together. The Scot and I rode on alone to Guivry, another seven kilometres. As we neared it so the sound of guns increased again, as though a military band had died away round one corner and came presently marching back round another, playing the same air, getting louder as it came.

In a small room lit by oil lamps, Generals and Staffs were bending over huge maps scored heavily with red and blue pencils. Telephones buzzed and half conversations with tiny voices coming from back there kept all the others silent. Orderlies came in motor overalls with all the dust of France over them.

They gave us food, — whisky, bully and bread, apples with which we filled our pockets. Of our Corps they knew nothing, but after much telephoning they "thought" we should find them at Château Beines.

The Scot and I looked at one another. Château Beines was ten minutes from the burning hangars. We had passed it on our way down, empty, silent, hours ago, in another life. Would the horses get us back up that interminable climb? Who should we find when we got there — our people or Germans? We rode back to Buchoire and distributed apples to the Babe, the Stand-by and the others and broke it to them that we had to go back on the chance of finding our brigade. The horses had been watered but not fed.

We turned about and caught up French transport which had blocked the road in both directions. We straightened them out, a wagon at a time, after endless wagging of hands and tongues and finally got to Chateau Beines to find a French Headquarters installed there who knew nothing about our brigade. There were English artillery in the farm a mile farther.

We went there. The farm was a ruin wreathed in fog, but from beneath the now smoking hangars a battery of ours was spitting shells into the night. Headquarters was somewhere in the farm cellar. We followed up a chink of light to its source and found a row of officers lying on wooden beds of rabbit netting, a signaller squatting on a reel of wire in the corner over a guttering candle, the concrete roof dripping moisture upon them. It was 3 A.M.

Orders were to come into action at once and open fire on a certain main-road junction.

The Scot and I went out and scoured ploughed fields waist-deep in drifting mist, looking for a position, found a belt of turf on the edge of a road and fetched the guns up. Locating the position on the map, working out the angle of the line of fire and the range with protractors took us back to the cellar where those lucky devils who were not commanding batteries were lying stertorous. Horses and men sweated their heart's blood in getting the guns into position on the spongy ground and within an hour the first ear-splitting cracks joined in the chorus of screaming resistance put up by the other two batteries, with gunners who lost their balance at the weight of a shell and fell upon their faces, picking themselves up without even an oath and loading up again in a stupor by a process of sub-conscious reflex energy.

What are the limits of human endurance? Are there any? We had three more days and nights of it and still those men went on.

24.

Sometime or other the Babe, the Stand-by and the other lad got some tea down in the cellar and fell asleep over their cups. Sometime or other I too got some tea, closed my eyes and fell off the box on which I was sitting. Sometime or other we got the order to cease fire and seek covered positions for the day's work. Time, as one ordinarily recognises it, had ceased. There was no night, marked by rest, nor day divided off into duties and meals. Time was all one, a blurry mixture of dark and cold; light, which hurt one's eyes, and sweat. Sleep and rest were not. What was happening we did not know. It might have been the end of the world and we shouldn't have known till we were in the next. There were just guns to be fired at given points for ever and ever, always and always, world with or without end, amen. Guns, guns and nothing but guns, in front, behind, right and left, narrowing down to those of mine which grew hot and were sponged out and went on again and still on, unhurriedly, remorselessly into the German advance, and would go on long and long after I was dead.

One's mind refused to focus anything but angles and ranges and ammunition supply. There was nothing of importance in the world but those three things, whether we moved on or stayed where we were, whether we walked or whether we rode, whether we ate or whether we starved. In a sort of detached fog one asked questions and gave orders about food and forage and in the same fog food eventually appeared while one stared at the map and whispered another range which the Stand-by shouted down the line of guns.

With spades we cut a gap in a hedge which shut off an orchard from the road. The ditch was filled with stones and bricks from the farm. The horses took the guns in one by one, and other gaps were cut in the front hedge for the gun muzzles. Platforms were dug and trail beds, and ammunition began to pile up beside each gun as the sun came out and thinned the fog.

A telephone line ran away across the fields and a new voice came through the receiver, tickling one's ear, — that of an uncaptured Colonel of a captured brigade who honoured us by taking command of our brigade. With a shaven face and washed hands he had looked upon our bearded chins and foul appearance and talked of the condition of our horses.

In front of the guns a long line of French machine gunners had dug themselves in and we were on the top of a high ridge. Below us the ground sloped immediately away to a beautiful green valley which rose up again to a feathery wood about to burst into green and ran past it in undulations like the green rollers of the Atlantic. Away in the distance were the great bulbous ever-watching eyes of the enemy, — balloons, which as the sun came up, advanced steadily, hypnotically, many of them strung out in a long line. Presently from the wood below came trickling streams of men, like brown insects coming from a dead horse. The sun glinted on their rifles Steadily they came, unhurriedly, plodding up to the ridge, hundreds of them, heedless of the enemy barrage which began climbing too in great hundred-yard jumps.

"What news?" said I, as one trickle reached me. It was led by a Colonel.

He shook his head. "We've been relieved by the French," said he, not stopping.

"Relieved? But, God's truth, isn't there a war on?"

"Who the hell are you talking to?" He flung it over his shoulder and his men followed him away.

Somehow it didn't seem credible. And yet there all along the ridge and the valley was the entire British infantry, or what looked like it, leisurely going back while the French machine gunners looked at them and chattered. I got on the 'phone to Brigade about it. The Colonel said, "Yes, I know."

We went on firing at long range. The teams were just behind the guns, each one under an apple tree, the drivers lying beside their horses. The planes which came over didn't see us. The other batteries were in the open behind the crest tucked into folds of the ground, all the wagon lines clinging to a farmhouse about a mile back where the headquarters was. The Hun barrage was quickly coming nearer.

A troop of cavalry trotted down into it and took cover under one end of the wood. They had only one casualty. A shell struck a tree and brought it crashing down on top of a horse and rider. The last of our infantry had passed behind us and the wood was empty again. The opposite ridge was unoccupied; glasses showed no one in the country that stretched away on the left. Only the balloons seemed almost on top of us. The cavalry left the wood and trotted over the ridge in a long snake of half sections, and then the fringe of the barrage reached us. It splashed into the orchard. Drivers leaped to the horses' heads. No man or animal was touched. Again one heard it coming, instinctively crouching at its shriek. Again it left us untouched as with an inattentive eye I saw the cavalry come trotting quietly back. It was followed by a chattering of the French. The reason was obvious. Out of the wood other streams came trickling, blue this time, in little parties of four and five, momentarily increasing in number and pace.

The first lot reached the battery and said they were the second line. The Boche was a "*sale race, b'en zut alors!*" and hitching their packs they passed on.

The machine gunners began to get ready. The battery began to look at me. The Stand-by gave them another salvo for luck and then ordered ten rounds per gun to be set at fuze 6 — the edge of the wood was about fifteen hundred.

The next stream of poilus was hotter. They sweated much all among the orchard and told me with a laugh that the Boche would be here in five minutes. But when I suggested that they should stay and see what we could do together they shrugged their shoulders, spat, said "*En route!*" and en routed.

The gunners had finished setting the fuzes and were talking earnestly together. The machine gunners weren't showing much above ground. The barrage had passed over to our rear.

I called up the Colonel again and told him. He told me I could drop the range to three thousand.

The Stand-by passed the order. It got about as far as the first gun and there died of inanition. The battery was so busy talking about the expected arrival of the Boche that orders faded into insignificance. The Stand-by repeated the order. Again it was not passed. I tried a string of curses but nothing more than a whisper would leave my throat. The impotence of it was the last straw. I whispered to the Stand-by to repeat word for word what I said. He megaphoned his hands and you could have heard him across the Channel, — a lovely voice, a bull of Bashan, that rose above the crash of shells and reached the last man at the other end of the line of guns. What he repeated was totally unprintable. If voice failed me, vocabulary hadn't. I rose to heights undreamed of by even the Tidworth sergeant major.

At the end of two minutes we began a series which for smartness, jump, drive, passing and execution of orders would have put a Salisbury depot battery into the waste-paper basket. Never in my life have I seen such gunnery as those fellows put up. Salvos went over like one pistol shot. Six rounds battery fire one second were like the ticking of a stop watch. Gun fire was like the stoking of the fires of hell by demons on hot cinders.

One forgot to be tired, one forgot to look out for the Hun in the joy of that masterly performance, a fortissima cantata on a six-pipe organ of death and hate. Five minutes, ten minutes? I don't know, but the pile of empty shell cases became a mountain behind each gun.

A signaller tugged at my arm and I went to the 'phone.

"Retire immediately! Rendezvous at Buchoire!"

I was still caught up with the glory of that shooting.

"What the hell for?" said I. "I can hang on here for ages yet."

"Retire immediately!" repeated the Colonel.

I came to earth with a bang and began to apologise. Somehow it doesn't do to talk like that to one's Colonel even in moments of spiritual exaltation.

We ceased fire and packed up and got mounted and hooked in like six bits of black ginger, but the trouble was that we had to leave the comparative safety of our orchard and go out into the barrage which was churning up the fields the other side of the hedge. I collected the Stand-by and gave him the plan of campaign. They were to follow me in column of route at a trot, with twenty yards between guns, — that is, at right angles to the barrage, so as to form a smaller target. No man can have failed to hear his voice but for some unknown reason they failed to carry out the order. The leading gun followed me over the ditch on to the field, shells bursting on every side. About sixty yards across the field I looked over my shoulder and saw that they were all out of the orchard but wheeling to form line, broadside on to the barrage.

The leading gun, which the Stand-by took on, was the only one that got safely away. The five others all stuck with horses dead and men wounded, and still that barrage dropped like hail.

We cut out the dead horses and shot the badly wounded ones and somehow managed a four-horse team for each gun. The wounded who couldn't walk were lifted on to limbers and held there by the others, and the four-horse teams nearly broke their hearts before we got the guns off that devilish bit of ploughed land on to a road, and after another twenty minutes had got out of the shell fire. Three sergeants were wounded, a couple of drivers and a gunner. The road was one solid mass of moving troops, French and English, infantry, gunners and transport. There was no means of going cross-country with four-horse teams. One had to follow the stream. Fortunately there were some R.A.M.C. people with stretchers and there was a motor ambulance. Between the two we got all our casualties bandaged and away. The other batteries had been gone already three quarters of an hour. There was no sign of them anywhere.

My own battery was scattered along a mile of traffic; one gun here, another there, divided by field kitchens and French mitrailleuse carts, marching infantry and limbered G.S. wagons. Where the sergeant major was with the wagon line was beyond the bounds of conjecture. One hoped to find him at the rendezvous at Buchoire. There was nothing with us in the way of rations or forage and we only had the limbers full of ammunition. Fortunately the men had had a midday ration issued in the orchard, and the horses had been watered and fed during the morning. In the way of personnel I had the Quartermaster sergeant, and two sergeants. The rest were bombardiers, gunners and drivers, — about three men per gun all told. The outlook was not very optimistic.

The view itself did not tend to lighten one's depression. We climbed a fairly steep slope which gave a view of the country for miles on either side. The main roads and every little crossroad as far as the eye could carry were all massed with moving troops going back. It looked like the Allied armies in full retreat, quite orderly but none the less routed. Where would it end? From rumours which ran about we were almost surrounded. The only way out was south. We were inside a bottle which we could not break, all aiming for the neck.

And yet everywhere on that slope French infantry had dug themselves in, each man in a little hole about knee-deep with a tiny bank of mud in front of him, separated from the next man by a few yards. They sat and smoked in their holes, so like half-dug graves, waiting for the enemy, watching us go back with a look in their eyes that seemed to be of scorn. Now and again they laughed. It was difficult to meet those quiet eyes without a surge of rage and shame. How much longer were we going to retreat? Where were our reinforcements? Why had our infantry been "relieved" that morning? Why weren't we standing shoulder to shoulder with those blue-clad poilus? What was the brain at the back of it all? Who was giving the orders? Was this the end of the war? Were we really beaten? Could it be possible that somewhere there was not a line of defence which we could take up and hold, hold for ever? Surely with magnificent men like ours who fought till they dropped and then picked themselves up and fought again, surely something could be done to stop this appalling débâcle!

25.

The tide of traffic took us into Guiscard where we were able to pull out of the stream one by one and collect as a battery, — or at least the gun part of it. While studying the map a mounted orderly came up and saluted.

"Are you the — Brigade, sir?" he said.

I said yes.

"The orders are to rendezvous at Muiraucourt instead of Buchoire."

To this day that man remains a mystery. The rest of the brigade did rendezvous at Buchoire and fought twice again that day. The Colonel never gave any order about Muiraucourt and had never heard of the place. Where the orderly came from, who he was, or how he knew the number of the brigade are unsolved problems. I never saw him again. Having given the message he disappeared into the stream of traffic, and I, finding the new rendezvous to be only about three kilometres away in a different direction to Buchoire and out of the traffic road, led on again at once.

We passed French gunners of all calibres firing at extreme range and came to Muiraucourt to find it absolutely empty and silent. While the horses were being watered and the wounded ones bandaged I scouted on ahead and had the luck to find an A.S.C. officer with forage for us and a possibility of rations if we waited an hour. It was manna in the wilderness.

We drew the forage and fed the starving horses. At the end of the hour an A.S.C. sergeant rode in to say that the ration wagons had been blown up. — We took up an extra hole in our Sam Brownes. It appeared that he had seen our headquarters and the other batteries marching along the main road in the direction of Noyon, to which place they were undoubtedly going.

The Quartermaster whispered something about bread and tea. So we withdrew from the village and halted on a field just off the road and started a fire. The bread ration was a snare and a delusion. It worked out at about one slice per every other man. He confided this to me sadly while the men were spread-eagled on the bank at the roadside, enjoying all the anticipation of a full stomach. We decided that it wasn't a large enough quantity to split up so I went over and put the position to them, telling them that on arrival at Noyon we hoped to find the brigade looking out for us with a meal for everybody ready. Meanwhile there wasn't enough to go round. What about tossing for it? . . . The ayes had it. They tossed as if they were going to a football match, the winners sending up a cheer, and even the losers sitting down again with a grin.

I decided to ride on into Noyon and locate the brigade and find out where to get rations. So I handed the battery to the Stand-by to bring on when ready, left him the Babe and the other lad, and took the Quartermaster on with me.

It was a nightmare of a ride through miles and miles of empty villages and deserted country, blown-up bridges like stricken giants blocking every way, not a vehicle on the roads, no one in sight, the spirit of desertion overhanging it all, with the light failing rapidly and Noyon apparently as far off as ever. The horses were so done that it was difficult to spur them out of a walk, we ourselves so done that we could hardly raise the energy to spur them. At last after hours of riding we came to the main Roye-Noyon road but didn't recognise it in the dark and turned the wrong way, going at least half an hour before we discovered our mistake! It was the last straw.

A thing that added to our anxiety was the sight of big guns on caterpillars all coming away from the place we were going to and as we got nearer the town the roar of bursting shells seemed to be very near. One didn't quite know that streams of the enemy would not pour over the crest at any minute. Deep in one's brain a vague anxiety formed. The whole country was so empty, the bridges so well destroyed. Were we the last — had we been cut off? Was the Hun between us and Noyon? Suppose the battery were captured? I began to wish that I hadn't ridden on but had sent the Stand-by in my place. For the first time since the show began, a sense of utter loneliness overwhelmed me, a bitter despair at the uselessness of individual effort in this gigantic tragedy of apocalyptic destruction. Was it a shadow of such loneliness as Christ knew upon the cross when he looked out upon a storm-riven world and cried, "My God, my God, why hast thou forsaken me?" All the evil in the world was gathered here in shrieking orgy, crushing one to such mental and physical tiredness that death would only have been a welcome rest.

Unaided I should not have regretted that way out, God knows. But two voices came to me through the night, — one from a little cottage among the pine trees in England, the other calling across the Atlantic with the mute notes of a violin.

"Your men look to you," they whispered. "*We* look to you. . . ."

26.

We came to Noyon!

It was as though the town were a magnet which had attracted all the small traffic from that empty countryside, letting only the big guns on caterpillars escape. The centre of the town, like a great octopus, has seven roads which reach out in every direction. Each of these was banked and double-banked with an interlocked mass of guns and wagons. Here and there frantic officers tried to extricate the tangle but for the most part men sat silent and inert upon their horses and vehicles beyond effort and beyond care.

Army Headquarters told me that Noyon would begin to be shelled in an hour's time and gave me maps and a chit to draw food from the station, but they had never heard of the brigade and thought the Corps had been wiped out. As I left, the new lad came up and reported that the battery had halted on the outskirts of the town. We went back to it and collected the limbers and tried to take them with us to the station, with hearts beating high at the thought of food. It was impossible, so we left them on the pavement and dodged single file between wagon wheels and horses' legs. After an hour's fighting every yard of the way we got to the station to find a screaming mob of civilians carrying bundles, treading on each other in their efforts to enter a train, weeping, praying, cursing, out of all control.

The R.S.O. had gone. There was no food.

We fought our way back to Army Headquarters where we learned that a bombardier with two wagons of rations destined to feed stray units like us had gone to Porquericourt, five kilometres out. If we found him we could help ourselves. If we didn't find him — a charming smile, and a shrug of the shoulders.

I decided to try the hotel where I had spent a night with my brother only three weeks ago. Three weeks, was it possible? I felt years older. The place was bolted and barred and no amount of hammering or shouting drew an answer. The thought of going back empty-handed to my hungry battery was an agony. The chances of finding that bombardier were about one in a million, so small that he didn't even represent a last hope. In utter despair one called aloud upon Christ and started to walk back. In a narrow unlit street we passed a black doorway in which stood a soldier.

"Can you give me a drink of water?" said I.

"Yes," said he. "Come in, sir. This is the officers' club."

Was it luck? Or did Christ hear? You may think what you like but I am convinced that it was Christ.

We went in. In one room were sleeping officers all over the floor. The next was full of dinner tables uncleared, one electric light burning. It was long after midnight. We helped ourselves to bits of bread from each table and drank the leavings of milk which had been served with the coffee. Then a waiter came. He said he would cook us some tea and try and find a cold tongue or some ham. I told him that I had a starving battery down the road and wanted more than tea and ham. I wanted food in a sack, two sacks, everything he could rake up, anything.

He blinked at me through his glasses. "I'll see what I can do, sir," he said and went away.

We had our tea and tongue and he brought a huge sack with loaves and tins of jam and bits of cheese and biscuits and packets of cigarettes and tins of bully. Furthermore he refused all payment except two francs for what we had eaten.

"That's all right, sir," he said. "I spent three days in a shell hole outside Wipers on one tin o' bully. — That's the best I can do for you."

I wrung him by the hand and told him he was a brother and a pal, and between us the lad and I shouldered the sack and went out again, thanking God that at least we had got something for the men to eat.

On returning to the battery I found that they had been joined by six wagons which had got cut off from the sergeant major's lot and the entire wagon line of the Scotch Captain's battery with two of his subalterns in charge. They too were starving.

The sack didn't go very far. It only took a minute or so before the lot was eaten. Then we started out, now a column about a mile long, to find Porquericourt, a tiny village some two kilometres off the main road, the gunners sleeping as they walked, the drivers rocking in the saddle, the horses stumbling along at a snail's pace. None of us had shaved or washed since the 21st. We were a hollow-eyed, draggled mob, but we got there at last to be challenged by sentries who guarded sleeping bits of units who had dropped where they stood all over the place. While my two units fixed up a wagon line I took the Quartermaster with me and woke up every man under a wagon or near one, asking him if he were Bombardier So and So, — the man with the food. How they cursed me. It took me an hour to go the rounds and there was no bombardier with food. The men received the news without comment and dropped down beside the wagons. The Babe had collected a wagon cover for us to sleep under and spread it under a tree. The four of us lay on it side by side and folded the end over ourselves. There was a heavy dew. But my job wasn't over. There was to-morrow to be considered. I had given orders to be ready to move off at six o'clock unless the Hun arrived before that. It was then 3 A.M.

The Army had told me that if our Corps was not completely wiped out their line of retreat was Buchoire, Crissolles and so back in the direction of Lassigny. They advised me to go to Crissolles. But one look at the map convinced me that Crissolles would be German by six o'clock in the morning. So I decided on Lagny by the secondary road which went straight to it from Porquericourt. If the brigade was not there, surely there would be some fighting unit who would have heard of them, or who might at least be able to spare us rations, or tell us where we could get some. Fighting on scraps of bread was all right but could not be prolonged indefinitely.

At six o'clock we set out, as a squadron of cavalry with slung lances trotted like ghosts across the turf. We had been on the march only five minutes when a yell from the rear of the battery was passed quickly up to me as I walked in the lead.

"Halt! Action rear!"

My heart stood still. Were the Germans streaming up in the mist? Were we caught at last like rats in a trap? It *couldn't* be. It was some fool mistake. The Babe was riding just behind me. I called him up. "Canter back and find out who gave that order and bring him here. — You, lead driver! Keep on walking till I give you the order to do anything else."

We went on steadily. From moment to moment nothing seemed to happen, no rifle or machine-gun fire. — The Babe came back with a grin. "The order was 'All correct in rear,' sir."

Can you get the feeling of relief? We were not prisoners or fighting to the last man with clubbed rifles in that cold grey dawn on empty stomachs.

I obeyed the natural instinct of all mothers who see their child snatched from destruction, — to slap the infant. "Find out the man who passed it up wrongly and damn his soul to hell?"

"Right, sir," said the Babe cheerily and went back. Good Babe, he couldn't damn even a mosquito properly!

The road was he most ungodly track imaginable, blocked here and there by 60-pounders coming into action. But somehow the horses encompassed the impossible and we halted in the lane outside the village at about seven o'clock. The Stand-by remained in charge of the battery while the Babe and I went across gardens to get to the village square. There was an old man standing at a door.

He gazed at us motionless. I gave him *bon jour* and asked him for news of British troops, gunners. Yes, the village was full. Would we care for some cider? Wouldn't we! He produced jugfuls of the most perfect cider I've ever drunk and told us the story of his life. He was a veteran of 1870 and wept all down himself in the telling. We thanked him profusely, shook his trembling hand and went out of his front door into the main street.

There were wagons with the brigade mark! I could have wept with joy.

In a couple of minutes we had found Headquarters. The man I'd dosed with champagne on the road corner two days before fell on my neck with strong oaths. It appeared that I'd been given up as wiped out with the whole battery, or at least captured. He looked upon me as back from the dead.

The Colonel had a different point of view. He was no longer shaved and washed, and threatened to put me under arrest for not having rendezvoused at Buchoire! Relations between us were strained, but everybody was in the act of getting mounted to reconnoitre positions so there was no time for explanations or recriminations. Within three quarters of an hour the battery was in action, but the Quartermaster had found the sergeant major, who, splendid fellow, had our rations. He functioned mightily with cooks. Tea and bacon, bread and butter, — what could the Carlton have done better than that?

And later, when the sun came out, there was no

firing to be done, and we slept beside the gun wheels under an apple tree, slept like the dead for nearly a whole hour.

27.

The Hun was indeed at Crissolles, for the brigade had fought there the previous evening. So much for Army advice.

The day was marked by two outstanding events; one, the return of the Major of the Scotch Captain's battery, his wound healed, full of blood thirst and cheeriness; the other, that I got a shave and wash. We advanced during the morning to cover a village called Bussy. We covered it, — with gun fire and salvos, the signal for each salvo being a wave from my shaving brush. There was a hell of a battle in Bussy, street fighting with bayonets and bombs. The brigade dropped a curtain of fire on the outer fringe of the village and caught the enemy in full tide. Four batteries sending over between them a hundred rounds a minute of high explosive and shrapnel can make a nasty mess of a pin-point. The infantry gloated, — our infantry.

On our right Noyon was the centre of a whirl-wind of Hun shells. We were not out any too soon. The thought added zest to our gun fire. Considering the amount of work those guns had done in the last five days and nights it was amazing how they remained in action without even breaking down. The fitter worked like a nigger and nursed them like infants. Later the Army took him from me to go and drive rivets in ships!

We pulled out of action again as dusk was falling

and the word was passed that we had been relieved and were going out of the line. The brigade rendezvoused at Cuy in a field off the road while the traffic crept forward a yard and halted, waited an hour and advanced another yard, every sort of gun, wagon, lorry, ambulance and car, crawling back, blocked at every crossroads, stuck in ditches, sometimes abandoned.

All round the sky glared redly. Hour after hour we sat in that cup of ground waiting for orders, shivering with cold, sleeping in uneasy snatches, smoking tobacco that ceased to taste, nibbling ration biscuits until the night became filled with an eerie strained silence. Jerky sentences stopped. Faint in the distance came the crunch of wheels, a vague undercurrent of sound. The guns had stopped. Now and again the chink of a horse mumbling his bit. The tail end of the traffic on the road below us was silent, waiting, the men huddled, asleep. And through it all one's ear listened for a new sound, the sound of marching feet, or trotting horses which might mean an Uhlan patrol. Bussy was not far.

Suddenly one voice, far away, distinct, pierced the darkness like a thin but blinding ray. "Les Boches! — Les Boches!"

A sort of shivering rustle ran over the whole brigade. Men stirred, sat up, muttered. Horses raised their heads with a rattle of harness. Hands crept to revolvers. Every breath was held and every head stared in the direction of the voice.

For a moment the silence was spellbound.

THE WESTERN FRONT

Then the voice came again, "*A gauche! A gauche! Nom de Dieu!*" and the crunch of wheels came again.

The brigade relaxed. There came a laugh or two, a mumbled remark, a settling down, a muttered curse and then silence once more.

Eventually came a stir, an order. Voices were raised. Sleeping figures rolled over stiffly, staggered up. Officers came forward. The order "Get mounted!" galvanised everybody.

Wagon by wagon we pulled out of the field. My battery was the last. No sooner on the road, with our noses against the tailboard of the last vehicle of the battery in front, than we had to halt again and wait endlessly, the drivers sleeping in their saddles until pulled out by the N.C.O.'s, the gunners flinging themselves into the ditch. At last on again, kicking the sleepers awake, — the only method of rousing them. It was very cold. To halt was as great an agony as to march, whether mounted or on foot. For five days and nights one had had one's boots on. The condition of feet was indescribable. In places the road was blocked by abandoned motor lorries. We had to extemporise bridges over the ditch with rocks and tins and whatever was in the lorries with a tailboard placed on top, to unhook lead horses from a four-horse gun team and hook them into a loaded wagon to make a six-horse team, to rouse the drivers sufficiently to make them drive properly and get the full team to work together, and at last, having reached a good metalled road, to follow the battery in front, limping and blind, hour after hour. From time to time the gunners and drivers changed places. For the most part no word was spoken. We halted when the teams bumped their noses on the wagon in front, went on again when those in front did. At one halt I sat on a gun seat, the unforgivable sin for a gunner on the line of march, — and I was the Battery Commander. Sprawled over the breech of the gun in a stupor I knew no more for an indefinite period when I woke again to find us still marching. The sergeant major confided to me afterwards that he was so far my accomplice in that lack of discipline that he posted a gunner on either side to see that I didn't fall off. We had started the march about five o'clock in the afternoon.

We didn't reach our destination till nine o'clock next morning. The destination consisted of halting in the road outside a village already full of troops, Chevrincourt. The horses were unhooked and taken off the road, watered, and tied to lines run up between trees. Breakfast was cooked, and having ascertained that we were not going to move for the rest of the day we spread our valises, and got into pyjamas, not caring if it snowed ink.

28.

We stayed there two days, doing nothing but water and feed the horses and sleep. I succeeded in getting letters home the first morning, having the luck to meet a junior Brass Hat who had done the retreat in a motor car. It was good to be able to put an end to their anxiety. Considering all things we had been extraordinarily lucky. The number of our dead, wounded and missing was comparatively slight and the missing rolled up later, most of them. On the second night, at about two in the morning, Battery Commanders were summoned urgently to Brigade Headquarters. The Colonel had gone, leaving the bloodthirsty Major in command. It transpired that a Divisional brigade plus one battery of ours was to go back into the line. They would take our best guns, some of our best teams and our best sergeants. The exchanges were to be carried out at once. They were.

We marched away that day, leaving one battery behind. As it happened, it didn't go into the line again but rejoined us a week later.

The third phase of the retreat, marching back to the British area — we were far south into the French area at Chevrincourt which is near Compiègne, and all its signboards showed Paris so many kilometres away — gave us an impression of the backwash of war. The roads were full, not of troops, but of refugees, women, old men, girls and children, with what possessions they could load into a farm wagon piled sky high. They pulled their cattle along by chains or ropes tied round their horns. Some of them pushed perambulators full of packages and carried their babies. Others staggered under bundles. Grief marked their faces. The hope of return kept them going. The French have deeper roots in the soil than we. To them their *"patelin"* is the world and all the beauty thereof. It was a terrible sight to see those poor women trudging the endless roads, void of a goal as long as they kept away from the pursuing death, half starved, sleeping unwashed in leaky barns, regardless of sex, begging milk from the inhabited villages they passed through to satisfy their unhappy babies, managing somehow to help the aged and infirm who mumbled bitter curses at the "*sale Boche*" and "*soixante-dix.*" I heard one woman say "*Nous savons c'qu, c'est que la guerre! Nous avons tout fait excepté les tranchées.*" "We know what war is. We have done everything except the trenches." Bombarded with gas and long-range guns, bombed by aeroplanes, homeless, half starved, the graves of their dead pillaged by ghoul-like Huns, their sons, husbands, and lovers killed, indeed they knew the meaning of war.

England has been left in merciful ignorance of this side of war, but woe unto her if she ever forgets that these women of France are her blood-sisters, these peasant women who later gave food to the emaciated Tommies who staggered back starving after the armistice, food of which they denied themselves and their children.

On the third day we reached Poix where only three months previously we had spent a merry Christmas and drunk the New Year in, the third day of ceaseless marching and finding billets in the middle of the night in villages crowded with refugees. The whole area was full, British and French elbowing each other, the unfortunate refugees being compelled to move on.

Here we exchanged old guns for new, received reinforcements of men and horses, drew new equipment in place of that which was destroyed and lost, found time to ride over to Bergicourt to pay our respects to the little Abbé, still unshaved, who was now billeting Moroccan troops, and who kissed us on both cheeks before all the world, and in three more days were on our way to their firing line again.

It was here that the runaway servants were dealt with; here too that my brother came rolling up in his car to satisfy himself that I was still this side of eternity or capture. And very good it was to see him. He gave us the number of divisions engaged against us, and we marvelled again that any of us were still alive.

We went north this time for the defence of Amiens, having been joined by our fourth battery, and relieved a brigade in action behind the village of Gentelles. The Anzacs were in the line from Villers-Bretonneux to Hangard where their flank touched the French. The spire of Amiens cathedral peeped up behind us and all day long-range shells whizzed over our heads into the stricken city.

Some one was dissatisfied with our positions behind the village. The range was considered too long. Accordingly we were ordered to go forward and relieve some other batteries down the slope in front of Gentelles. The weather had broken. It rained ceaselessly. The whole area was a mud patch broken by shell holes. The Major who had remained behind at Chevrincourt and I went forward together to locate the forward batteries. Dead horses everywhere, and fresh graves of men marked our path.

Never have I seen such joy on any faces as on those of the officers whom we were coming to relieve.

On our return we reported unfavourably, urging strongly that we should remain where we were. The order was inexorable. That night we went in.

We stayed there three days, at the end of which time we were withdrawn behind the village again. Our dead were three officers — one of whom was the Babe — half the gunners, and several drivers. Our wounded were one officer and half the remaining gunners. Of the guns themselves about six in the brigade were knocked out by direct hits.

Who was that dissatisfied "some one" who, having looked at a map from the safety of a back area, would not listen to the report of two Majors, one a regular, who had visited the ground and spoke from their bitterly-earned experience? Do the ghosts of those officers and men, unnecessarily dead, disturb his rest o' nights, or is he proudly wearing another ribbon for distinguished service? Even from the map he ought to have known better. It was the only place where a fool would have put guns. The German artillery judged him well.

Poor Babe, to be thrown away at the beginning of his manhood at the dictate of some ignorant and cowardly Brass Hat!

"Young, unmarried men, your King and country need you!"

29.

So we crawled out of that valley of death. With what remained of us in men and guns we formed three batteries, two of which went back to their original positions behind the village and in disproof of their uselessness fired four thousand rounds a day per battery, fifty-six wagon-loads of ammunition. The third battery tucked itself into a corner of the village and remained there till its last gun had been knocked out. One S.O.S. lasted thirty-six hours. One lived with a telephone and a map. Sleep was unknown. Food was just food, eaten when the servants chose to bring it. The brain reeled under the stupendousness of the strain and the firing. For cover we lived in a hole in the ground, some four feet deep with a tarpaulin to keep the rain out. It was just big enough to hold us all. The wings of the angel of death brushed our faces continuously. Letters from home were read without being understood. One watched men burned to death in the battery in front, as the result of a direct hit, without any emotion. If there be a hell such as the Church talks about, then indeed we had reached it.

We got a new Colonel here, and the bloodthirsty Major returned to his battery, the Scotch Captain having been one of the wounded. My own Captain rolled up again too, having been doing all sorts of weird fighting up and down the line. It was only now that we learned the full extent of the retreat and received an order of the day from the Commander in Chief to the effect that England had its back up against the wall. In other words the Hun was only to pass over our dead bodies. He attempted it at every hour of the day and night. The

Anzacs lost and retook Villers-Bretonneux. The enemy got to Cachy, five hundred yards in front of the guns, and was driven back again. The French Colonials filled Hangard Wood with their own and German dead, the wounded leaving a trail of blood day and night past our hole in the ground. The Anzacs revelled in it. They had never killed so many men in their lives. Their General, a great tall man of mighty few words, was round the outpost line every day. He was much loved. Every officer and man would gladly have stopped a shell for him.

At last we were pulled out of the line, at half an hour's notice. Just before hooking in — the teams were on the position — there was a small S.O.S. lasting five minutes. My battery fired four hundred rounds in that time, — pretty good going for men who had come through such an inferno, practically without sleep for fifteen days.

We sat under a haystack in the rain for forty-eight hours and the Colonel gave us lectures on calibration. Most interesting!

I confess to having been done in completely. The Babe's death had been a frightful shock. His shoulder was touching mine as he got it and I had carried him spouting blood to the shelter of a bank. I wanted to get away and hide. I was afraid, not of death, but of going on in that living hell. I was unable to concentrate sufficiently to dictate the battery orders. I was unable to face the nine o'clock parade and left it to the Orderly Officer. The day's routine made me so jumpy that I couldn't go near the lines or the horses. The sight of a gun filled me with physical sickness. The effort of giving a definite order left me trembling all over.

The greatest comfort I knew was to lie on my valise in the wet straw with closed eyes and listen to "Caprice Viennois" on the gramophone. It lifted one's soul with gentle hands and bore it away into infinite space where all was quiet and full of eternal rest and beauty. It summed up the youth of the world, the springtime of love in all its fresh cleanness, like the sun after an April shower transforming the universe into magic colours.

I think the subalterns guessed something of my trouble for they went out of their way to help me in little things.

We marched north and went into the line again behind Albert, a murdered city whose skeleton melted before one's eyes under the ceaseless rain of shells from our heavy artillery.

During and since the retreat the cry on all sides was "Where the devil are the Americans?" — those mysterious Americans who were reported to be landing at the rate of seven a minute. What became of them after landing? They seemed to disappear. Some had seen them buying up Marseilles, and then painting Paris all colours of the rainbow, but no one had yet heard of them doing any fighting. The attitude was not very bright, until Pershing's offer to Foch. Then everybody said "Ah! *Now* we shall see something." Our own recruits seemed to be the dregs of England, untrained, weedy specimens who had never seen a gun and were incapable of learning. Yet we held the Hun all right. One looked for the huskies from U.S.A., however, with some anxiety.

At Albert we found them, specimens of them, wedged in the line with our infantry, learning the game. Their one desire was to go out into No Man's Land and get to close quarters. They brought Brother Boche or bits of him every time. One overheard talk on one's way along the trenches to the O.P. "Danger?" queried one sarcastically, "Say, I ain't bin shot at yet." And another time when two officers and I had been shelled out of the O.P. by a pip-squeak battery to our extreme discomfort and danger, we came upon a great beefy American standing on the fire step watching the shells burst on the place we had just succeeded in leaving. "If that guy don't quit foolin' around with that gun," he said thoughtfully, "some one'll likely get hurt in a minute."

Which was all to the good. They shaped well. The trouble apparently was that they had no guns and no rifles.

Our own positions were another instance of the criminal folly of ignorance, — great obvious white gashes in a green field, badly camouflaged, photographed and registered by the Hun, so placed that the lowest range to clear the crest was 3500 and the S.O.S. was 3550. It meant that if the Germans advanced only fifty yards we could not bring fire to bear on them.

The dawn of our getting in was enlivened by an hour's bombardment with gas and four-twos. Every succeeding dawn was the same.

Fortunately it proved to be a peace sector, comparatively speaking, and I moved out of that unsavoury spot with no more delay than was required in getting the Colonel's consent. It only took the death of one man to prove my point. He was a mere gunner, not even on proficiency pay, so presumably it was cheap knowledge. We buried him at midnight in pouring rain, the padre reading the service by the light of my electric torch. But the Colonel wasn't there.

From the new position so reluctantly agreed to we fired many hundreds of rounds, as did our successors, and not a single man became a casualty.

What is the psychology of this system of insisting on going into childishly unsuitable positions? Do they think the Battery Commander a coward who balks at a strafed emplacement? Isn't the idea of field gunners to put their guns in such a place as will permit them to remain in action effectively for the longest possible time in a show? Why, therefore, occupy a position already accurately registered by the enemy, which he can silence at any given moment? Do they think that a Major of two years' experience in command of a battery in the line has not learned at least the rudiments of choosing positions for his guns? Do they think it is an attempt to resent authority, or to assert their own importance? Do they think that the difference of one pip and a foot of braid is the boundary between omniscience and crass stupidity?

In civil life if the senior partner insists on doing

the junior's job and bungles it, the junior can resign, — and say things.

While we were outside Albert we got our first leave allotment and the ranks were permitted to return to their wives and families for fourteen days, provided always that they had been duly vaccinated, inoculated, and declared free from vermin and venereal disease by the medical officer.

A delightful game, the inoculation business. Army orders are careful not to make it compulsory, but if any man refuses to be done his commanding officer is expected to argue with him politely, and, if that fails, to hound him to the needle. If he shies at the needle's point then his leave is stopped, — although he has sweated blood for King and country for eighteen months or so, on a weekly pay with which a munitioneer daily tips the waiter at the Carlton. If he has been unlucky enough to get venereal disease then his leave is stopped for a year.

In the next war every Tommy will be a munition maker.

30.

The desire to get out of it, to hide, refused to leave me.

I wrote to my brother and asked him if he could help me to become an R.T.O. or an M.L.O.; failing that, a cushy liaison job miles away from shambles and responsibility and spit and polish. He knew of the very thing, and I was duly nominated for liaison. The weeks went by and the nomination papers became a mass of illegible recommendations and signatures up to the highest Generals of the English Army and a Maréchal of France. But the ultimate reply was that I was a Battery Commander and therefore far too important to be allowed to go. Considering that I was half dead and not even allowed an opinion in the choosing of a position for my own battery, Gilbert and Sullivan could have conceived no more priceless paradox.

Somewhere about the end of May we were relieved and went to a rest camp outside Abbeville which was being bombed every night. A special week's leave to England was granted to "war-weary officers." I sent a subaltern and, prepared to pawn my own soul to see England again, asked if I might go too.

The reply is worthy of quotation. "You don't seem to understand that this is a rest camp, the time when you are supposed to train your battery. You'll get your leave in the line."

The camp was on turf at the edge of a deep lake. All day the horses roamed free grazing, and the men splashed about in the water whenever they felt inclined. The sun shone and footballs appeared from nowhere and there were shops in the village where they could spend money and Abbeville was only about a mile and a half away. In the morning we did a little gun drill and cleaned vehicles and harness. Concerts took place in the evenings. Leslie Henson came with a theatrical company and gave an excellent show. The battery enjoyed its time of training.

Most of those officers who weren't sufficiently war-weary for the week in England, went for a couple of days to Tréport or Paris-Plage. For myself I got forty-eight hours in Etaples with my best pal who was giving shows to troops about to go up the line, feeding train-loads of refugees and helping to bandage wounded; and somehow or other keeping out of the way of the bombs which wrecked the hospital and drove the reinforcement camps to sleep in the woods on the other side of the river. We drove out to Paris-Plage and lunched and dined and watched the golden sea sparkling and walked back in a moonlight filled with the droning of Gothas, the crashing of bombs and the impotent rage of an Archie barrage.

Not only were there no horses to look after nor men to handle but there was a kindred spirit to talk with when one felt like it, or with whom to remain silent when one didn't. Blessed be pals, for they are few and far between, and their value is above rubies.

Our rest camp came to an end with an inspection from Field Marshal Sir Douglas Haig and once more we took the trail. The battery's adventures from then until the first day of the attack which was to end the war can be briefly summed up, as we saw hardly any fighting. We went back to Albert and checked calibrations, then entrained and went off to Flanders where we remained in reserve near St. Omer for a fortnight or so. Then we entrained once more and returned to Albert, but this time south of it, behind Morlancourt.

THE WESTERN FRONT

There was an unusual excitement in the air and a touch of optimism. Foch was said to have something up his sleeve. The Hun was reported to be evacuating Albert. The Americans had been blooded and had come up to expectations. There was a different atmosphere about the whole thing. On our own sector the Hun was offensive. The night we came in he made a raid, took two thousand yards of front line on our right, and plastered us with gas and four-twos for several hours. No one was hurt or gassed except myself. I got a dose of gas. The doctor advised me to go down to the wagon line for a couple of days but the barrage was already in for our attack and the Captain was in England on the Overseas Course. The show started about 4 P.M. right along the front.

It was like the 21st of March with the positions reversed. South of us the whole line broke through and moved forward. At Morlancourt the Hun fought to the death. It was a sort of pivot, and for a couple of days we pounded him. By that time the line had ceased to bulge and was practically north and south. Then our infantry took Morlancourt and pushed the Hun back on to the Fricourt ridge and in wild excitement we got the order to advance. It was about seven o'clock at night. All Battery Commanders and the Colonel dashed up in a car to the old front line to reconnoitre positions. The car was missed by about twelve yards with high explosive and we advanced in the dark, falling over barbed wire, tumbling into shell holes, jumping trenches and treading on corpses through a most unpleasant barrage. The Hun had a distinct sting in his tail.

We came into position about three hundred yards northwest of Morlancourt. The village and all the country round stank of festering corpses, mostly German, though now and again one came upon a British pair of boots and puttees with legs in them, — or a whole soldier with a pack on his back who looked as if he were sleeping until one saw that half his face was blown away. It made one sick, sick with horror, whether it was our own Tommies or a long trench chaotic with rifles, equipment, machine guns and yellow, staring and swollen Germans.

The excitement of advancing died away. The "glory of victory" was just one long butchery, one awful smell, an orgy of appalling destruction unequalled by the barbarians of pre-civilisation.

Here was all the brain, energy and science of nineteen hundred years of "progress", concentrated on lust and slaughter, and we called it glorious bravery and rang church bells! Soldier poets sang their swan songs in praise of dying for their country, their country which gave them a period of hell, and agonising death, then wept crocodile tears over the Roll of Honour, and finally returned with an easy conscience to its money-grubbing. The gladiators did it better. At least they were permitted a final sarcasm, "*Morituri, te salutant!*"

Even gentle women at home who are properly frightened of mice and spank small boys caught ill-treating an animal, even they read the flaming headlines of the papers with a light in their eyes and said, "How glorious! We are winning!" Would they have said the same if they could have been set down on that reeking battlefield where riddled tanks splashed with blood heaved drunkenly, ambulances continuously drove away with the smashed wrecks of what once were men, leaving a trail of screams in the dust of the road, and always the guns crashed out their pæan of hate by day and night ceaselessly, remorselessly, with a terrible trained hunger to kill and maim and wipe out?

There was no stopping. I was an insignificant cog in that vast machine but no man could stop the wheels in their mighty revolutions. Fate stepped in, however.

We advanced again to Mametz and there mercifully I got another dose of gas. The effects of the first one, seven days previously, had not worked off. This was the last straw. Three days later it toppled me over. The doctors labelled me and sent me home.

PART IV

THE ARMISTICE

IV. THE ARMISTICE

1.

THE battery, commanded by I know not whom, went on to the bitter end in that sweeping advance which broke the Hindenburg line and brought the enemy to his knees. Their luck held good, for occasional letters from the subalterns told me that no one else had been killed. The last I heard of them they were at Tréport, enjoying life with the hope of demobilisation dangling in front of their eyes. May it not dangle too long.

For me the war was over. I have never fired a gun again, nor, please God, will I ever do so.

In saying the war was over I was wrong. I should have said the fighting. There were other and equally terrible sides of this world-tragedy which I was destined to see and feel.

Let me sketch briefly the facts which led to my return to duty.

The Medical Authorities sent me to a place called The Funkhole of England, a seaside town where never a bomb from airships or raiding Gothas disturbed the sunny calm, a community of convalescent hospitals with a list of rules as long as your arm, hotels full of moneyed Hebrews who only journeyed to London by day to make more money and retired by night to the security of their wives in the Funk-hole, shopkeepers who rejoiced in the war because it enabled them to put up their prices two hundred per cent, and indecent flappers always ready to be picked up by any subaltern.

The War Office authorities hastened to notify me that I was now reduced to subaltern, but somehow I was "off" flappers. Another department begged me to get well quickly, because, being no longer fit to command a battery, I was wanted for that long-forgotten liaison job.

The explanation of degrading from Major to subaltern is not forthcoming. Perhaps the Government were thinking of the rate payers. The difference in pay is about two shillings and sixpence a day, and there were many thousands of us thus reduced. — But it does not make for an exuberant patriotism. My reply was that if I didn't go out as a Major I should not hurry to get well. This drew a telegram which stated that I was re-appointed acting-Major while employed as liaison officer, but what they gave with one hand they took back with the other, for the telegram ordered me to France again three weeks before the end of my sick leave.

It was a curious return. But for the fact that I was still in uniform I might have been a mere tourist, a spectator. The job was more "cushy" even than that of R.T.O. or M.L.O. Was I glad? Enormously. Was I sorry? Yes, for out there in the thick of it were those men of mine, in a sense my children, who had looked to me for the food they

THE ARMISTICE

ate, the clothes they wore, the pay they drew, the punishments they received, whose lives had been in my keeping so long, who for two years had constituted all my life, with whom I had shared good days and bad, short rations and full, hardships innumerable, suffering indescribable. It was impossible to live softly and be driven in a big Vauxhall car, while they were still out there, without a twinge of conscience, even though one was not fit to go back to them. I slept in a bed with sheets and now and again had a hot bath, receiving letters from home in four days instead of eight, and generally enjoying all the creature comforts which console the back-area officer for the lack of excitement only found in the firing line. It was a period of doing little, observing much and thinking a great deal among those lucky ones of the earth whose lines had been cast in peaceful waters far behind even the backwash of that cataclysmic tidal wave in which so many less fortunate millions had been sucked under.

My first job was to accompany a party of French war correspondents to the occupied territory which the enemy had recently been forced to evacuate, — Dunkerque, Ostend, Bruges, Courtrai, Denain, Lille. There one marvelled at the courage of those citizens who for four years had had to bow the neck to the invader. From their own mouths we heard stories of the systematic, thought-out cruelty of the Germans who hurt not only the bodies of their victims, but their self-respect, their decency, their honour, their souls. How they survived that interminable hopeless four years of exaggerated brutality and pillage, cut off from all communication with the outside world; fed with stories of ghastly defeats inflicted upon their countrymen and allies, of distrust and revolt between England and France; fined and imprisoned for uncommitted offences against military law, not infrequently shot in cold blood without trial; their women submitted to the last indignities of the "*Inspection sanitaire*", irrespective of age or class, wrenched from their homes and deported into the unknown interior, sent to work for the hated enemy behind the firing line, unprotected from the assault of any German soldier or officer, — for those women there were worse things than the firing trenches.

We saw the results of the German Official Department of Demobilisation which had its headquarters in Alsace-Lorraine at Metz under a General, by whose direct orders all the factories in the occupied regions were dismantled and sent back piecemeal to Germany, the shells of the plant then being dynamited under pretence of military necessity. We saw a country stripped of its resources, gutted, sacked, rendered sterile.

What is the Kultur, the philosophy which not only renders such conduct thinkable but puts it into the most thorough execution? Why do any of us make any pretensions to civilization if this is the best we can do as soon as the veneer cracks? Didn't Lloyd George bow to herd-hysteria when he stood for re-election on the "Hang-the-Kaiser!" plank? Didn't Clemenceau, like Pilate, wash his

THE ARMISTICE

hands of Woodrow Wilson, dismissing his ideals with a jest, "Ce Monsieur est plus exigeant que le Bon Dieu!"

2.

French General Headquarters, to which I was then sent as liaison officer, was established in a little old-world town, not far from Paris, whose walls had been battered by the English centuries ago. Curious to think that after hundreds of years of racial antagonism we should at last have our eyes opened to the fact that our one-time enemies have the same qualities of courage and endurance, a far truer patriotism and a code of honour which nothing can break. No longer do we think of them as flippant and decadent. We know them for a nation of big-hearted men, loyal to the death, of lion-like courage, with the capacity for hanging on which in our pride we ascribed only to the British bulldog. We have seen Verdun. We have stood side by side with them in mud and blood, in fat days and lean, and know it to be true.

In this little town where the bells chimed the swift hours and market day drew a concourse of peasant women, we sat breathless at the 'phone, hourly marking the map that liberated each time a little more of France. Days of wild hope that the end was at hand, the end which such a short time back had seemed so infinitely remote, days when the future began to be a possibility, that future which for four years one had not dared to dream about. Will the rose colours ever come back? Or will the memory of those million dead go down with one to the grave?

The Armistice was signed. The guns had stopped. For a breathless moment the world stood still. The price was paid. The youth of England and France lay upturned to the sky. Three thousand miles across the ocean American mothers wept their unburied sons. Did Germany shed tears of sorrow, or rage?

The world travail was over, and even at that sacred moment when humanity should have been purged of all pettiness and meanness, should have bowed down in humility and thankfulness, forces were astir to try and raise up jealousy, hatred and enmity between England, France and America.

Have we learnt *nothing*? Are these million dead in vain? Are we to let the pendulum swing back to the old rut of dishonest hypocritical self-seeking, disguised under the title of that misunderstood word "patriotism"? Have we not yet looked into the eyes of Truth and seen ourselves as we are? Is all this talk of world peace and league of nations mere newspaper cant to disguise the fear of being out-grabbed at the peace conference? Shall we return to lying, hatred and all malice and re-crucify Christ? What is the world travail for? To produce stillborn through our own negligence the hope of Peace? The leopard cannot change his spots, you say. My answer is that the leopard does not want to. What does the present hold out to us who have been through the Valley of the Shadow? What does it look like to us who gaze down upon it from the pinnacle of four years upon the edge of eternity? This is what it looks like: this, what it

THE ARMISTICE

holds out: a corpse of what was once the most beautiful woman, fast entering into decomposition. The elements of that decomposition are what it holds out to us, a Body-politic surging with clamouring voices, all striving after self, filled with the lust of power at any price, even that of honesty and truth, who would sell their country for a mess of pottage; a Church which has denied God, pandering to snobbery, reeking of hypocrisy and cant, spoon-feeding its people with a comfortable, easy-going effete creed whose resemblance to real religion is a mockery, revelling in sin on week-days and salving its conscience by a half crown in the bag on Sundays, dealing in superstition to any who will buy; a Justice, well-represented blind whose scales are rusty, and whose weights are false; a Press which crawls down the foul gutters of life like a mangy dog raking over muck heaps for stray bones, battening upon the backstairs of divorce courts, gloating over sexual intrigue, illustrating it pornographically, suppressing truth as though it were a plague, already quarreling over unmourned dead as to who won this battle and that, filled with jealousy and hatred; a Faculty of Medicine more charlatan than any negro witch-finder, hushing up its abortions, leaving a trail of death and broken hearts on its way to Harley Street, that marketplace of lies; a Theatre whose stage doors are the tombs of virtue, virginity the price of entrance to the race for success; a Eugenics based on mock-modesty, a shocked screening of facts, leaving the young to grope their way to knowledge through the satisfying of a curiosity which sends our sons to Piccadilly and our daughters to promiscuous country houses; an Education like a foundry which pours off the liquid gold of our youth through one mould into square bars all the same shape, lacking in ideals, practising a sneaking immorality counteracted in part by athleticism, already imbued with the spirit of *laisser faire*, fired with ambition, the ambition to sow wild oats. — On the night of the Armistice, Allied officers went out from prison camps and debauched with German prostitutes. They defiled the Roll of Honour.

We have gone through the greatest war of all time and looked back upon the country that bred us. That is something of what we saw.

Your old men shall see visions and your young men shall dream dreams.

The vision of the old men has been realised. In the orgy of effort for world domination they have dug up a world unrest fertilised by the sightless faces of youth upturned to the sky. Their working hypothesis was false. The result is failure. They have destroyed themselves also in the conflagration which they started. It has burnt up the ancient fetishes, consumed their shibboleths. Their day is done. They stand among the still-smoking ruins, naked and very ugly.

The era of the young men has begun. Bent under the Atlas-like burden loaded upon their shoulders they have stood daily for five years upon the edge of eternity. They have stared across into the eyes of Truth, some unrecognising, others with disdain, but many there are in whose returning faces is the dawn of wisdom. They are coming back, the burden exchanged. On them rests the fate of the unborn. Already their feet are set upon the new way. But are they strong enough unaided to keep the pendulum from swinging back? No. It is too heavy. Every one of us must let ourselves hear the new note in their voices, calling us to the recognition of the ideal. For five years all the science, philosophy and energy of mankind has been concentrated on the art of dealing death. The young men ask that mankind should now concentrate on the art of giving life. We have proved the power within us because the routine of the world's great sin has established this surprising paradox, that we daily gave evidence of heroism, tolerance, kindliness, brotherhood.

Shall we, like Peter who denied Christ, refuse to recognise the greatness within ourselves? We found truth while we practised war. Let us carry it to the practice of peace.

www.ingramcontent.com/pod-product-compliance
Lightning Source LLC
Chambersburg PA
CBHW020808100426
42814CB00014B/372/J